Saint Oscar and Other Plays

For Trevor Griffiths

Saint Oscar
and Other Plays

TERRY EAGLETON

First published 1997

2 4 6 8 10 9 7 5 3 1

Blackwell Publishers Ltd
108 Cowley Road
Oxford OX4 1JF, UK

Blackwell Publishers Inc.
238 Main Street
Cambridge, Massachusetts 02142, USA

British Library Cataloguing in Publication Data

A CIP catalogue record for this book is available from the British Library.

Library of Congress Cataloging-in-Publication Data

Eagleton, Terry, 1943–
Saint Oscar and other plays / Terry Eagleton.
p. cm.
Contents: Saint Oscar – The white, the gold and the gangrene – Disappearances – God's locusts.
ISBN 0-631-20452-0 (hardbound : alk. paper). – ISBN 0-631-20453-9 (pbk. : alk. paper)
1. Wilde, Oscar, 1854–1900–Drama. 2. Authors, Irish–19th century–Drama. 3. Ireland–Drama. I. Title.
PR6055.A44S198 1997
822'.914–dc20
96-26957
CIP

Typeset in 10 on 12 pt Aster
by Best-set Typesetter Ltd., Hong Kong
Printed in Great Britain by Hartnolls Limited, Bodmin, Cornwall.

This book is printed on acid-free paper

Contents

———◆———

Introduction

———◆———

An academic who turns to so-called creative writing should always choose drama, since like bingo or bowling it gets you out of the house. Writing novels or poetry is as solitary a task as writing theoretical textbooks, whereas theatre is a practical, collective affair in which the writer is just one component among many, and not necessarily the most central. In its collaborative, experimental, trial-and-error nature, staging a play is the humanist's equivalent of the scientist's laboratory. It is a therapeutic experience for intellectuals accustomed to being at the controlling centre of their own work to sit slumped in the stalls at rehearsal, silenced and sidelined, experiencing the death (or at least decentring) of the author as brute reality rather than fancy idea.

In other ways, however, the whole distinction between 'intellectual' and 'creative' writing is surely rather bogus. Modernism was the period in which theorizing itself came to be a poetic act, and works of art came to include quasi-theoretical reflections upon themselves. How arrogant of some Romantics to reserve the word 'creative' for art, as though there was no creative chemical engineering or political theory! People have sometimes congratulated me, when they heard I was a critic who also wrote plays, on putting my money where my mouth was, trying it with the ball, laying myself rashly open to the kind of criticism I professionally doled out to others. But I had never seen literary theory or criticism in the first place as just something secondary, a consolation prize for those who couldn't rise to the real thing. There is no reason, as Wilde himself argued, why writing criticism or theory shouldn't be an art in itself, just as enthralling and fulfilling as fashioning fiction. The prejudice to the contrary has been lurking around Europe only for a mere two hundred years or so.

It isn't, perhaps, a prejudice quite so easy to sustain in Ireland, where the line between fictional and non-fictional writing, drama and politics, art and ideas, has for all sorts of historical reasons never been quite so indelibly drawn. A lot that sees itself as transcending intellectual or political argument in the metropolitan world gets inexorably sucked into it in the (post-)colonial sphere, for both good and ill. All of these plays but one have Irish themes, and the odd one out, *Disappearances*, is about what I suppose we must nowadays call neo-colonialism. The three Irish pieces were first produced in that country, and the fact that they try to transgress the jealously patrolled frontiers between 'art' and 'ideas' is probably relevant to that setting. *Saint Oscar* and *The White, the Gold and the Gangrene* toured Ireland in the thick of the Troubles, produced by Northern-based theatre companies (Field Day of Derry and Dubbeljoint of Belfast respectively) which regard drama as part of a wider range of discourses. When *Saint Oscar* came to London, it instantly became a different play, as Stephen Rea, who played Wilde with rare brilliance, found to his cost. 'Was Wilde really Irish, or is Eagleton making that up?', I heard a woman enquire of her companion, faintly indignantly, during the interval on the opening night. A lot of tedious spadework there, as the character in P. G. Wodehouse remarked when his interlocutor seemed not to understand the word 'pig'.

But the ignorance is not uncommon. In fact I first thought of writing about Wilde when I discovered that hardly any of the Oxford students who asked to study him with me realized that he was Irish. Since Wilde himself realized this only fitfully, this is hardly a grievous crime, though it might be said to be evidence of one. English students of literature would know of course that Yeats and Joyce were Irish, and probably – thinking of those tasty babies of *A Modest Proposal* – Jonathan Swift; but it is more doubtful whether they could name the national home of Sterne, Sheridan, Goldsmith or Burke, and they might even hesitate over Bernard Shaw. British cultural imperialism has long since annexed these gifted foreigners to its own literary canon, and Wilde himself was in many ways glad enough to be recruited. 'English' stage comedy would be poor indeed without the Irish, who were able to exploit the fact that they were at once familiar with English conventions, and relative strangers to them, to expose that arbitrariness of what is taken as natural which lies at the root of so much comic art. Several of the characteristics which make Wilde himself appear most typically upper-class English – the scorn for bourgeois normality, the flamboyant self-display, the verbal *brio* and iconoclasm – are also, interestingly enough, stereotypical Irish traits; and pondering this odd paradox was one point of origin of *Saint Oscar*.

Another such point was my sense of how astonishingly Wilde's work prefigured the insights of contemporary cultural theory. Or perhaps it would be more accurate to say that such theory, for all its excited air of novelty, represents in some ways little advance on the *fin de siècle*. Language as self-referential, truth as a convenient fiction, human identity as an enabling myth, criticism as a form of creative writing, the body and its pleasures pitted against a pharisaical ideology: in these and other ways, Wilde looms up for us more and more as the Irish Roland Barthes. The parallel is not fortuitous: somewhere behind Wilde, as somewhere behind modern literary theory, lurks the gigantic shadow of Friedrich Nietzsche. But for me personally this was more than just an intriguing intellectual conjuncture. As an Oxford academic of Irish provenance, working with these cultural notions, writing about the Irish Oxfordian socialist proto-deconstructionist Wilde came after a time to feel less like a possibility than a necessity. As Wilde had impudently hijacked the artistic forms of the English for his own devious ends, so I would try to turn his own dramatic parodies back on himself, finding some way of reinventing him without, with a sole exception, actually quoting him.

As I moved more deeply into this work, I began to discover that the two factors which had triggered my fascination with Wilde – his Irishness and his curious anticipation of some present-day cultural theory – were in fact closely related. The ideas of several of the leading avant-garde theorists of our own day need to be seen in the context of their socially marginal status, whether as ex-colonials (Jacques Derrida), women (Julia Kristeva) or homosexuals (Barthes, Foucault). It wasn't difficult to see just how this might illuminate Wilde, or to begin to fumble for some of the connections between modernism and colonialism. If, like Wilde, your history has been largely one of colonial disruption, you are less likely to be enamoured of stable representational forms, which are usually, so to speak, on the side of Caesar. You will find yourself a parodist and a parasite, bereft of any imposingly continuous tradition, cobbling one together as you go along. Your writing will tend to set up home with anti-realist fantasy and imaginative extravagance, for which one word is simply 'wit', forced often enough into these modes as a kind of compensation in spirit for a harsh social reality. If the language in which you write is, like Wilde's, that of your colonial masters, it is unlikely that you will avoid an intense verbal self-consciousness, of a 'modernist' kind; and language may come to figure as the sole surviving space in which you might momentarily be free, in an inexorably determining history. The Wildean epigram takes a piece of conventional English wisdom and tears it apart, turns it inside out, stands it on its head. Wilde was inverted in much more than a sexual sense, and his fetish from beginning to end was language itself.

The colonial subject, pitched into a permanent crisis of identity, will not be overimpressed by the solid, stable, well-rounded characters of classical realism, but is likely to feel itself fluid, provisional, diffuse; and a similar sense of provisionality will tend to apply to social forms and conventions, breeding an ironic awareness of their ungroundedness. Wilde was aware of the self as a sort of fiction, and in this he had the edge over the Establishment, who were deluded enough to believe that they knew exactly who they were. In these as in other ways, then, there is a kind of secret compact between artistic or theoretical experiment and the experience of colonialism, one still much in evidence today. 'Magic realism' was a phrase used by the great Irish radical Michael Davitt about the writings of the Young Irelander John Mitchel. For me, Wilde was one vital place where all this could be explored. He inherits a tradition of Anglo-Irish writing which is ironic about realism, sportive, satirical and fantastic, ecstatically comic with a dark sobering subtext, and, in its contradictions and subversive wit, deeply perverse. It is a style of writing to which I find myself spontaneously attracted, whatever inferior version of it I may churn out; and it is one which runs completely against the grain of my English academic training. Writing *Saint Oscar* was an attempt to rediscover something of my own suppressed voice in that respect, something bred in the bone, as though what I had been trying for some time to do in theory had finally to culminate logically in art. What at one level is a question of style is at another level a matter of identity. Examining the doubleness of Oscar Wilde, Oxford dandy and son of the dirtiest man in Dublin, then felt unavoidably like a stage of self-exploration.

If Wilde is not usually thought of in Britain as Irish, neither is he commonly seen as a particularly political figure. Yet Wilde is political in all kinds of ways, some of them fairly obvious and some of them not. He wrote finely about socialism, spoke up for Irish republicanism when the British sneered at it, and despite his carefully nurtured flippancy displayed throughout his life a tenderness and compassion towards the dispossessed, who no doubt plucked some faint chord in himself. But he is also political in some more elusive senses of the term – political, for example, because he is very funny, a remorseless debunker of the high-toned *gravitas* of Victorian England. The Irish have often found the high Arnoldian seriousness of the English irresistibly comic. Wilde is a radical because he takes nothing seriously, cares only for form, appearance and pleasure, and is religiously devoted to his own self-gratification. In Victorian society, such a man did not need to bed the son of the Marquess of Queensberry to become an enemy of the State, though it can't be said to have helped. If he sometimes displays the irresponsibility of the aesthete, he also restores to us something of the true political depth of that term, as a rejection of mean-spirited utility, and a devotion to human self-fulfilment as an end in itself, which is surprisingly close to the thought of Karl Marx. Wilde's concern with rhetoric, humour, self-irony, the mask, theatrical self-display, is in one sense the fruit of an Irish lineage at odds with English middle-class moralism, even if, contradictorily, they also reproduce something of the style of the English upper class.

Wilde hailed from the city which his compatriot James Joyce spelt as 'Doublin', and everything about him was doubled, ambiguous, unstable. He was English and Irish, upper class and underdog, socialite and sodomite, bohemian and *bon viveur*, aesthete and republican, a respectable paterfamilias who sported with rent boys in cheap hotels. *Saint Oscar* occasionally portrays his sexuality as a kind of doubleness, not of course because homosexuals are actually 'half man and half woman', but because this provided me with a way of linking that dimension of him to his other contradictions. In the end, the paradoxes of his sexual, social and national identities are deeply interrelated, and this, I imagine, lies somewhere near the heart of the play.

If *Saint Oscar* focuses on a hero of modernism, *The White, the Gold and the Gangrene* is a much more postmodernist affair, as the historical figure James Connolly, executed for his part in the anti-British Easter Rising in Dublin of 1916, finds himself up against a couple of highly contemporary sceptics, tricksters and debunkers. But the two pieces strike me as having a lot in common too; in writing a second play, you begin to discover what it is that consistently grips you, what styles or preoccupations spontaneously turn up again in a different context. A writer is in one sense the first reader of his own work, as surprised by strange affinities and recurrent obsessions as if he were scanning someone else's texts. And if the second play shares some of the limits of the first, as I think this one does, then you have now at least learnt what it is you can't do, what incapacities are constitutional rather than accidental, and how best to conceal them in future.

James Connolly may have been mythologized after his death, as an Irish revolutionary martyr, but he was a tough case to heroize during his lifetime. Stubby, bow-legged, squint-eyed and short-tempered, he was hard to mistake for a Finn or an Oisin. Being shot by the British while sitting in a chair is at once a moving image and a faintly farcical one. Connolly wasn't even a plastered saint, of whom the labour movement has had a fair few; so it was left to others to mythologize him, in contrast to Willy Yeats and Maud Gonne, who were dab hands at mythologizing themselves.

In our own day, the language of heroism and martyrdom has grown tarnished, suspect, for both creditable and discreditable reasons. The more creditable ones may be summarized in a paraphrase of Connolly's socialist colleague James Larkin: revolutionaries only appear great because we are on our knees. No man is a hero to his valet or his partner. If some thinkers hadn't idealized Connolly in the first place, others wouldn't have to make such a fuss about his feet of clay. The less creditable reasons for the unfashionableness of heroes spring from a hard-boiled, street-wise age for which virtue could only be a publicity stunt. 'I detest all heroism,' a distinguished Irish historian once remarked to me. But of course he wasn't thinking of Emily Pankhurst or Nelson Mandela. And those who can find in martyrdom nothing but a squalid cult of masochism are obviously not thinking of Steve Biko or Martin Luther King.

Heroism and martyrdom, which are also themes of *Saint Oscar*, can indeed be specious names for the macho, the self-aggrandizing, the zealously bigoted, but the current distaste for them seems a mite selective. Other people's martyrs, like other people's spouses, sometimes seem more attractive than one's own. Some gory events (the world wars) are to be solemnly memorialized, others (the Easter Rising, or even the Great Famine) to be tidied embarrassedly away. But a tragic figure like James Connolly, who was both ordinary and exceptional, is neither quite hero nor anti-hero, neither vulgar self-publicist nor cynic, and so offers us a way of reaching beyond the terms of this stale debate. Certainly the view from his execution chair can't have seemed all that upbeat: Europe plunged into military conflagration, its socialists everywhere cravenly selling out to their masters, the Irish Citizen Army numbering a derisory couple

of hundred, and the torch of Irish republicanism about to pass to a
bunch of bourgeois nationalists who had much to say of Cuchulain
but little about the festering slums which encircled them.

All Connolly could do in these circumstances was to sit it out –
clear a space in which some sort of alternative future might germi-
nate, with absolutely no guarantees. Connolly offered himself up to
the fortunes and misfortunes of a history he couldn't foresee, as a
kind of blank text which would be endlessly rewritten by the future
according to its own agendas. 'The words of a dead man,' as Auden
wrote of Yeats, 'are modified in the guts of the living.' *The White, the
Gold and the Gangrene* ponders among other things these questions
of (mis)interpretation, of how you can't really control your own
meaning for others.

Whether the Easter Rising was a courageous *coup* or a piece of
insane adventurism, whether it needed to happen at all, are matters
hotly debated by the historians. But it remains true that the actions
which we perform at the point of death, even if they are misguided,
are also in a way our freest and most authentic. Whatever we find
worth affirming then, despite the sheer futility of it (since we won't
be around to reap the fruits of that affirmation), had an authority, if
not necessarily a truth, which commands respect. What we find
ourselves unable to relinquish even at the point of death, when it is
ourselves that we relinquish, is in a sense most definitive of who we
are. In the end, what we are is what we can't walk away from; and
this is not on the whole something we can choose, like a hat or a
hair-style. Tragic protagonists may be woefully self-deluded, as
Yeats considered the men of 1916 to be; but the way they find themselves incapable of walking away from themselves, even if we happen to reject the beliefs which bind them to those selves, can then
bear a kind of fruit in the lives of others. Yeats's great poem on the
Rising understands this well enough, however politically hostile to
the insurrection it may be.

The real tragedy is that anyone should have to die for their beliefs
in the first place. 'Unhappy the land in need of martyrs' is not a slo-
gan of which many of the Irish need reminding. A just society would
be one without either heroes or radicals, since it would need neither. There are those who make an unsavoury cult of self-sacrifice,
and others who reject martyrdom because nothing for them could
ever be that precious in the first place. The alternative to both camps
is a figure like Connolly, who clearly did not want to die, who
seemed free (unlike his colleague Patrick Pearse) of any such self-

squandering sentimentalism, yet who discovered that death was the consequence of what he took to be the logic of his life. The genuine martyr is not only distinct from the suicide, but the exact opposite. The suicide gives away his life willingly because it has become worthless; the martyr abandons the most valuable thing he or she possesses. The mark of a just society would be one in which this was no longer necessary – not because value had been forgotten, but because it had been realized.

A society which is unable to remember is just the flip side of one which is unable to do anything else. Amnesia and nostalgia are terrible twins, inverted mirror images of each other. Happy the society which no longer needs to remember, not the one which needs to forget. We know that we are *en route* to a more healthy condition when it is the victors who start remembering, painfully lifting their self-willed repression, and the victims who begin mercifully to forget. There are ways of commemorating the past which are also ways of calling to mind the future, and this is certainly true of James Connolly, some of whose ideas we have still to catch up with. The past and the future have at least this much in common, that neither of them actually exists. The future is as much an unintelligible enigma as a dead body. But there are ways of mourning the violence of the past which might help to undo it in the future, and other ways which will simply ensure its ritual repetition.

Perhaps in this sense there is no unambiguous mourning or memory: if we plant gravestones to honour the dead, it is also to prevent them from rising again. The sorrow of the wake is mingled with the boisterous relief that we at least are still on our feet, whatever we can say of the corpse. Ireland has not yet completed its mourning, and so still cannot put Connolly to rest; but there are styles of remembrance which might speed that process on. Once it is complete, Connolly will no longer need to be used, abused, assailed, defended, commemorated. He can then be decently buried, as a sign that the reconciliation he fought for has finally arrived.

I won't say anything here about *Disappearances*, but will add a comment or two about my drama of the Irish Famine, *God's Locusts*, which may help to forestall some misunderstandings. The play's central figure, Hamish McClintock, is a transformed version of Sir Charles Trevelyan, the British official in charge of the famine relief operation; and although there is a good deal of fantasy in the portrayal, and the dramatic situations themselves are entirely fictional, most of what is factually asserted in the play about the Great Famine is in my view historically accurate. That this is sometimes hard to credit is testimony to the surreal nature of history itself, rather than to the play's free-wheeling fancies. Like any drama, *God's Locusts* is selective in its focus: it concentrates on the astounding shambles and callous inhumanity of key aspects of the British relief project, in reaction to historical accounts which have in my view largely whitewashed that operation. But it does not, for the most part, *invent* its evidence. It does not of course offer a comprehensive account of the Great Famine; but it tries to dramatize a reasonably accurate, if imaginatively intensified, account of one major dimension of that tragedy, in the belief that without an attempt to see the past as it actually happened, the writing of Irish history will continue to swing between sanitization on the one hand and sectarianism on the other.

T.E.

Saint Oscar

There is one quotation from the works of Oscar Wilde in this play: 'All women become like their mothers. That is their tragedy. No man does. That's his' (*The Importance of Being Earnest*).

Saint Oscar was first performed by Field Day Theatre Company in the Guildhall, Derry, on 25 September 1989. The cast was as follows:

OSCAR WILDE	Stephen Rea
LADY WILDE	Eileen Pollock
RICHARD WALLACE	Seamus Moran
EDWARD CARSON	Stanley Townsend
LORD ALFRED DOUGLAS	Peter Hanly
JUDGE	Jim Queally
JAMIE	Aidan McCann
Director	Trevor Griffiths
Set and costume designer	Bob Crowley
Lighting designer	Christopher Toulmin

Music by Neil Martin and the Pogues
Lyrics by Terry Eagleton

ACT ONE

The Chorus gathers on stage to sing 'The Ballad of Oscar Wilde' (to the tune of 'The Old Orange Flute'):

(Chorus)
    Well I'll tell you the tale of a quare Irish bard
    Who feared that old Ireland was Europe's backyard
    So he donned a cravat, wrote a lyric or two,
    Like a cross between Byron and Brian Boru.
      Too-ree-oo, too-ree-ay,
      From Portora to prison is quite a long way.

    His da was a doctor who poked in the ear
    While Oscar poked anything pleasantly queer.
    His ma was a Fenian, ferociously brave
    She was one part O'Connell and one part Queen Maeve.
      Too-ree-oo, too-ree-ay,
      From Portora to prison is quite a long way.

    But the Irish were deaf to this masterful wit
    Half man and half woman, part Paddy part Brit –
    'If you can't see I'm Shakespeare arisen to power
    Then I'm off on the boat to the ivory tower.'
      Too-ree-oo, too-ree-ay,
      From Portora to prison is quite a long way.

    So he hopped off to Oxford, his mammy in tears
    To learn how to mimic patricians and peers.
    He pranced down the High in magenta and blue
    Crying 'I'm Oscar Wilde, don't you wish you were too?'
      Too-ree-oo, too-ree-ay,
      From Portora to prison is quite a long way.

    'Sweet Jasus' said Oscar 'now why should I work?
    If there's brass in big business there's silver in talk.'
    So he wisecracked his way into stealing the spoons
    And he kissed the fine arses of titled buffoons.
      Too-ree-oo, too-ree-ay,
      From Portora to prison is quite a long way.

They thrilled to his words and they roared to his wit,
Their buttons were bursting, their corsets were split.
He showed them as shysters from top hat to toe
And the eejits cried 'Splendid!' 'Encore!' and 'Bravo!'
   Too-ree-oo, too-ree-ay,
   From Portora to prison is quite a long way.

His sallies they sparkled, his gibes were a gas,
He was jester-in-chief to the governing class
But a quare feckless Mick's never strictly true blue
For a man's got to do what a man's got to do.
   Too-ree-oo, too-ree-ay,
   From Portora to prison is quite a long way.

So they put him on trial and they slung him inside
Just to make England safe for the groom and the bride.
He rotted in Reading, he flaked out in France
'Twas a fitting demise for a fat foreign ponce.
   Too-ree-oo, too-ree-ay,
   From Portora to prison is quite a long way.

The moral of our tale it is plain for to tell:
Unnatural practices land you in hell
If you're quare and you're Irish and wear a daft hat
Don't go screwing the son of an aristocrat.
   Too-ree-oo, too-ree-ay,
   From Portora to prison is quite a long way.

(*Chorus exit. The stage in darkness. The cry of a new-born child.* WILDE's *voice speaks through the cry.*)

WILDE: A monstrous birth. When they pulled me out, they screamed and tried to kill me on the spot. A cock and a cunt together, the one tucked neatly within the other. A great blood-stained blob of words filling my mouth like mucus. They left me for dead in a handbag on Victoria railway station. A handbag! I was born queer, of the dirtiest man in Dublin and a poor imitation of Deirdre of the Sorrows. But I knew my true parents were princes.

(*Lights up on* WILDE *centre-stage. He is gorgeously attired: heavily made up, fat but sleek. Grins.*)

Or at least, let's say, extremely well-heeled landed gentry from Gloucestershire with a place in Berkeley Square. They called me Ernest. Ernest Wilde! It's everything I'm not. How can a man spend a lifetime at odds with his own name and not be a little bent? No, that's not true; they called me Oscar. Oscar Fingal O'Flahertie Wills Wilde. Others have names; I have a whole sentence. (*Pause.*) I was born with a sentence hanging over me.

I've set aside this evening for myself. From time to time a few other figures will stroll in and out of this little charade, purely to create the illusion of dramatic action. I wouldn't go as far as to call them characters. They're there to provide some visual distraction, in case you get bored with me. Not that anyone ever has. Foils to my wit, feeders of lines. Speaking of feeding, you may be wondering why I'm so unpleasantly fat. It's mainly to compensate for the starvation of the Irish race. I eat, so to speak, vicariously, on their behalf. It's nothing personal. I take hardly any pleasure in it. What you can't see is that inside this obese body an even fatter man is struggling to get out. Just as outside every slim man there's a fat man struggling to get in. Epitaph 56. Or do I mean epigram? Strange how I always confuse those words. (*Picks up a small handbell and tinkles it.*) No, that's not true. There's nothing *inside* a man at all. Always judge by appearances, they're far more reliable than reality. The English think that's hypocrisy. Do you wonder they distrust appearances when you see what they've done to half the world? They escape instead to an inner place called the truth. It's very deep – like a sewer. Whereas I'm superficial: profoundly so. There's nothing skin-deep about *my* superficiality.

(JAMIE *enters*.)

This is my man, Jamie. I can't really afford him, but he's pretty to look at. He helps me dress. (*Knowing look.*) And undress.

(JAMIE *begins to help him off with his clothes and into a new set.*)

You must forgive me, I have to change my clothes. I'm not going anywhere, it's just that I've been wearing these things for a good three hours. Don't bother about Jamie, he won't be saying much. In fact he won't be saying anything at all. I'm the only character around here.

My mother is coming to see me. She calls herself Speranza these days. Speranza! Sounds like a brand of mineral water. Before that she called herself Francesca; her real name is Jane. Do you wonder I'm such a phoney? My mother's quite as unreal as I am, but in a more vigorous sort of way. We both spend our lives in the theatre; it's just that mine is called the Haymarket and hers is called Ireland. I have a cast of ten, she has one of millions. She's currently trying to stage-manage the Irish revolution; I'm into comedy, she's into farce. She writes inflammatory nationalist verse and throws five dinner parties a week. You may observe a strangely aquiline look about her features; she says it comes from having been an eagle in a previous life.

(*Exit* JAMIE *with Wilde's old clothing.*)

She's an admirable woman; maybe that's what I dislike about her.

(*Sits in armchair and begins to smoke.*)

My aim in life is to be extraordinarily interesting. If you start off with a brogue, an arse my size and a face like a lump of dough, that's not easy. I was a socially disadvantaged child: public school, Trinity College, Dublin, Magdalen College, Oxford. Enough to drive any poor bugger to the bad. I try not to feel social resentment, but I can't help envying the privileges of the poor. Almost total freedom from indigestion, no need to panic about what to wear, no time to indulge in fruitless metaphysical speculation. It's their naturalness I envy. No, that's not true, I detest Nature. It seems to me somehow – inept. Clichéd. I watch some little seagull pecking perfunctorily around and find it singularly unconvincing. Oh, they do their best no doubt, but animals are such atrocious actors. They always botch things up. Nature lacks the knack of improvising; it just keeps doing the same dreary thing. Whereas I never do the same thing twice, which is what makes me so fascinating. My whole life has been one long unnatural practice. You can't predict me as you can a cauliflower.

It's the same with history: I find it impossible to take it at all seriously. Have you ever read a history of the human race? Don't bother, the plot is appallingly thin. I was reading one only the other day and could hardly contain my incredulity. The author's imagination was ludicrously narrow: almost all of his French characters were called Louis. No narrative thrust: just a lot of sub-plots carelessly abandoned, themes left hanging in mid-air, a mishmash of sensational occurrences. Wars, famines, massacres, revolutions: I've never read anything more improbable in my life. Nobody would believe a word of it for a second. Maybe that's what I dislike about Ireland: too much Nature and too much history. They both just go round and round, like mice on a wheel. Whereas I experiment – make it up as I go along. I've always been into make-up, of one kind or another. Speaking of Ireland, here she comes.

(LADY WILDE *enters, dressed exotically in green.*)

LADY WILDE: (*Melodramatically*) My son!

WILDE: She always had an excellent memory.

LADY WILDE: (*Laying her hands on his shoulders*) You are thin, my child. Getting thinner and thinner.

WILDE: And you, mother, are getting blinder and blinder.

LADY WILDE: Tell me about this dreadful trial, Oscar. How have they been persecuting you?

WILDE: Oh, the usual stuff. Laughing in the wrong places; not laughing in the right places. Sending me buff-coloured curtains when I particularly ordered dull lemon gold. How's my father?

LADY WILDE: Your father is – your father.

WILDE: I wasn't asking for evidence of my legitimacy, I was enquiring after his health.

LADY WILDE: He ails, Oscar; he ails as our whole nation ails. How can he not be sick in a land where only the rivers run free?

WILDE: Don't be ridiculous, mother: free is the last thing rivers are. Have you ever seen a river uncork a bottle of vodka? Still poking around in people's ears, is he?

LADY WILDE: You're a little out of date, Oscar. Your father has been appointed Surgeon Oculist to the Queen in Ireland.

WILDE: I'm glad to hear it; she could do with her eyesight improving where Ireland's concerned.

LADY WILDE: And he's writing still: he's just published a little book on Irish superstitions.

WILDE: I'm surprised to hear it's little.

LADY WILDE: Oscar, I want to talk to you about your father. He really isn't well, dear; he's growing old and fretful and nostalgic. And his gout has flared up again. He misses you, my dear; it would cheer him so much if you'd come back home, after all this terrible business is over. He's hardly seen you since Oxford.

WILDE: When I think of my father, I think of a shirt front stained with tobacco, a hairy belly and a hand wielding a fish-knife like a scalpel. Strange how we're both so clumsy in life and exact in art.

LADY WILDE: Will you come home, Oscar? Just for a little while?

WILDE: Why should I come home? There can't be anything *happening* there; nothing ever does.

LADY WILDE: Do you want to know what's happening in Ireland, Oscar?

WILDE: Please don't give me any facts, mother; they're fatal to the imagination.

LADY WILDE: When the potato crop failed, your father and I travelled out to the west. In Galway we saw a young couple feeding grass to their baby by the roadside. We saw scores of tenants evicted from their farms – thrown out empty-handed on to the highways by landlords who had never set foot in Ireland.

WILDE: You have tenants of your own, mother; I remember how you were always complaining about their rents being late.

LADY WILDE: But it didn't stop there; the Fenians were organizing the farmers out in Mayo; Parnell was sweeping the country. They hunted Parnell to death, but they killed him too late, too late to stop Home Rule. And now we're fighting with new weapons – with poetry and drama and music. We have our own theatre at last, we have writing in Irish again. You could have a part in all that, Oscar; instead you leave it all to that bogus old mystic Willy Yeats.

WILDE: Mother, neither you nor I can speak a word of Irish; I don't quite see how I'm supposed to spearhead the Celtic revival. Perhaps they could supply me with an interpreter.

LADY WILDE: Yeats can't speak Irish either.

WILDE: Well, ignorance never deterred him from anything.

LADY WILDE: The British are dithering, Oscar; they don't know whether to stay or leave. In just a few years we shall be a nation once again.

WILDE: Hmm. It's a long time since we've been a nation; we're a bit out of practice. Do you think we'll remember how to do it? Or is it innate knowledge, like scratching yourself?

LADY WILDE: It'll happen despite your mockery or anyone else's. Do you think the British can stop the grass from growing?

WILDE: I imagine they could have a pretty good try. They managed to stop Wolfe Tone in his tracks; I shouldn't think a little thing like the grass would prove much of a problem.

LADY WILDE: I never saw so clearly before how London's corrupted you. You've grown so precious you could be sold for a fortune. I can just see you, smirking with your friends in the Pall Mall clubs about the benighted Irish. I'm sure they're good for a few smart epigrams.

WILDE: That's not true. I always speak up for Ireland, whenever the God-forsaken English scoff at it. Anyway, we were never Irish, mother: we're Protestant gentlefolk with a house in Merrion Square and four others in Bray. What do we have in common with a clodhopper from Kinsale?

LADY WILDE: You could lend him your tongue, your pen, as I do. You could put your wit at the service of your own people, rather than casting it before Kensington swine.

WILDE: A writer has no people. The least whiff of an audience is fatal to art; it's almost as disastrous as the truth. All the great artists have had one foot in and one foot out.

LADY WILDE: Of what?

WILDE: I don't know; of something or other. I have a number of feet in and out. I'm a racial hybrid; I might as well be a sexual one too.

LADY WILDE: You'll never create anything without a root, Oscar. Your art's brilliant, but it's brittle too: it's lush and exotic and empty. You'll never be a major writer if you don't come home.

WILDE: My dear mother, I haven't the slightest desire to be a major writer; my ambition is to be a major minor writer. Anyway, if I'm a hybrid, I'm afraid it's because of you – you who prate of the peasantry and run the most fashionable literary salon in Dublin.

LADY WILDE: At least I'm not afraid to appear ridiculous – whereas you'd rather die than be seen on Oxford Street in the wrong colour of trousers. They call me a lunatic: a spoilt woman dabbling in politics as others dabble in porcelain. The mad Speranza, with her Fenian verse and her fancy-dress balls. Well, let them sneer. Better a rich rebel than no rebel at all; better a moonstruck romantic than an obedient servant of the

Crown. Whereas you, Oscar, have always lacked one kind of courage – the courage to appear a fool.

WILDE: Speaking of which, are you still busy ignoring my father's amorous affairs?

LADY WILDE: How dare you!

WILDE: I heard that he operated on the eyes of the King of Sweden, and when the King was temporarily blinded seduced the Queen.

LADY WILDE: (*Striking him on the face*) You puppy! Who are you to talk about affairs? Your father's one of the great men of Dublin – loyal and steadfast as you'll never be. You aren't worth his little finger. What have you ever done for your country?

WILDE: I got out, didn't I? At least they could be grateful to me for that. And if I did get out, it was because you forced me out. Who brought me up to imitate the English? Who was secretly overjoyed when I lost my Irish accent? My dear mother, you hardly brought me up sleeping with the pigs. So I've been faithful to you: I've turned myself into what you wanted. Even the cabmen can quote my lines. I did what you urged, entered the belly of the beast and made my name there. Do you wonder if I've had to take on a little protective colouring to survive in the guts of the Empire?

LADY WILDE: So I was ambitious for you – is that such a crime? I wanted you to flourish over here as your own man, as Oscar Wilde of Dublin, proud of your heritage; instead you went and sold it for a mess of caviare. And now you're just another high-society sycophant: half man, half Irish, half nothing.

WILDE: And who was it unmanned me? Who cowed me with her absurd histrionics? Do you think a child wants Queen Maeve as his mother? It was you I wanted, not Mother Ireland. If I met that old hag on a dark night, I'd cheerfully throttle her.

LADY WILDE: It wasn't me you wanted, Oscar; it was a bigger stage. There wasn't enough of an audience for you in Ireland.

WILDE: You were an activist, so I became an actor. All action is fictitious; actors are just those who make a profession of the fact.

LADY WILDE: Nonsense. You were a strong, fearless child. It's England that's crippled you.

WILDE: I got out because I preferred frivolity to Fenianism. Anything rather than the hairy-kneed Gael; better an effete aristocrat than a wife-beating peasant. So I took a piece of your body with me, brought it over here as a keepsake; that's what you can't forgive.

LADY WILDE: You're not fleeing the Gael, Oscar; you're just acting out that old weakness over the water. The strength of Ireland has always been her womenfolk; it's her manhood that's feeble. Who took over the leadership of the Land League when the men were thrown in gaol? Anna Parnell. The most feared revolutionary in the country today is Maud Gonne.

WILDE: You said it once yourself, mother: a woman will give a man the top of the milk till the end of the chapter. The Queen Maeves are all in the cowsheds, labouring for their menfolk.

LADY WILDE: Not any more. There's a new breed of women in Ireland, who can wield a rifle as well as a man. Don't talk to me about the virile Gael: our men have always been babes in arms, terrified of leaving go of the breast for all their swaggering and swearing. So I pushed you away from me, however much it hurt me. And you collapsed from that moment on – just like any Irishman adrift in London without his mammy.

WILDE: I hardly had one in the first place; you were too busy negotiating with your publishers.

LADY WILDE: My God, what a fantasist you are, Oscar.

WILDE: It runs in the family.

LADY WILDE: We were happy together when you were a child; is that too inconvenient to remember? Any mother can give a child a home; I wanted to give you a history too. But you had to have a drama all of your own; you couldn't make an issue out of Ireland, so you made a theatre out of yourself.

WILDE: Oh, I learned all my drama from you, mother. You passed on your illusions to me; it's just that we put them to different uses. You're playing an Irishwoman, I'm playing an Englishman; what's the difference?

LADY WILDE: All the difference! The difference between a real theatre and a puppet show. The finest drama of your life was there on your own doorstep; instead you had to go and write about croquet and cucumber sandwiches to flatter the British.

WILDE: Ireland is a third-rate melodrama in an infinite number of acts; I think I'll stick to croquet.

LADY WILDE: Yes, they say *I'm* melodramatic; why shouldn't I be? Why shouldn't I proclaim what's happening in Ireland from the rooftops, when the British want to tidy it away into a corner? Why shouldn't I run wild on the streets with my hair hanging loose?

WILDE: That wasn't the way I heard you appeared at the Lord-Lieutenant's ball. What was it you were wearing? Three skirts of white silk hooped up with bouquets of gold flowers and green shamrocks. I suppose you left your rifle in the cloakroom.

LADY WILDE: So I'm extravagant – just like you. But if I call attention to myself it's for a good cause. If *I* blow my own trumpet, it's to call for volunteers.

WILDE: I plead exemption on the grounds of incurable perversion. Not that I wouldn't quite fancy the uniform.

LADY WILDE: (*Taking his hand*) Oscar, it isn't Mother Ireland you're so angry with – it's me. You think I've injured you somehow; that's why you're so bitter, poor boy. It wasn't I who hurt you, my dear, don't you see that? It was you who maimed yourself when you broke with the body of your country. And you've never stopped punishing yourself for it. You abuse your body because you loathe it, you drape it in finery to hide it from sight; you shelter behind your wit like a wounded animal.

WILDE: The body of my country! Countries have bogs and bridges, mother, not bodies. They're made up of the same people living in the same place – or in the case of Ireland the same people trying to get out of the same place. I detest all this mythology: all those seven-foot young heroes wedded to the bride of their land. All those bog-screwers and soil-shafters. It's shockingly decadent stuff; it's even more perverted than I am. At least I don't couple with corpses.

LADY WILDE: It's easy to sneer at mythology in the middle of Chelsea, Oscar. Myths are what ordinary people have to live by. Anyway, what else are you but a myth for fashionable London?

WILDE: A fiction: that's entirely different. Myths are fictions that have forgotten that they're such; whereas I never forget for a moment how ludicrously unreal I am. I suppose that's the only real thing about me. We're both illusions, mother; the only difference between us is that I admit it.

LADY WILDE: Which saves you from having to look at yourself.

WILDE: The only self I have is my latest mood. I'm the runaway son of the Surgeon Oculist and the great Speranza – an imitation

Englishman. Well, what else are the Irish but imitation Irish? The whole nation's an imposture. I'm not false, mother; I'm true to the sham of my country. You can't be a traitor to an illusion.

LADY WILDE: Cromwell was an invention; the penal laws were a fantasy; the famine was a bad dream.

WILDE: The Irish have no history. It belongs entirely to the British.

LADY WILDE: I'm afraid for you, Oscar. I'm afraid that without convictions you're going to die.

WILDE: Don't think I despise your convictions. I even hold one or two extreme opinions myself – moderately, of course. It's just that I find my beliefs rather hard to believe in. What have we Irish ever had to be assured of? Least of all the potato crop.

LADY WILDE: Tell me about the trial, Oscar.

WILDE: What do you want to know? Whether I'm guilty or not?

LADY WILDE: I took that for granted.

WILDE: How tender is a mother's trust.

LADY WILDE: I was wondering how you proposed to defend yourself.

WILDE: Oh, by a well-tried legal device; it's known as lying.

LADY WILDE: I should be sorry to see my son lie in public.

WILDE: That's how I earn my living, mother; I'm a playwright. What do you suggest I do – tell them the truth?

LADY WILDE: Of course. Stand up in court and defy them. Stand up and exult in your own being – in your own difference.

WILDE: Oh, I see. Your final chance to turn me into one of your Celtic heroes. The Cuchulain of the Old Bailey, my nostrils flared like spacious caverns within which the woodlark might build her nest. Around my rough jerkin a belt of sheep's entrails, and my voice bellowing like the sound of many waters. No, mother, I refuse this last theatre of yours. I'll answer to the charges in my own way, with wit and cunning; I won't muff my big moment by playing to anybody's script but my own. If I go to my doom, then I go as myself – which means, roughly speaking, whatever part of me isn't you.

LADY WILDE: Then Ireland has lost a poet, and I have lost a son.

WILDE: What nonsense. The Irish lose their poets as often as they lose their virginity. And you've lost an illusion, not an infant.

LADY WILDE: If you want to be true to my body, then be true to yourself. Stand up and tell them who you are.

WILDE: Ah, if I could only do that, I doubt any of this would have happened. You speak up for women, mother; I've learnt from you there. I've laid aside my manhood: that ought to please you. Instead it's the very weakness you can't abide.

LADY WILDE: Will you come back with me, Oscar, when all this is over? For your father's sake?

WILDE: I'm sorry, mother. I won't serve; I can't. Give my father my dear love. And yourself too. (*Takes her hand and kisses it.*) Yourself above all.

LADY WILDE: Be careful, Oscar. They'll break you as they broke Parnell. You think you despise them, but you don't; your mockery is a form of love, a hunger. You need their applause like a drunk needs his whiskey, because without it you're just a phantom. They see in you all that terrifies them in themselves, and to be rid of that they'll tear you apart. You're like them yet you're not, and that unnerves them, and when they're uneasy they're vicious. None of this need have happened: you could have come home, where there's a place for you, where you could root and settle and thrive. But you can't tear yourself away: you could have slipped across to France, your friends even had a boat waiting, but you wouldn't leave.

WILDE: There wasn't time.

LADY WILDE: That's a lie. Even the Public Prosecutor delayed issuing the warrant until after the last boat-train had left.

WILDE: What do you want me to do, mother? Stand up in court like Cuchulain or slink off to Calais?

LADY WILDE: I want you just for one moment to stop lying to yourself about why it is you have to stay.

WILDE: You tell me why.

LADY WILDE: Because you need to destroy yourself; because you won't rest happy till they've hacked you to pieces. Because you need to expiate.
(*Pause.*)

WILDE: They take away our land and language and make us feel terribly guilty about it. As though it's we who've betrayed them. As though someone's in pain somewhere, but nobody quite knows who.

LADY WILDE: I know, my dear. And as long as you feel like that, they'll always be victorious. (*Kissing him*) Goodbye, Oscar. I'll tell your father that you were in good spirits.
(*Exit* LADY WILDE.)

WILDE: 'All women become like their mothers. That's their tragedy. No man does. That's his.' How potent cheap generalities are! Remarkably easy, too. You just have to think up a well-sounding phrase, and in a few days you'll have half of London believing it. Or repeating it, which comes to the same thing.

There are times when I get thoroughly sick of my own brilliance. I could go on like this all night. Genius can be such a bore. How consoling it would be to be some sweaty shite-shovelling peasant – not to be plagued by this incessant flow of insight, like a permanent haemorrhage. I've always yearned after simplicity, in a complicated kind of way. I find my own conversation so enthralling I can't bear going to sleep. They accuse me of self-love: always adore yourself, it's much less painful than adoring others. More enjoyable too. Others waver, cool off, sell you out, whereas I'm pledged in perfect fidelity to myself. I find other people somehow disappointing – I mean, just the fact they aren't me. I wonder how they can tolerate it. At least I know that when I go to bed I'll still be there for myself in the morning. Unlike Bosie. Sweet Bosie, how I love him. What bollocks. No, I mean what bollocks I'm talking. A savage squalid grasping little sod. But his sins are mainly venial; it isn't his fault he's the most brutal egoist since his father. One flash of his eyes, or better still his thighs, and I fall instantly to appreciating his finer points. Hard though they are to remember. I love him as the torturer's victim loves the knife that will put him out of his agony; as Saint Sebastian loved the arrows.

At least we've known some pleasure – that word which turns the English sick in the face. They'd rather have typhoid than a good time. Masochists the lot: someone tells them they have to suffer and they proffer their buttocks as obediently as whores. I've never been able to understand this insatiable appetite they have for reality. Reality has always seemed to me overrated: once you've seen one bit of it you've seen it all. Fantasy is so much more substantial.

My wife doesn't understand me. Talking of clichés, my life has known no greater enemy. Whole nations have perished of them. Fucking a woman has always struck me as somehow . . . banal. Oh, I can do it all right, but it's only

slightly more exciting than chewing a carrot. I invert plati-
tudes like I lay boys on their bellies. I have to come at things
back to front; all the best blows are struck with the left hand.
My wife doesn't understand me. We finish dinner together,
discuss our failing finances in low courteous tones over a
glass of Chablis. Then I tiptoe upstairs to gaze on the faces of
my sleeping children, get Jamie to call me a cab and rattle off
to the brothel to wank off some hairy little Mancunian who
says 'grass' and 'bath' (*short vowels*). I ask him to say 'I love
you', just to savour the slovenly vowel. *Luv*. His pronunci-
ation is as inept as his show of passion. As to the passion I
couldn't give a shit, but the English language is to be handled
more reverently than the male organ. Do we still have to teach
the English how to speak their own language? Do we have to
write *all* their great literature for them? Being a queer, you
can take the body and let the soul go screw itself; none of this
marital mush. It's the nearest I ever come to the plain truth,
which is why it disgusts me so much. Afterwards I drive back
home and peep in on the children again, just to make sure
they're asleep. No, that's not true, just to make sure they're
real. If they are, then I am too. How did these manhandled
loins come to breed such tender flowers? I've always taken a
great interest in innocence – it reminds me so irresistibly of
corruption. Children and Irishmen: the English can't tell the
difference.
(*Towards the end of this speech* RICHARD WALLACE, *one hand
bandaged, has entered. Wilde turns and sees him.*)
Richard, how delightful to see you! You must excuse me, I
was monologuing. I always do it at this time of day – it serves
me for exercise.

WALLACE: You monologue at any time of day, Oscar – not least in
company.

WILDE: My dear boy, you're injured. Come and sit down at once;
what can I get you?

WALLACE: I'm all right; I hit a policeman in the truncheon, that's all.

WILDE: A policeman?

WALLACE: At the demonstration. (*Pause.*) Don't tell me you haven't
heard about the demonstration.

WILDE: You know I don't read the newspapers. I've quite enough
trouble keeping abreast of my own eventful life without bur-
dening myself with public affairs.

WALLACE: It was yesterday: a mass rally of the unemployed in Trafalgar Square. The police rode their horses straight into the crowd. I saw one of them bend down and lash a young girl across the mouth; he was laughing at the time.

WILDE: I always avoid Trafalgar Square – those moronic-looking lions. You know I can't stand naturalistic art.

WALLACE: You'd miss the Second Coming, Oscar, if they didn't arrange a private showing. No doubt you were rollicking with one of your rent boys.

WILDE: I suppose I might have enjoyed the spectacle. If I'd dropped in on that loathsome little toady Henry James I could have had a splendid view of it from his balcony.

WALLACE: Important things are happening, Oscar. For the first time since the Chartists the workers are starting to organize. Look what's happened since the dock strike: thousands flooding into the seamen's union, the birth of the miners' federation – even the white-collar workers are getting themselves organized. I hear there are new dockers' unions in Glasgow and Liverpool, and over in Belfast –

WILDE: Please, please, my dear fellow! I really can't keep track of all these hideous organizations. Dockers are charming fellows, but I refuse to associate with more than one at a time, and certainly not in public. What is this, stir-Oscar's-conscience day? I've just had my mother in here snarling at me for not wearing a shamrock between my teeth. Can't we talk about something important – Baudelaire, for example?

WALLACE: There's a new alliance forming between the intellectuals and the working class. Why do you think the State sent the police in? Because the political consensus is crumbling and they're powerless to oppose it with anything but their truncheons.

WILDE: The police are certainly shockingly ill-mannered. How unfair they get to wear those rather fetching uniforms.

WALLACE: All this concerns you, Oscar; your cause and the workers' struggle are the same.

WILDE: But I don't have any cause, Richard; you must be mistaking me for that frightful Bernard Shaw. I know all Irishmen look alike to the English, but this is absurd. The only struggle I have is how to get out of bed without rupturing myself, which is hardly of interest to the proletariat.

WALLACE: I was thinking about the trial.

WILDE: That has to do with my getting into bed, not getting out of it.

WALLACE: Why are the ruling class after your balls, Oscar? Because you're a living affront to the sex-and-property market. Who's going to inherit the land if all the sons are inverted? Who's going to marry the débutantes? You've been egging on the frog-spawn of the aristocracy to forget that their pricks are strictly for begetting. You have the upper class by the balls, the workers have them by the pocket: it's a powerful combination.

WILDE: What nonsense. The workers are a lot of muscle-bound little beasts who raise one fist against their employers and the other against their wives. They reek of pure masculinity; that's what I find so delectable about them.

WALLACE: The wives are on the move too. The feminists are the other link in the chain.

WILDE: Some of my best friends are feminists; my mother, for example. I'm only here because she didn't take her views entirely seriously. Anyway, please don't lecture me about politics, Richard; I find just supporting socialism exhausting enough, let alone having to do anything about it. Certainly not if it involves looking at those unspeakable lions.

WALLACE: Your pamphlet on socialism's magnificent, Oscar; it's been read by some of the union leaders.

WILDE: Have the workers really read my little gem? Somehow I thought they were all illiterate. I hope they appreciate the sinuous modulations of its prose.

WALLACE: They appreciate support from an unlikely quarter.

WILDE: Well, I'm delighted they like it – as long as I don't have to meet any of them.

WALLACE: Are you really a socialist, Oscar? Or is it just another of your poses, like wearing a parrot on your shoulder in the Athenaeum?

WILDE: Of course I'm a socialist: haven't you read my fairy stories for children? They're all revolutionary tracts. I'm a fifth columnist, Richard: a spy, a changeling, an alien smuggled into the upper class to corrupt their offspring. I dine with dukes and prowl the slums at night. Sometimes I get a bit confused about which side I'm on. My side, perhaps.

WALLACE: And how do you square dining with dukes with supporting the proletariat?

WILDE: I'm an egalitarian: I find all social classes equally vulgar.

WALLACE: Or maybe you're just an old-fashioned individualist.

WILDE: I'm a socialist *because* I'm an individualist. How can anyone be an individual in this cesspit of a society? In my saintly devotion to my own ego I'm prefiguring the New Jerusalem, in which everyone will be able to be purely themselves. That's why I'm so bone idle: to bear witness to a time when nobody will need to work.

WALLACE: You can't run socialism as a private enterprise. Until everybody's free, nobody is.

WILDE: Maybe so. But my idleness doesn't come at all naturally; I have to work fearfully hard at it. It's not easy, you know, being a symbol of the socialist future. There are times when I catch myself positively itching to work and have to be quite severe with myself. Jamie has to physically restrain me.

WALLACE: Well, it's certainly an original strategy: just lie in bed all day sipping absinthe and be your own communist society.

WILDE: Work's the only crime. What's robbing a bank compared to founding one? As long as drudgery exists, we'll be plagued by this fatiguing altruism. As long as there's poverty, we'll never be able to be ourselves.

WALLACE: So the point of socialism is to relieve you of your guilt?

WILDE: Of course: what more noble aim? Socialism isn't an end in itself, Richard: it's just a device for turning us all into Michelangelos.

WALLACE: The dockers threaten the bosses' profits; you mock at their morality. You have a certain solidarity there.

WILDE: The only thing I share with the upper class is that they're as queer as I am. You mustn't forget I'm a foreigner: they'll never entirely accept me because of that.

WALLACE: And you'll never work out whether you want to be accepted or not.

WILDE: Of course I want to be accepted. You can't bite the hand that doesn't feed you.

WALLACE: You don't fool anybody, Oscar; your accent's too polished for a start. You should slur a bit more. You're much too perfect to be the real thing.

WILDE: Oh, that's just to rub their noses in it: to show them I can handle their preposterous conventions even better than they can. That's what infuriates them so much; they can't tell whether it's praise or parody. I subvert their forms by obeying them so faithfully.

WALLACE: I've never been sure whether you're an upper-class wastrel or a feckless Mick. Maybe there's not much difference.

WILDE: Ah, if only you knew how I've laboured to transform myself from one to the other. The highest form of art is to be an artist of oneself. I've spent a whole lifetime sculpting myself into shape, chipping away at the old rough patch, erasing the last traces of Nature. I think I can safely say that I'm now more precious than the Venus de Milo, who could have taken a bit more chipping in my opinion. I want them to write on my tombstone: 'He may not have paid his bills, but that was because he was a work of art.' Perhaps they could add: 'He was completely useless.'

WALLACE: 'He was an ardent socialist and completely useless.'

WILDE: Of course: that's the whole point of socialism. Use a man and you violate his being. Listen, Richard: I've dedicated my life to flouting that bizarre deviation the English call normality, which is enough to make any decent pervert puke. If their normality is a lie, then so is my perversion. No depths, then no surfaces either. It's strange, when I think of the English, I sometimes begin to feel quite normal. It's a hideous experience. Then I rush out and hire myself some rough little tart from Bermondsey and begin to feel myself again.

WALLACE: Those rough little tarts will be laying evidence against you at the trial. That old maniac Queensberry is out to crucify you, Oscar; it's a miracle they've given you bail.

WILDE: Don't be alarmed, dear boy. So far in my life I've talked my way out of marriage, debt, blackmail, physical assault, being sent down from Oxford and a number of exorbitant hotel bills. I don't see why I shouldn't talk my way out of this.

WALLACE: You amaze me, Oscar. You pamper yourself from top to toe and you're hell-bent on self-destruction. You must find danger incredibly erotic. That's because you don't really understand what they're like; when it comes down to it, old friend, you're still a bloody foreigner. You don't realize that you're feasting with panthers – not in your heart. You're too soft-hearted, Oscar. You say surface is all there is: that's what you'd *like* to think, that they're as civilized as they look. Well, they're not: they're barbarians. They'll skewer you in the guts as they're helping you on with your overcoat. Do you think they can subjugate India and not bat you like a fly?

WILDE: My dear boy, I'm mortally offended that you should think me soft-hearted. It's true I occasionally give money to beggars, but purely for aesthetic effect. I may be inverted but nobody has ever accused me of being nice.

WALLACE: Are you really out to destroy yourself, Oscar? Is that what you want?

WILDE: How do I know what I want? Why am I so fascinated by pimply little railway porters? To humiliate myself, perhaps. To expiate my sins as a social fraud. To encounter something a little more real than cucumber sandwiches. To find the nearest thing to fucking myself.

WALLACE: You've become the repository of their fantasies, Oscar, and that's terribly dangerous. Sex is the truth around which this nation turns: touch that and they'll kick and howl and hunt you to death. They scramble over each other to kiss your arse: that means they're after your guts.

(*Pause.*)

WILDE: Richard – if things go wrong . . . you will . . . you will come and see me, won't you?

WALLACE: Of course I will. Nobody's going to run out on you, Oscar.

WILDE: And make sure I can have just one of my green Romanian claret decanters with me?

WALLACE: I'll do my best.

WILDE: And perhaps my grey-plumaged Java parrot?

WALLACE: Anything you like. Provided you promise to come with me on the next unemployed demonstration.

WILDE: When's that?

WALLACE: Three weeks after the trial.

WILDE: My dear fellow, Her Majesty permitting I'll be up there on the front row.

WALLACE: (*Shaking hands*) I'll see you there. Goodbye, Oscar; good luck.

(*Exit* WALLACE.)

WILDE: I find these emotional scenes so exhausting. Maybe I could space them out a bit more – say one every ten years. (*Tinkles bell.*) Dear Richard: what a monstrous egoist he thinks me. He's quite wrong, of course: it's this wretched altruism that's driving me to distraction. This compulsion to entertain. I'm a martyr to my own pathetic hunger to please. Maybe it's the woman in me. I can't take a cab without trying to charm the driver into an erotic frenzy. The humblest ticket clerk isn't allowed to get off without an indelible impression of my genius. And it's no better when I'm alone: I'm the most pitiless audience I ever had. I flog myself ruthlessly to new heights of performance, crawl exhausted into the wings, then whoop myself back on stage.

(JAMIE *enters*.)

It's a kind of insanity. Still, better insanity than spontaneity. As for spontaneity, our servants can do that for us.

Time for a change of costume, I think, Jamie. I feel myself growing a little predictable around the armpits.

(JAMIE *helps him into new clothes*.)

Curious how human beings still disapprove of wearing clothes, after all these millennia. They regard nakedness as somehow more authentic. I can't imagine a more perverted frame of mind. Nakedness has always seemed to me so artificial. To appear in the courtroom stark naked – ah, that would be the ultimate pose. Take away my clothes and my soul comes away with them. What was it my mother said? – that I draped my body with finery to hide it from sight. As if the body wasn't just another mask. And beneath that the soul: appearance layered on appearance, curled upon nothing. Like Salome's veils, there's no end to them. Strip off one after the other and you never get down to the dark pubic secret. My mother urges me to be myself and can't even remember her own Christian name. Ah yes, to be oneself: the final play-acting.

I should take a notebook to court with me, in case things get tedious. I could dash off a comedy about my life; or a verse tragedy, depending on the verdict. Yes, a notebook; what an excellent idea. If I have to go down, I'll go down writing.

(*While he is dressing the* CHORUS *comes on-stage and sings*.)

(Chorus) Oscar's in a pickle but he doesn't give a sod
He sometimes thinks he's Baudelaire and sometimes
    that he's God
He strolls down Piccadilly with a lily in his hand
And every earl he ogles is instantly unmanned.
   Oscar, beware! A man who's slightly quare
   Will never get to heaven 'cos he's really not all there.
   Oscar, look pale! You're not a proper male

*There's better crack in Cricklewood than down in
   Reading Gaol.*

He's got a sack of epigrams to see him through his life
He fondles them at midnight 'stead of sleeping with
   his wife
He pulls them out at parties and the lads begin to
   shout
'Oh, look at Oscar's epigram, he's flashing it about.'
   Oscar, beware! . . .

You've never met a genius so bouncy and so bold
But in the silent attic his portrait's growing old
The rats are creeping closer, the cops are closing in
Oh, say you're not at home today or swear you've got
   a twin.
   Oscar, beware! . . .

They've shut the silver plate away, they've counted all
   the spoons
They've turned off the applauding and they've locked
   up all their sons
You may talk of Michelangelo, of art for fine art's sake
But you'd better run for cover when Lord Alfred burns
   the cakes.
   Oscar, beware! A man who's slightly quare
   Will never get a knighthood 'cos he's really not all
   there.
   Oscar, look pale! You're not a proper male
   There's better crack in Cricklewood than down in
   Reading Gaol.

(*During the final chorus* WILDE *has finished dressing; he walks
off-stage, head ostentatiously high.*)

———◆———

ACT TWO

A courtroom: slightly surrealist, perhaps, to indicate that the scene is only tenuously realist. WILDE, JUDGE, EDWARD CARSON.

JUDGE: You may proceed, Mr Carson.

CARSON: Thank you, my lord. My lord, the prosecution will establish that between April 23rd and May 16th last year the accused engaged in acts of sodomistic intercourse with Frederick Atkins, a male prostitute, in the Salisbury Hotel in Kensington. The chambermaid will testify that fecal stains were discovered on the bed linen. We will further establish that on June 6th and June 23rd of last year the accused engaged in oral and sodomistic intercourse with Alfred Wood, also a male prostitute, in the Malvern Hotel in Bloomsbury, and underwent a mock form of marriage with the youth, dressed as a bride. We also submit that on January 12th of this year the accused performed simultaneous acts of buggery with Herbert Tankard and Ernest Scarfe, also in the Malvern Hotel.

JUDGE: Did you say simultaneous, Mr Carson?

CARSON: I mean in rapid succession, my lord.

JUDGE: I see.

CARSON: And further, my lord, that between March 3rd and March 7th of this year he engaged in recurrent acts of buggery with Alfonso Harold Conway, also a male prostitute, in the Davenant Hotel in Knightsbridge. Conway will testify that he was persuaded by pecuniary inducements to dress as Salome and to treat the accused as John the Baptist.

JUDGE: How do you mean, Mr Carson, treat him as John the Baptist?

CARSON: I mean, my lord, that the accused smeared his neck with a cosmetic substance resembling blood and stuck his head through a paper platter procured from the hotel dining-room, thus simulating decapitation, while Conway held the platter and executed an erotic dance.

JUDGE: Why should he do that?

CARSON: Because he is depraved, my lord.

JUDGE: I see.

CARSON: And furthermore, my lord, that for several years the accused has conducted a sodomistic relationship with Lord Alfred Douglas, younger son of the Marquess of Queensberry.

JUDGE: Very well. You may proceed with your questioning, Mr Carson.

CARSON: Thank you, my lord. Is your name Oscar Fingal O'Flahertie Wills Wilde?

WILDE: It is. As to my identity, that's quite another matter.

CARSON: Do you admit to having had sexual relations with these so-called rent boys in the hotels mentioned?

WILDE: I wouldn't be seen dead in the Davenant, let alone debauched in it. None of the hotels you mention is in the least in fashion. (*Turning to* JUDGE) My lord, you must understand that I am more a creature of fashion than of passion. It would be quite unthinkable for me to set foot in any of these dreary establishments; my reputation would suffer irreparable harm.

CARSON: You have spent your life as a man of the theatre?

WILDE: Not exactly: my life *is* a theatre.

CARSON: Would you tell the court something of how you pass your time?

WILDE: Harmlessly, for the most part. Aping the English upper classes. Dressing: I spend much of my time dressing. And then undressing, which leaves me little time in between for any sort of mischief.

CARSON: You are a friend of Lord Alfred Douglas?

WILDE: We are acquainted.

CARSON: Oh, come now, Mr Wilde, you can do better than that. Is it not the case that there has been for several years a relationship of sexual intimacy between you?

WILDE: The only people who are on intimate terms with Lord Alfred are his creditors.

CARSON: I put it to you, Mr Wilde, that the relationship between you and Lord Alfred is of a sodomistic nature.

WILDE: Of a what nature?

CARSON: Sodomistic. You are a bugger, Mr Wilde, are you not?

WILDE: Not at all, sir; I am Irish. There are no buggers in Ireland; the Church would not allow it. We are a God-fearing people, pious to a fault; we even dance chastely, arms pinned to sides. We are also one of the most sexually prolific nations in the world. Simple arithmetic will indicate that Irish sodomites must be unusually thin on the ground, otherwise whence all those great hordes of children? We are, moreover, a people characterized by what I might venture to call a dialectical habit of thought – the unity of opposites. Unlike the English, we tend to believe that one thing is true, but also its antithesis. It is not that we are illogical, merely economical. A belief in the unity of opposites is quite incompatible with any form of homo-eroticism.

CARSON: Would it be accurate to say, Mr Wilde, that you are talking an unbelievable amount of utter drivel?

WILDE: I am a dramatist, sir; old habits die hard.

JUDGE: I must warn you, Mr Wilde, to give your answers truthfully and sincerely.

WILDE: I'll do my best, my lord. But to be frank, I've always had difficulty with both of those terms. I'm afraid philosophy was never my strongest point. I read Divinity when I was at Oxford.

JUDGE: You studied Divinity?

WILDE: Indeed, my lord. I took first-class honours in a special paper on the forty-nine Articles.

JUDGE: Thirty-nine, Mr Wilde.

WILDE: My mathematics were somewhat poorer. My lord, would it be permissible for me to give the most rhetorically effective answers to these questions? I think I could do that pretty well.

JUDGE: I'm afraid not, Mr Wilde. You must answer the questions as Counsel puts them to you. Carry on, Mr Carson.

CARSON: Mr Wilde, I have here a statement from a so-called rent boy of your acquaintance, Alfred Wood, describing one of your encounters in the Malvern Hotel. (*Reads*) 'He gave me a glass of red stuff and called me his lily and gave me another glass of red stuff and put his hand on my thigh and interfered with my integrity.' Is that true, Mr Wilde?

WILDE: I fail to see how anyone capable of such atrocious English can have any integrity to be interfered with.

CARSON: You admit that you called him a lily?

WILDE: Not at all: I called him Lily. Lily is a whore in an Oxford brothel, as your lordship is no doubt aware. I caught the clap from her at the age of twenty.

CARSON: What was your purpose in associating with these youths?

WILDE: I'm concerned for the education of the proletariat. I regard it as the duty of a gentleman to share his cultivation with those less fortunate. My purpose was pedagogy, not pederasty.

CARSON: So I suppose you spent your time discussing Shakespeare with them.

WILDE: Oh, indeed; we passed many an hour analysing the structure of his sonnets. I'm glad to say that many of these youths developed quite remarkably under my tutelage. Some came on apace; absolutely none of them failed to put forth a frail bud. It was an experiment in the crossing of class barriers. Indeed, I can confidently say that the working classes of this country are with me to a boy.

CARSON: Are you mocking the court, Mr Wilde?

WILDE: Not at all. It's true that we Irish are inveterate satirists, but we reserve most of our mockery for ourselves. That way we can assure ourselves that we exist.

CARSON: Call Alfred Wood, Herbert Tankard and Ernest Scarfe.

(*Three* RENT BOYS *enter, with cloth caps, raggedly dressed.*)

You may proceed with your evidence, gentlemen.

Song of the Rent Boys

(*First Boy*)
> Before I was beguiled I was a most delightful child,
> A chubby-cheeked angelic little mite
> But, my lord, to put it mild, I've been defiled by Mr Wilde
> And I'm ruined entirely for my wedding night.

(*All Three*)
> If you can't get a job
> Find yourself a nob
> Who'll call you sweetie-pie and quote you Shelley.
> When the frost makes you cough
> Have it off with a toff
> And stroll through life a-lying on your belly.

(*Second Boy*)
> I didn't have a pal, so I stared in the canal
> Considering a watery demise
> When I met this queer old geezer who said 'Would a fiver
>   please yer?'
> And looked me most politely in the thighs.

(*All Three*)
> If you can't get a job
> Find yourself a nob
> And nick his wallet while he lies a-snoring.
> If you need a sugar-daddy

Find a big soft-hearted Paddy
The work is skilled though sometimes rather boring.

(*Third Boy*)

Before I was unmanned, I flogged matches in the Strand
I've never been so perishingly cold
When I met a little chum, who said 'Why not flog your bum?
Each cheek is worth a hundredweight in gold.'

(*All Three*)

Yes, find yourself a toff
And knock the bastard off
We're surgeons to the Englishman's disease.
If they had it off at Harrow
They're queer right to the marrow
One saucy smile will bring them to their knees.
So bend over for your betters
Forget the old French letters
It beats a lifetime sleeping on the Strand.
Bend over for the gentry
So they can make their entry
I'm sure me dear old mum would understand.

JUDGE: Thank you, gentlemen. I will see you all in my chambers later.

(*The* RENT BOYS *wink hugely in unison to the audience and march off, with furtive waves to* WILDE.)

CARSON: Mr Wilde, to turn to the matter of Lord Alfred Douglas. You will admit, will you not, that your behaviour with him was outrageous enough to provoke his father into branding you as a sodomite?

WILDE: Mr Carson, Lord Alfred Douglas's father is a sadistic dwarf. The latter misfortune is perhaps not in his power to change; the former certainly is. He hunts me down in my club with a dog whip; he sends me uncouth letters threatening to kill me. He is a brutal psychopath who ought to be chained to the floor for his own safety, and who would most certainly be confined to an asylum did he not own half of Scotland. My lord, there is a conspiracy against me. Nobody will speak out on my behalf because they are terrified of that mad dog's violence.

CARSON: It is true, even so, that your illicit relationship with his son drove him to the lengths of calling you a sodomite?

WILDE: Not at all. The Marquess of Queensberry left a card for me at my club on which was inscribed the word 'somdomite'. I have no objection to being called a sodomite, but I have a proper respect for the English language, which is to be safeguarded from illiterate oafs like the Marquess. How can one credit the word of a man who can't even spell the crime he accuses me of? Is this court to give credence to the testimony of a man whose only achievement in life has been to draw up the rules by which imbeciles batter each other senseless?

CARSON: Mr Wilde, is it not the case that you have spent the whole of your adult life engaged in homosexual relationships? That you indulged in them with fellow students when at Oxford; that you have regularly hired male prostitutes for your pleasure; that you are known to associate with a number of notoriously homosexual artists and actors; and that you have set about with calculated intent to corrupt the son of the Marquess of Queensberry?

WILDE: Mr Carson, I am accused of homosexual relations by an Establishment for whom such practices are as habitual as high tea. Homosexual behaviour is as English as morris dancing, if somewhat less tedious. My lord, I repeat, there is a conspiracy against me. When I lost a libel suit against the Marquess of Queensberry, the Judge who presided in the case sent a note of congratulation to the Prosecuting Counsel. Is this what is known as British justice? The young man with whom I am accused of buggery will never be brought to court because he is the son of an aristocrat. I am told that one of the rent boys with whom I am accused of consorting will not be called to bear witness in this trial because he is the nephew of the Solicitor-General. Soliciting would seem to run in his family. My lord, this is not justice; this is pure vindictiveness.

CARSON: Mr Wilde, you bring innocent young men to ruin; you indulge in the most vile and shameful practices known to humanity; you flaunt your degeneracy on the open streets, and you expect to be treated with respect?

WILDE: Mr Carson, I expect to be treated with the same respect that I showed to the youths on whom I was imprudent enough to bestow my friendship. I treated them with courtesy and

consideration, as they have all been good enough to acknowl-
edge. My lord, I have done nobody harm; throughout my life
I have tried to help those less fortunate than myself. It's a
weakness which runs in my family.

CARSON: I put it to you, Mr Wilde, that you are idle, inverted, debauched and degenerate.

WILDE: I reject the accusation but admire the alliteration. I suppose
you mean I'm an artist; there's no need to put it in such
euphemistic language. Where I come from, we have rather
more respect for artists than the English do: we drive them
out.

CARSON: You are a foreigner in this country?

WILDE: That's so. But I speak the language fairly fluently; you were
kind enough to teach it to me. Like Caliban, your reward is
that I know how to curse. Anyway, Ned, you're not exactly a
true-born Brit yourself. Have you forgotten how we used to
stroll arm in arm around St Stephen's Green when we were
students together?

JUDGE: Is this true, Mr Carson?

CARSON: It's true that the accused and I were students at Trinity
College together, my lord. It's not true that we used to stroll
arm in arm.

WILDE: (*Camp*) Oooh, the fibber! Don't you remember how we used
to tickle each other's tummies?

JUDGE: Tickle each other's tummies?

WILDE: Well, not when we were at Trinity; that was a long time
before, when we used to play together as boys on the beach
at Dungarvan. Ned and I used to have the most delicious
wrestles. Still, I have no hard feelings about him. If one
Irishman is to be basted, it's easy enough to find another to
turn the spit.

CARSON: I have here a record of your movements in the first part of
this year. In the early part of January you spent a week with
Lord Alfred Douglas in the Abermarle Hotel in London; after
that you spent a fortnight or so in the Lake District at work on
a play. In February you were with Lord Alfred for two weeks
in Algiers, and spent some time with him in Cannes on the
way home. In early March you were with him again in the
Imperial Hotel in Brighton, and after that you were in
Gloucestershire for a while at the home of your friend Mr
Robert Ross. Is this correct?

WILDE: It sounds vaguely familiar.

CARSON: Mr Wilde, where was your wife throughout this period?

WILDE: My wife?

CARSON: Yes.

WILDE: She was at home.

CARSON: In Chelsea?

WILDE: Yes.

CARSON: Alone?

WILDE: Yes; well, the children were with her.

CARSON: Your children are very young, I believe?

WILDE: Yes.

CARSON: Is it true that your wife is an invalid?

WILDE: She is.

CARSON: Would you tell the court what is the matter with her?

WILDE: She has an illness of the spine; a curvature. She fell downstairs.

CARSON: And she has therefore to spend a good deal of time in bed?

WILDE: Yes.

CARSON: She walks with great difficulty?

WILDE: That's right.

CARSON: And how often, during this period, did you see your wife?

WILDE: I really don't know.

CARSON: For a week? More? Less?

WILDE: I really can't remember.

CARSON: I put it to you that you saw your wife during this period, when she was sick and solitary and bedridden, for a sum total of half a day. Is that correct?

WILDE: I've no idea.

CARSON: You have two children – two young boys?

WILDE: I have.

CARSON: How often did you see them in the first part of this year?

WILDE: I don't know. Perhaps for an afternoon or so.

CARSON: For one afternoon in a period of three months?

WILDE: Probably; I don't keep any record.

CARSON: Is it true that your wife has been in considerable financial difficulty?

WILDE: She has enough money for her purposes.

CARSON: But it's true that throughout this period she frequently complained to others of having too little money to manage her domestic affairs?

WILDE: She did, yes.

CARSON: Are you aware that in the first three months of this year you spent the sum of approximately five thousand pounds on your travels with Lord Alfred Douglas?

WILDE: I didn't keep any check.

CARSON: That would sound more like the sum of money a man would spend on a mistress than on a friend, would it not?

WILDE: I haven't a clue; I know nothing of mistresses. (*Turning to* JUDGE) My lord, am I on trial here for being an indifferent husband?

CARSON: You seem to have rather a high opinion of your own generosity. It doesn't seem to extend to your own family. Do you regard your conduct towards them as defensible?

WILDE: Not in the least; though I'd like to say something else in my defence, if I may. My lord, my defence is that I should very much like not to go to prison, if it can possibly be arranged. I'm afraid it wouldn't suit my temperament at all, especially the hard labour. Any form of physical exercise is fatal to my health; the only outdoor sport I have occasionally indulged in is a spot of dominoes outside French cafés. I should very much prefer it if you could arrange to have me deported to my native city. I assure you that that would be punishment enough.

(*Lights down, and instantly up again.*)

JUDGE: Mr Carson, would you like to sum up?

CARSON: Thank you, my lord. It is clear, I believe, how the accused would wish to present himself to the world. He is enlightened, we are benighted; he has thrown off the chains of common morality, whereas we are still its helpless dupes. He has been known to declare that there is no such thing as a moral or an immoral book, only a well-written or badly-written one. This is the kind of maxim which trips easily from his tongue, and for which he is fêted throughout fashionable society. He spins one vacuous paradox after another and calls it genius; and those who fawn on him affect to find such flippancy profound, because they are terrified of being thought conventionally minded. Does Mr Wilde then believe that a book which, shall we say, advocated the massacre of an entire race, or one which gloated over the systematic mutilation of a human being, is not immoral? Or is he so enraptured by his own glib tongue that he will say anything whatsoever for the infantile pleasure of creating an effect?

Mr Wilde urges us to reject the idea of truth – another dreary shibboleth of the so-called Establishment. Very well, let us take him at his word. Let us inform him here and now that we are not concerned to weigh the evidence in this case, but are intent on sentencing him to imprisonment with hard labour whether he is guilty or not. Let us decide that it is of no consequence whether he is in truth the father of his own children, and remove them for ever from his sight. Would not this wipe something of the smugness from his lips? Would he then be so eager to instruct us that truth is nothing but mood, impression, opinion?

Mr Wilde is a professional mocker, who has the knack of making us lesser mortals feel commonplace and gauche. His life has been one long gesture of contempt for those ordinary men and women who, lacking his leisure and privilege, must work for their living, nurture their children, exercise responsibility for one another – men and women who have neither the time nor the education to appreciate the doctrines of Mr Walter Pater. Mr Wilde thinks of these anonymous individuals as nothing – as inferior, obtuse, fodder for his wit, foils to his own flamboyance. They are the lesser breeds who exist to cook his food, tailor his clothes, fill his bed. And all this from a man who has the impudence to call himself a socialist. He is an iconoclast who lives off the fat of the land, a bohemian who will frequent only the very best restaurants, a born rebel who cannot pull a shirt over his head without the help of a servant. He is vain, arrogant and self-deluded; he believes himself impregnable, beyond the reach of common human judgement, contemptuous of the opinions of others, heedless of the warnings of his friends, convinced that he is so godlike that nothing can harm him. He is so besotted with himself that he would sell his own mother for the sake of a smart quip. He is a spoilt brat who has never done a decent day's work in his life, and who at the ripe age of forty presents the grotesque spectacle of one striving to perpetuate his undergraduate years. He has done nothing in his life for others, ruthlessly dedicated as he is to his own supremely trivial pleasures.

My lord, it is time that Mr Wilde had a little seriousness introduced into his futile existence. It might indeed prove to be the making of him. I therefore ask that he be sentenced to the fullest term of imprisonment with hard labour which the law sees fit to prescribe for the offences in question.

JUDGE: Mr Wilde, have you anything to say?

WILDE: I have, my lord. My lord, I can say only this in my defence. The only power which has ever enthralled me is the power of words. I know nothing of law and politics but the rhetoric of them. I have a wife called language, to whom I am faithfully wedded, and with whom I occasionally play fast and loose – it's known as poetry. I speak of course metaphorically, but there's no other way of speaking. I thrill exquisitely to Shelley but can find nothing but tedium in *Hansard* or the penny catechism. I have never understood the meaning of the term morality, other than as a ploy for oppressing others. I am, in short, a decadent. But I fear that your health may be more diseased than my decadence. Better a sensationalist than an imperialist. I fear for the moral health of an entire nation obsessed with which hole to put it in. You subjugate whole races, you condemn the mass of your own people to wretched toil, you have reduced my own nation to misery and despair, and all you can think about is which sexual organ goes in where. You prate of liberty and crush anything that differs from you as soon as it stirs. You look about you and can tolerate no image but your own; the very sight of otherness is intolerable to you. You bow your knee to art and give not a fart in your corduroys for it. You preach of the family and abandon your children as soon as they can crawl to nurse-maid and prep school. You worship God and would crucify his daughter along with his son were they rash enough to appear next time in tandem. You crucify your own women and dub it marital duty. I am the son of Lady Wilde of Dublin, who is proud to bear the name of feminist, along with that of republican.

You disgust me. You disgust me most of all because you tempt me into seriousness, a temptation to which I refuse to yield because to do so would be to play your own game. My lord, I object to this trial on the grounds of a fundamental incompatibility between the English and the Irish notions of truth. Truth for you means whatever is the case; I am afraid that we Irish have very little idea any longer of what is the case, if indeed we ever knew. I object to this trial on the grounds that no Irishman can receive a fair hearing in an

English court, because the Irish are figments of the English imagination. I am not really here; I am just one of your racial fantasies. You cannot manacle a fantasy. I do not believe in your morality and I do not believe in your truth. I have my own truth and morality, which I call art. I am not on trial here because I am a pervert but because I am an artist, which in your book comes to much the same thing. You hold that a man is a man and a woman is a woman. I hold that nothing is ever purely itself, and that the point where it becomes so is known as death. I therefore demand to be defended by metaphysicians rather than by lawyers, and that my jury should be composed of my peers – namely, poets, perverts, vagrants and geniuses.

(*Pause.*)

JUDGE: Have you anything to add, Mr Wilde?

WILDE: Yes. Have I got off?

(*Black-out.*)

Lights up on prison scene. The CHORUS *enters dressed as prisoners, in two stately files, solemnly intoning the Dies Irae:*

(Chorus)

> Dies irae, dies illa,
> Solvet saeclum in favilla:
> Teste David cum Sibylla.
> Quantus tremor est futurus,
> Quando judex est venturus,
> Cuncta stricte discussurus!
> Tube mirum spargens sonum
> Per sepulcra regionum
> Coget omnes ante thronum.
>
> Mors stupebit et natura,
> Cum resurget creatura,
> Judicanti responsura.
> Liber scriptus proferetur,
> In quo totum continetur,
> Unde mundus judicetur.
> Judex ergo cum sedebit,
> Quidquid latet apparebit:
> Nil inultum remanebit.

Quid sum miser tunc dicturus?
Quem patronum rogaturus?
Cum vix justus sit securus.
Rex tremendae majestatis,
Qui salvandos salvas gratis,
Salva me, fons pietatis.
Recordare Jesu pie,
Quod sum causa tuae viae:
Ne me perdas illa die.

(WILDE *enters in prison uniform, grey and haggard. He passes between the two ranks of prisoners, occasionally extending his hand to be kissed in the manner of a bishop. Then he sits on a chair, head buried in hands, while the prisoners gather around him and sing.*)

(Prisoners)

Poor old Oscar,
All passion spent.
That's what befalls you
When you're old and bent.

Poor old Oscar,
Bosieless and bust.
That's what comes of mixing
With the upper crust.

Mouse shit on the mattress,
Rats' tails flick his toes
Abscesses adorn his jaw,
Sparrows peck his nose.

Poor old Oscar,
Only tried to please.
Tattered rags of epigram
Billow round his knees.

Strewn around his stony cell
Broken shards of wit.
Poor old Oscar's
Landed in the shit.

Dorian's become his portrait,
Jekyll is Mr Hyde
The happy prince has lost his eyes
And the applause has died.

If you let such monsters loose
They'll give the world a fright.
So stuff him back in the handbag
And shut the lock up tight.

(*The* CHORUS *exit, bending down in front of* WILDE *to whisper* '*Poor old Oscar*' *as they pass.*)

WILDE: (*Leaping up briskly*) What a splendid place prison is! Forget all that whining I did in the ballad I wrote about it. A momentary aberration: I was missing my amber-coloured silk chasuble with the embroidered peacocks. Ridiculous: it would have clashed horribly with the walls. But I've seen through all that now. The secret of life is humility. To be purged, washed up, clean as a whistle; to know you can fall no further: there's no finer liberation than that. To be smelted down inch by inch, pose by pose, mask by mask. And whatever few drops of precious metal linger on in the crucible of the self – that's the only truth you'll ever find.

The Irish have always understood about failure. They need to: there's a lot of it over there. No nation was ever so much in love with losing; they can't get enough of it. But they know the meaning of sacrifice: to be immolated on the altar of oneself. The martyr will always worst the conqueror. Power the conqueror can understand; it's sheer helplessness which leaves him disarmed. Helplessness was always Ireland's secret weapon.

I have no poses left any more; I've shed them one by one. Got down to rock bottom at last. I never would have thought I had so much humility. It's positively inexhaustible; the stuff just keeps gushing out of me. I can't believe how long-suffering I've become: calm, meek, self-possessed, willing to endure any insult, every indignity. They nail me up to the tree of my agony and I look down on them from that lonely height with infinite forbearance. What a marvellous thing humiliation is.

To think I've had the seeds of sainthood inside me all these years and never known it. Evil always seemed to me so much more alluring. But I've seen through that now; my sinning was just a perverse form of saintliness. To come to God through his negation; to run to him by running away. The sinner was always the most precious of his children. In the hierarchy of the Church there are the sinners at the top, then the saints, then the lapsed, then the simple faithful. The simple faithful a long way behind.

Saint Oscar. It doesn't sound too impressive. But then most of the saints' names are fairly hideous. Hideousness is what I've come to embrace. True art lies in the gutter, not in the stars. The only true artists are stinking scabby syphilitic vagrants with halitosis. That's where real beauty belongs – in destitution. To embrace nothingness; to come to the grave burnt out, dispossessed, empty-handed. My God, what a superb exit that would make. I hope I'll be there to see it.

Bosie is coming to see me. Dear little Bosie, he'd make a model prison visitor. They allow me one visitor every three months, just in case I get overexcited. But I must put him behind me now. When I get out of here I think I'll become a pig farmer. Pigs have their elusive beauty. Perhaps on some rocky strip of land in Connemara, overlooking the ocean. Of course leaving England for good might be a bit of a wrench. Dear old England: you may find it heartless, snobbish, philistine, but when you think of those quaint little tea-shops with their mullioned windows and those sun-drenched cathedral closes you know in your heart you detest it. Yes, a strip of land in Connemara; alone, except perhaps for a young shepherd boy as companion. No, no, I mustn't think of that. Down, you old devil. I'm beyond the body now; suffering has refined my flesh to nothing, to a mere phantom.

I wish to hell it had. What a fucking awful place prison is. Since I've been here I've had ulcers, abscesses and gumboils; now I've got the shits. Can you imagine what it's like to have dysentery locked up in a cell twenty-four hours a day? The stink is abominable. I fell last week and hurt my ear; it's still bleeding. I can't hear much on this side (*indicates left ear*). I must confess I was quite looking forward to prison at first. Being locked up with a lot of young men of indifferent moral character didn't seem the worst punishment they could devise for me. But – my God – the stench, the food, the boredom, the brutality.

I used to believe that all experience was valuable. To catch each exquisite nuance and savour its unique intensity. Well, I've got all the unique intensities I ever needed in here: earache, gut ache, heartache, the lot. Anyone who believes all experience is valuable can't have been punched in the kidneys by a warder for not slopping out fast enough.

(BOSIE *enters*.)

Bosie! My sweet little flower.

BOSIE: Hello, Oscar. (*Looks around*.) Christ, this is a bit of a hole.

WILDE: What did you expect, my love? Queen Anne furniture?

BOSIE: Do you get anything decent to eat in here?

WILDE: Gruel, suet and water, black bread. I can only eat the gruel; I've got mouth ulcers.

BOSIE: God, it's a bit grim, isn't it? I think I'd go mad in here. Do they make you wear those pyjamas all the time?

WILDE: These aren't pyjamas, my angel, they're my daily attire. I thought of asking for a matching waistcoat, but evidently the request would have had to go all the way up to the Home Office.

BOSIE: Is that right? How are you then, old bean? Bearing up?

WILDE: Couldn't be more content. And yourself?

BOSIE: Oh, can't grumble. Bit short of the old ready, you know the kind of thing.

WILDE: I suppose, dear boy, that this is the one time in your life you can't ask me for money. Been backing the gee-gees again?

BOSIE: On and off. How do you spend your time in here?

WILDE: I read – voraciously. I'm reading the Bible at the moment.

BOSIE: The Bible? Christ almighty, have you turned religious or something?

WILDE: My dear Bosie, you must remember I'm an Irishman. We're a deeply religious nation; it's just that in some of us religion takes the form of rampant atheism. I sometimes think I've always loved God in my inner being.

BOSIE: Huh. Fancied him, maybe.

WILDE: Speaking of divine authority, how's your dear father? Still revelling in his triumph over me?

BOSIE: Don't talk to me about that old turd. He won't let me have a bean.

WILDE: My darling, when I get out of this place you can have all the beans you desire – from my own personal supply.

BOSIE: Forget it, Oscar.

WILDE: Well, that's the first time I've ever known you turn down an offer of money.

BOSIE: I said, forget it, Oscar. Haven't you learnt your lesson? You
    don't seriously think we can get together again, do you? The
    old bastard would cut me off entirely.
    (*Pause.*)

WILDE: You do realize, my sweet, how I came to land up in here?

BOSIE: You mean I should feel obliged to you? Is that it?

WILDE: You might be a teeny bit more tender to your old Oscar. I'm
    having rather a rough time because of you, my petal.

BOSIE: Oh, come on, Oscar, let's face it, I can't spend the rest of my
    life tied to a . . .

WILDE: Gaolbird? Minor poet? Ageing queen?

BOSIE: Anyway, you must be crazy. If we start up anything again,
    they'll have you inside for good. They'll be watching you for
    the rest of your life.

WILDE: My precious, listen to me for just a moment. I've showered
    you with affection, money, meals, clothes, hotel rooms,
    travel.

BOSIE: You're not the only one who's given me those things.

WILDE: No, but I've given you something they couldn't: I've given you
    my mind. I've shared my soul with you, Bosie, not just my
    bed. It's not every undergraduate who's lucky enough to live
    in the company of a great artist.

BOSIE: You're not a great artist, Oscar; you're just an entertainer.
    Your work won't survive.

WILDE: *I* will survive; I'm my finest work of art.

BOSIE: Well, you wouldn't fetch much on the market right now, old
    friend.

WILDE: And what did I get back? I got your rages, your infidelities,
    your extravagances, your intolerable egoism. You sucked me
    dry, my angel; you sucked me dry like you do everybody.

BOSIE: You were glad enough to be sucked.

WILDE: You leeched on me, Bosie; you put my head on a platter. It
    was like living with a tiger: I knew if I took my eye off you for
    one second you'd tear me to pieces.

BOSIE: Well, you're well out of it then, aren't you?

WILDE: Don't leave me, Bosie; don't run out on me. Deny all the
    others but not me; not your cuddly old Oscar. Not your sweet
    faithful old Oscar – you wouldn't deny him, would you?
    (*Pause.*)

BOSIE: I'm off to Marseilles for a couple of weeks.

WILDE: Really? What are you going to live on?

BOSIE: Oh, that's being laid on.

(*Pause.*)

WILDE: I see. You've found yourself another sugar-daddy, have you?

BOSIE: I'm going with a friend, if that's what you mean.

WILDE: Who is he?

BOSIE: Nobody you know.

WILDE: I see. Some noble lord with a big cock and a place in the country, is that it?

BOSIE: I said, nobody you know.

WILDE: Some poor besotted wretch who'll let himself be screwed for all he's worth and still come crawling after you with his tongue hanging out. Someone else you can batten on, suck dry, kick in the balls. You bastard.

BOSIE: I do pretty well, Oscar; I always did.

WILDE: You bitch. You rotten little queer.

BOSIE: Bye bye, Oscar.

WILDE: No, don't go – please, Bosie. I didn't mean it. (*Reaching out to him*) Stay for a while. Just let me . . .

BOSIE: (*Leaping back*) Get your hands off me! Do you think I'm going to spend the rest of my life tied to an old scumbag like you? You're finished, Oscar, washed up, can't you see? You've lost all your friends, you're bankrupt, you couldn't even walk down the street without being spat on. If you so much as smile at anybody ever again they'll string you up. You're better off in here, old pal – the moment you step outside they're going to tear you to pieces. You ought to get back on the boat – maybe those savages over there will take you in. Because nobody here will, old fruit: I can tell you that for sure.

(*Exit* BOSIE.)

WILDE: Little charmer. I told you what a tease he is. Always playing hard to get. He's just shy, really. He'll be back. Oh yes, he'll come running back to old Oscar. Anyway, what does he matter? I told you, I'm the only character around here. Worse luck. He doesn't mean it, it's just his eccentric manner. He's soft as a kitten underneath. I must summon the infinite forbearance of the Almighty. It's not easy, though: how can I practise Christlike forgiveness with shits like him around? (*Feels his jaw.*) These ulcers are killing me. I can't hear anything out of my left ear. When are they going to let me out of this shit-house? Ripeness is all; the arrows of Saint Sebastian. I shall grapple them to me.

Well, it's what I always wanted: to live my life like a work of art. I think it's known as Greek tragedy.

Lights down; up again on WILDE *sitting at a café table, drinking. Tattered cloak, battered hat. He is slightly drunk, drinks steadily throughout the scene, and is fairly far gone by the end of it.*

WILDE: If I'm not Jack the Ripper then maybe my father is. He has the requisite skills. He delves into bodies; so do I.

Banished. Washed up on the rue des Beaux Arts cadging drinks from old pals. Those of them who don't see me coming. I pay them in the only currency I have left: talk. I ran into Henry James the other day; he dived into a café like a man who hadn't eaten for a week. Ironic, really: he's as queer as I am. And Max Beerbohm cut me outside the Procope. He didn't make much of a job of it; if you're going to cut somebody, do it in style. Poor old Max: he'd bungle wiping his own arse. Ah well, there's no more distinguished place for an Irish writer to end up in than exile. It's our Westminster Abbey. Oedipus, bloody eyed, cast out of Thebes. He comes forward, pointing to his mask. It's only theatre after all. Strip off one mask and you find another.

I'm sitting here like a coroner, trying to establish the cause of death. Was it murder or suicide? Did they destroy me, or did I do it for them? I was always too eager to please. Always too enraptured by pain as well. The sweet beheading of the Baptist – the lovely shudder as the head drops from the body, the ecstatic spurt of blood. There's nothing more ravishing than torment.

No, no, I can't be a martyr: a martyr would like to live. I'd like to go on writing but not living; it's not easy to arrange.

(RICHARD WALLACE *enters, smarter in appearance than before, and looks across puzzledly at* WILDE.)

I have loved only two things in my life: the eternal beauty of art, and a certain sort of smooth tight bum. No doubt there's a connection between them somewhere, though I can't see it at the moment.

WALLACE: (*Coming over to the table*) It isn't . . . is it . . . is it Oscar?

WILDE: Richard! My dear fellow, how splendid to see you. What are you doing in Paris?

WALLACE: Oscar – I hardly recognized you, you've changed so much.

WILDE: I know; if I lose any more weight I won't need to use my pseudonym. I call myself Sebastian Melmoth these days; suitably mouth-filling, don't you think? I always think a pseudonym should sound like a pseudonym; one wouldn't want to deceive. What are you doing here, Richard?

WALLACE: (*Sitting at the table*) I'm with some people; we're on our way back to England. We've just come over from Monaco. How are you, Oscar? Where are you staying?

WILDE: I'm sitting here trying to work out how not to go back to my unspeakable hole of a lodging-house. And how to pay for this drink – and its four predecessors.

WALLACE: You don't have any money?

WILDE: Not a sou.

WALLACE: Let me pay for it, Oscar.

(*He places money on the table.*)

WILDE: My dear Richard, you're too kind.

WALLACE: We all feel awful about you, Oscar – you must know that. Is there anything I can do?

WILDE: You could invite me out to dinner.

WALLACE: I'd love to, Oscar, but I'm supposed to be dining with these friends of mine at the hotel.

WILDE: Are they English?

WALLACE: I'm afraid so.

WILDE: Then I quite understand. I was chatting up a rather pleasant young American in a café the other week when an Englishman came across to the table and dropped a card in front of the youth. It read, 'This is Oscar Wilde.' The lad made his apologies and vanished – before I could tackle him round the thighs and bring him to the ground, of course. Tell me, Richard, do I look to you like a seducer?

WALLACE: No, Oscar, you don't.

WILDE: How are things back in England? It's odd to think I'll probably never set foot in it again.

WALLACE: Bad. Thomas Hardy's just published a new novel.

WILDE: That's certainly unfortunate.

WALLACE: No, no, it's a fine piece of work – a blistering assault on the Church, the family, the educational system, the lot. The response has been astounding: the bishops up in arms, the Purity League on the rampage, Hardy dragged through the press like a child molester. He says it's been enough to cure him of any desire to write fiction again; he's beaten.

WILDE: Well, he shouldn't be; at least he's still got a home to go to. He should take a look at me: exiled, bankrupt, friendless, ulcerated, deaf in one ear. I'm not beaten.

WALLACE: You're not?

WILDE: Of course not. How's the dialectic these days, Richard? Still staggering on?

WALLACE: Ground to a halt would be more like it. There's nothing moving politically in Britain now; the Empire's doing a good job keeping the workers docile. At least they know they're better off than the nig-nogs and the Paddies.

WILDE: My dear Richard, don't tell me you've become a cynic. I thought you relied on me to play that role.

WALLACE: Things have changed, Oscar; the heady days of the dock strike are over. No more mass rallies, just a lot of soup kitchens. There's talk of a Labour party: you watch, it'll be a wonderful way of converting working-class militants into middle-class politicians.

WILDE: And what about this alliance between the intellectuals and the working class?

WALLACE: I think you and your rent boys just about summed it up. The most we can hope for is a rather more humane form of capitalism.

WILDE: Don't be absurd, Richard: that's not worth hoping for at all. That's like saying the most you can hope for is to get the pox in one ball only. If you're going to hope, do it on a grand scale: hope for a society where every man and woman will be allowed to be themselves.

WALLACE: You're not telling me you're still a utopianist, Oscar, after all you've been through? My God, that really would be the final perversion: Oscar Wilde, run out by the Establishment and starry-eyed about a socialist Britain.

WILDE: Oh, I have hope, Richard – a lot of it. Not for myself, of course. But you surely don't imagine that in a hundred years from now homosexuals in England will still be hounded? It's too absurd. There'll be an end to this long stupidity; we don't still burn witches, do we? In a century from now everyone will be androgynous, the workers will run society, and the government will be paying Ireland a million pounds' reparation a year. If the Archbishop of Canterbury still exists, he'll be a raving queen in fish-net stockings and a big floppy hat. Nobody will remember the Empire, industrial labour will be entirely automated, and everyone will just lie around all day in loose crimson garments reciting Dante to each other. That'll just be the working day; I won't begin to describe the leisure activities.

WALLACE: Well, Oscar, you never cease to amaze me. I suppose exile has given you a lot of time to dream.

WILDE: You used to dream too, Richard. I can dream because I've nothing to lose – I'm a man with a great future behind me. Whereas you look to me like a man with something to lose – that rather fine suit, for a start.

WALLACE: I inherited my father's business a couple of years ago.

WILDE: I see.

WALLACE: Well, Engels was a capitalist.

WILDE: And who's going to speak up for the workers?

WALLACE: Not me any longer, I'm afraid. And not you either, stuck out here in Paris.

WILDE: I'm speaking up for them just by sitting here. They've read about what happened to me, I suppose; that should open their eyes a bit wider.

WALLACE: They'd probably denounce you as a demon.

WILDE: I doubt it. They know the people who sentenced me are the same kind as their bosses. I told you once I was prefiguring the New Jerusalem by doing nothing; well, that's what I'm doing right now.

WALLACE: You don't look to me much like an image of the future, Oscar.

WILDE: I'm an image of the failure of the present. That's the only image of the future worth having. (*Pause.*) Have you heard anything of Bosie?

WALLACE: Not much. I heard he'd had the cheek to dedicate a volume of poetry to you. And that he sold an article about you both to a newspaper for some astronomical sum.

WILDE: I heard that too. He was never so fascinated by me when we were together.

WALLACE: Have you seen anything of him?

WILDE: A bit: we got back together for a while, in Naples. Then I ran out of money and he deserted me.

WALLACE: Oscar, that was madness. You might as well drink arsenic straight off.

WILDE: Oh, I know. He's a venomous little megalomaniac who deserves to burn in hell-fire. There's a kind of insanity about his rages; they're more like epilepsy than anger. He's not right in the head, just like his father. The whole of the English aristocracy is mentally ill; that's why they drawl so much. It's a symptom of mental disorder; if they were bank clerks they'd be sent for speech therapy.

WALLACE: But you still can't put him behind you.

WILDE: Oh no; he's my fate, my demon. I won't ever be able to shake him off. He once physically attacked me when I had high fever in a hotel room, and I managed to crawl to the manager and get him to hire me a cab. But even as I drove away I was missing him. I love him, Richard; it's entirely out of my hands.

WALLACE: I hear Queensberry still has private detectives on your trail.

WILDE: That's right – just in case I try to kidnap his little boy. They're probably hanging around out there right now.

WALLACE: Oscar, is there anything I can do? We all feel so desperate about you.

WILDE: Yes, you could do something, Richard. You could stay with me for a week – keep me company, take me to the theatre. I'm so much on my own. But of course that's the last thing I can ask you; it wouldn't be too good for business for the boss to be seen consorting with a notorious pederast.

WALLACE: Have you no other friends here? Nobody you can go to?

WILDE: It's the English I miss, and they're the ones who avoid me. Prison only starts once you come out; being inside's a picnic compared to that.

WALLACE: I have to go, Oscar; my friends'll be waiting. If there's anything else I can do . . .

WILDE: You could leave me a bit more money.

WALLACE: I'd be glad to.

(*He places more money on the table.*)

WILDE: And you could take a message to Bosie. Tell him . . .

WALLACE: What?

WILDE: No, it doesn't matter. Tell him nothing.

WALLACE: (*Taking his hand*) Goodbye, Oscar. God bless you.

(*Exit* WALLACE.)

WILDE: When I was in prison I used to think I was Jesus Christ. Well, I'm not, but then neither was he.

I'm dying out here. The clap has finally caught up with me. A legacy from Oxford, along with my MA; they both cost me a fiver. It's strange, hardly anyone knows how to die effectively; they just let it happen to them, like measles. A pity, really, since it's the only dramatic event in most people's lives. They ought to take lessons in it; they don't realize death is something you have to *do*. There are only two rules in life: the first is to make an aesthetically memorable exit. If they shoot you, remember to fall in an interesting posture; don't leave your arse in the air or your tongue lolling out. The second rule nobody's discovered yet. Well, death won't catch me napping. I'll watch it creep up on me out of the corner of my eye, pretend I haven't seen it, and then when it's about to pounce seize it by the neck and force it into my service. My last stage; my finest performance. What a magnificent pose: to disappear for ever and ever. Never to be at home to callers, refusing all invitations, playing impossible to get. I'll be the most sought-after man in Society; giving everybody the cold shoulder. The last mask is the death mask. I'll sail off into the artifice of eternity; emigration was always the Irish way out. The last thing I shall lose is my composure. No giving in; no surrender.

CARSON'S VOICE: That's right, Oscar. No surrender.

(*Lights up on* CARSON *in paramilitary uniform.*)

WILDE: So it's you, Ned. Well, I must say the cap suits you better than that silly old wig.

CARSON: The law's all very well in its place, Oscar. But there are times when it needs to arm itself with the sword.

WILDE: You always did adore dressing up, Ned. Barrister, preacher, politician. You're just like me, really: always the play-actor. There wasn't much dividing us in that courtroom. And how carefully you've hung on to your brogue. It must go down a treat at Westminster and the Inns of Court.

CARSON: I speak like the Irishman I am. That's more than can be said for you.

WILDE: A stage Irishman, Ned; like me in that too – except that you've made more money out of it. I speak for Ireland in an English accent; you defend the Crown in a Dublin one. We're both topsy-turvy.

CARSON: Was it reparation for Ireland you were talking about? Oh, there'll be reparation all right. If the British sell out the Union they'll be repaying with their blood down through the generations.

WILDE: Why did you put me away, Ned? Why did they need another Irishman to turn the spit? Do I threaten your manhood?

CARSON: I don't give a damn about your sex life. I took the brief because you had to be put out of harm's way. I had the best tongue for the purpose – the only one to vie with your own. The English do well to leave their rhetorical dirty work to us.

WILDE: Tell me why I do harm.

CARSON: Because you don't belong anywhere; because you have no faith. We're moving into dark times, Oscar; harsh times. There'll be no lying around all day reciting Dante. The people must stand fast: they need to work and believe and belong. Every word you write shits on their fidelity. There'll be no place for your kind in the new order.

WILDE: I didn't notice all that much elbow-room in the old.

CARSON: Do you know what I say to the people, Oscar? I tell them that this is our territory: British soil. Our fathers planted and nurtured it and handed it down to us as a sacred trust. When they ditched and ploughed, it was God's hand that worked through theirs. His sweat was in their sweat, his sinew in their sinew. There are no moral books, there are no immoral books, there is no boss and no worker, there is neither sexual normality nor sexual perversion. There is only loyalty and betrayal.

WILDE: I see you've been taking a bath in the blood of the Lamb, Ned. I preferred you when you were a vegetarian.

CARSON: The valleys of Ulster are his open book, the farmsteads of Ulster are his flesh. That's what I tell the people.

WILDE: And you don't believe a word of it.

CARSON: Maybe not. But I know what the people need, I know the truth they need. What are you offering them, Oscar? Freedom? They'd wither of it in six months. They ask for bread and you give them cake. Without vision the people perish.

WILDE: What are you defending them against, Ned? Irony?

CARSON: Yes. And wit and art and pleasure. All the precious things we talked of into the night at Trinity. You're an artist, Oscar, which means you're faithless. The people need their fictions of order and all you give them is chaos. What right have you to deprive them of their graven images? Your quips do well enough for the London theatre public – there's nothing at stake for them. There's no call for mythology in the middle of Chelsea. But we must keep your wit out of Ireland. I saw a chance to shut your mouth for ever, so I moved fast.

WILDE: So you hobnob with a bunch of thugs in orange sashes chanting 'Kick the Pope'. It's unworthy of you, Ned. We talked about Aristotle at Trinity.

CARSON: Oh yes, I can't stand the stink of them. But they believe in order. There's no meaning without order. Maybe there's no meaning anyway, but unless we have order we'll never find out.

WILDE: We talked about Shakespeare too.

CARSON: There's only one work of art, Oscar, and that's the future. One nation, one heart, one blood beating together. It's clear and luminous and it's beautiful. The future is a work of art, Oscar; artists have no place in that. That's why you're dying here; you're dying of your infidelity.

WILDE: I'm dying of the clap.

CARSON: It's all one.

(*He makes to move off.*)

WILDE: Don't go, Ned; don't leave me here in the darkness. You wouldn't abandon your old Oscar, would you? Give me your hand, Ned. (*Stretches out his arm.*) No loyalty, no betrayal; just friendship. *Our* friendship, Ned.

CARSON: You lived a fantasist, Oscar, and you'll die one. It's too late for that.

(*Lights down on* CARSON.)

WILDE: Poor Ned. It was all because I knocked his sand-castle over in Dungarvan. I want them to write on my tombstone: 'Here lies Oscar Wilde, poet and patriot.' No, that's a bit terse; not true either. How about: 'Here lie the two Oscar Wildes: social-ite and sodomite, Thames and Liffey, Jekyll and Hyde, aristo-crat and underdog.' I could have a double grave and a double monument; friends could choose which one to mourn at, or alternate between the two. Or perhaps I could select one of my epigrams; number 83 would do nicely, I think. Let's see, number 83; how does it go again? Number 83 . . . Don't say words are failing me; I refuse to believe it. I shall be declaim-ing as they shovel me down; in the grave I'll be crawling with words. My oratory will seep through the soil like snowdrops. If I have to go down, I'll go down writing.

Any epigram will do. Ah no, let them just write: 'He camped it up.' Oedipus, bloody eyed. My father blinded the King of Sweden. The body of my country. A cock and a cunt together. They screamed and tried to kill me. It took them a long time but they managed it in the end. Gone in the teeth, the testicles; poemless, penniless. I shall have the last word. I'm the only character in this little charade. I shall have the last . . . true . . . word. Let's see. (*Raises his head with an effort.*) Ah yes. 'The English believe that blood will out. Pity it had to be mine.'

(*He smiles to himself. The* CHORUS *enters in carnivalesque dress. They dance around the slumped figure of Wilde, singing.*)

(Chorus)
He's on his way to heaven to chase the cherubim.
He'll be chatting up Saint Anthony to tempt him into sin.
His tomb it lies in Paris, if you visit it one day
Sure you'll find the place is empty and the stone is rolled away.
  So here's a health to Oscar, here's looking at you kid,
  When you see just what you started you'll be proud of what you did.
  There's Prods and Papes together a-dancing in the street,
  The blind have got their eyesight and the cripples find their feet.

The babes kiss politicians and promise them the earth,
The women fill the boozers while the men are giving birth.
The duke leaves lipstick traces on the duchess's moustache,
The beggars ride in limos while the bankers shovel trash.
  So here's a health to Oscar . . .

The fox pursues the huntsman, the lion flees the lamb,
The Pope is six months' pregnant but he doesn't give a damn.
The Ayatollah's pissed again, the judge is doing time
And Wall Street's never been the same since work was made a crime.
  So here's a health to Oscar . . .

The Germans they've turned giddy, the French have jacked in sex,
There's passion down in Pimlico, desire in Middlesex.
The Japanese don't show for work, the Russians take the pledge,
Old Santa shoots the kiddies down and smashes up his sledge.
  So here's a health to Oscar . . .

The Brits are emigrating to Cashel and to Cork,
They dig the streets of Dublin though they're none too keen on
    work.
In Maidenhead and Margate the kiddies in their school
Are taught to speak the Irish and learn Churchill was a fool.
   So here's a health to Oscar . . .

The Dalai Lama's stripping twice nightly in Pigalle,
The Queen is turning somersaults and busking in the Mall.
The rich sleep under cardboard, the poor are off to Greece.
They're having fun in Brixton planting dope upon the police.
   So here's a health to Oscar, here's looking at you kid,
     When you look down from heaven you'll be proud of what you
      did.
   There's Prods and Papes together a-dancing in the street,
   The blind have got their eyesight and the cripples find their feet.

CURTAIN

———————◆———————

The White, the Gold and the Gangrene

———◆———

James Connolly was born in Edinburgh of Irish parents and became Ireland's greatest socialist thinker and organizer. He led the assault on the Dublin Post Office in 1916 and was shot in the foot by British forces. Unable to stand for his execution, he was shot sitting in a chair. The popular outcry which followed this event, along with the execution of the other leaders of the 1916 Easter Rising, led to the Irish war of independence and the founding in 1921 of the Irish Free State.

The White, the Gold and the Gangrene was first performed by Dubbeljoint Theatre Productions at An Chultúrlann, West Belfast, in March 1993. The cast was as follows:

McDAID	Dan Gordon
MATHER	Anthony Brophy
CONNOLLY	Tim Loane
LIAM	Ventriloquist's Dummy

Musical director	Neil Martin
Lighting and sound	Sean Pagel
Director	Pam Brighton

ACT ONE

The actors playing MCDAID, MATHER *and* LIAM *gather on stage with musical instruments. Back-projection: 'The Ballad of Big JC'. The verses are spoken not sung, by each actor in turn, in the drawling style of an American folk ballad; choruses sung in unison.*

The Ballad of Big JC

He stood five foot four in his Cuban heels
'Cos he spent his childhood short of meals
There wasn't much fat from the Forth to the Clyde
Except for the rats who were five foot wide
And chewed the babies till they died
Big Jim

(Chorus) *Big Jim, big Jim, big bold Jim.*

His daddy took him on his knee
Said son don't you take after me
Shovelling shit for the corporation
Find some cushier avocation
How about a hero of the Irish nation?
Jim

(Chorus) *Big Jim . . .*

Well being a hero I'll admit
'S got no more future than shovelling shit
But there's a deal of job satisfaction
Fighting the forces of reaction
You get canonized if you die in action
Jim

(Chorus) *Big Jim . . .*

So Jim hopped off to preach class war
In Mayo and in Mullingar
He read about profit and exploitation
Labour and class and state and nation
And a little bit of Hegel for recreation
Jim

(Chorus) *Big Jim . . .*

> An invite came from Patrick Pearse
> Who loved his country something fierce:
> 'We're having a rising tomorrow at three
> By ten past four we'll all be free
> Bring the kids and the missis RSVP'
> Big Jim

(Chorus) *Big Jim . . .*

> They had that old post office sussed
> But Britannia wouldn't bite the dust
> So they marched old Jimmy off to gaol
> For interfering with the mail
> Don't reckon there's much chance of bail
> Big Jim

(Chorus) *Big Jim . . .*

> So here he lies before your eyes
> If you don't die you'll never rise
> To rise in the world you carry a hod
> But Jim's gonna rise to a firing squad
> If Asquith don't act fast – or God
> Big Jim

(Chorus) *Big Jim, big Jim, big bold Jim.*

(A penny whistle pipes up chirpily with the first two lines of 'The Red Flag', moving directly into a quavering, tentative rendering of the first five notes of 'The Soldier's Song'.

Actors exit. Lights slowly up on a prison cell, of surreal appearance. Bed, table, a few chairs, a door left. To the right, a space representing the prison yard, with a bizarrely bullet-holed wall. Bring up distant sounds of gun-fire, shouting. CONNOLLY *is lying on the bed asleep, his left ankle heavily bandaged and blood-stained. Fade sounds of gun-fire.*

Enter MCDAID, *dressed like a cross between a warder and a soldier, a rifle slung over one shoulder, carrying a breakfast tray. He puts down the tray on the table, then unslings his rifle and places it on the table next to the tray.)*

MCDAID: *(To himself, meditatively, as if memorizing)* Now that's the breakfast *(points)* and that's the rifle *(points again)*.

(He comes over to the bed, looks down on CONNOLLY *for a while*

and releases a sentimental 'Aaaah', as one might over a sleeping child. Then he stoops suddenly, puts his mouth to CONNOLLY's *ear and lets out an ear-piercing yell.)*

CONNOLLY: (*Sitting up in fright, Scottish accent*) Whaa? What is it?

McDAID: Rise and shine, Jimmy; time to get up and be shot.

CONNOLLY: What time is it?

McDAID: Relax, Jim, I was only kidding. We can't shoot you without your consent. What do you think we are, savages?

CONNOLLY: What do you mean, consent?

McDAID: (*Pulling a form from his pocket*) Government issue C-stroke-8295-stroke-BW; Consent to be Executed. You have to sign it, it's regulations. (*Takes out pen and hands it with form to* CONNOLLY.) Here you are, scrawl your X on the bottom of this; press hard now, it has to come through underneath.

CONNOLLY: What are you playing at, McDaid?

McDAID: I told you, we need your consent to be shot – it's just routine. Come on, don't be awkward; I don't make the rules, I just execute them – and the prisoners. (*Brief laugh at own joke.*)

CONNOLLY: You need my consent to be executed?

McDAID: Well OK, strictly speaking we don't *need* it. I mean if you're going to get all bureaucratic and neo-scholastic about this, then no, technically speaking not. But there's more to life than bare necessity. An execution without the condemned man's consent is neither improper, invalid nor particularly unusual, but it's far from ideal. From the moral standpoint it leaves something to be desired.

CONNOLLY: (*Lying down again*) Why don't you just leave off?

McDAID: You see, Jim, you think of the law as impersonal, unfeeling, because you're a bastard rebel and a Marxist scumbag and all that (*unemotional*). But the law has its feelings: it likes a spot of affection, a spark of sympathy, a bit of a cuddle just like anyone else. It doesn't like having to wave a big stick; if it does, it's failed, people lose faith in it. The law wants your allegiance, Jim; it wants you to look it in the eyes and whisper that you've understood. You think it enjoys doing what it has to do? How would *you* like to go around with everybody pointing and jeering and saying look at that mad bastard, he takes people out and shoots them without their consent?

CONNOLLY: I'm not signing.

McDAID: You'll feel better if you do; you don't want to die all bitter and unregenerate.

CONNOLLY: I don't consent.

McDAID: You haven't got a drop of compassion in your body, have you? Callous bastard. (*Moves towards door.*) I'm going to have to take instructions from the Governor on this one. (*Takes rifle from table.*) Your breakfast's over there.

CONNOLLY: I can't reach it.

McDAID: I'll eat it myself, then.

CONNOLLY: Have you spat in it?

McDAID: Spat in it? Why should I do that if I'm going to eat it myself?

(MCDAID *exits, whistling a rebel song. In a few moments* MATHER *enters, whistling the continuation of the same tune. Same build, uniform and general appearance as* MCDAID; *as far as possible he keeps his face averted from the audience as he comes in. Sits down, takes an apple and a knife from his pocket and begins to peel the apple.*)

CONNOLLY: (*After a pause*) So?

MATHER: So what?

CONNOLLY: That was quick.

MATHER: What was quick?

CONNOLLY: I thought you were going to see the Governor.

MATHER: What would I be doing seeing the Governor? (*Comes over to bed.*) Are you hallucinating again?

CONNOLLY: You're not . . . are you . . . was I just talking . . . ?

MATHER: Sorry, I should introduce myself – Francis Xavier Mather. (*Shakes hands.*) Pleased to make your acquaintance, however brief. How's it going?

CONNOLLY: You look just like –

MATHER: (*Sharply*) No remarks of a personal nature!

CONNOLLY: Where's McDaid?

MATHER: He just slipped out. (*Pause.*) When are you due?

CONNOLLY: You tell me.

MATHER: You look pretty close to me.

CONNOLLY: How do you know?

MATHER: You get a nose for these things. What's your name?

CONNOLLY: James Connolly.

MATHER: (*Surprised*) What, *the* James Connolly?

CONNOLLY: I suppose so.

MATHER: The James Connolly who used to run a vegetable stall in
Moore Street?

CONNOLLY: No.

MATHER: Ah, well there you are. I thought you might have known my
uncle; he was a solicitor's clerk in Ballinasloe.
(*Re-enter* MCDAID; *places rifle on table.*)

MCDAID: It's alright, you can forget it, you had your chance. If you
won't sign you won't sign.

CONNOLLY: So what happens?

MCDAID: We're going to have to use coercion. It'll mean a lot of
rethinking – a lot of reorganizing.

CONNOLLY: I don't see why.

MCDAID: A consensual and a coercive execution may look the same
to the untutored eye, old son, but that's a blatantly superficial
judgement. The whole spirit of the thing is different, which
affects the various modes of strategic address, calibrations
and projections. There's a lot of technical retooling involved
here, Jim; you've just lobbed a spanner in the whole fucking
works.

CONNOLLY: Would you get me my breakfast?

MCDAID: (*To* MATHER) Get the man his breakfast. (MATHER *brings the
breakfast tray over to* CONNOLLY.)

MCDAID: You couldn't spare a piece of toast, could you?

CONNOLLY: Alright.

MCDAID: (*Comes over and takes a piece of toast; to* MATHER) Fancy a
piece of toast?

MATHER: Alright. (MCDAID *throws him one, leaving none for* CONNOLLY.
They munch in silence for a while.)

MCDAID: (*To* CONNOLLY) How's the foot?

CONNOLLY: It's bleeding.

MCDAID: Empty your sock.

MATHER: You were lucky they didn't amputate.

MCDAID: They couldn't.

MATHER: Too far gone?

MCDAID: Regulations. (*Pulls book of rules from pocket.*) Let's see.
(*Wets thumb and leafs through book.*) Aliens, Borstal, delirium
tremens, treatment of prisoners, escape, prevention and punishment of (*flicks back*), censorship, condemned prisoners.
Rule 534 (*reads*): 'For execution to be deemed effective life
must be extinguished absolutely and without reasonable

chance of retrieval in each and every part of the prisoner's person including all internal organs surfaces and orifices together with all extraneous tissue and external appurtenances not excluding pathological protuberances and excrescences but without detriment to all inorganic supplements and appendages such as dentures, prostheses and the like' – on to footnote 127 – 'The latter term to be taken as encompassing glass eyes and artificial hairpieces.' (*Shuts book.*) Well, that seems clear enough, right? No shilly-shallying there. But in this particular case it raises a nasty little problem.

MATHER: How do you mean?

McDAID: I mean how can you execute a man if there's a piece of him missing?

MATHER: You execute what's left; there's no problem in that.

McDAID: Not according to footnote 28. (*Reads.*) 'For the purposes of these regulations the prisoner's life shall be deemed to exist whole and entire in each and every portion of his person however peripheral, dysfunctional or otherwise rudimentary.' You see? You've got to kill the whole of him; the foot can't be allowed to escape. The foot can't be criminalized.

MATHER: The whole of him as at present constituted.

McDAID: You're not telling me that a man with his foot off constitutes a whole person?

MATHER: He's whole enough *for him*. That's the whole of him as of the present moment in time.

McDAID: So a pint with three sups out of it is a whole pint?

MATHER: It is so; it's whole and entire with respect to itself.

McDAID: A one-wheeled bicycle is a whole bicycle? An orange with no peel, pips, flesh or juice is still an orange?

MATHER: In a certain conception of it.

McDAID: Well I won't be accepting an invitation to *your* picnic.

MATHER: It's a question of time-scale: the condemned man possesses his organs *retrospectively*.

McDAID: So he still possesses the pimples he had at the age of fifteen? Do you execute those too? How far back do you stretch?

MATHER: To the moment of sentencing. The organs which are executed are all such as he was furnished with when he stood in the dock.

McDAID: What if he had a boil on his bum and now it's gone? Does that render the execution invalid?

MATHER: You can't push it that far. On that hypothesis you can never execute anybody.

McDAID: I don't see why.

MATHER: Because the man who stood in the dock is never exactly the man who faces the firing squad. His cellular structure has subtly altered in the interim.

McDAID: So no condemned prisoner is ever executed?

MATHER: Strictly speaking, that's the case.

McDAID: Hey, Jim, we've got some good news for you.

MATHER: I'm not saying it's unproblematic.

McDAID: It's a clear dilemma. If you kill the foot, you can't kill the prisoner, and if you don't kill it, you can't kill him because he'll probably die anyway.

MATHER: It takes a clear mind.

McDAID: You won't solve that little conundrum between biting your nails and spitting them out.

MATHER: That's another thing.

McDAID: What?

MATHER: Nails; hair.

McDAID: They come under extraneous tissue.

MATHER: They go on growing after he's dead. You can't blast a man's beard into eternity with a bullet. It'd be a fierce guillotine that could stop a full head of hair dead in its tracks.

McDAID: That's true enough. There's no way you can execute a man's toenails.

MATHER: They're beyond the jurisdiction of the law – an inherently anarchic appendage.

McDAID: It's a very shoddily framed regulation; I must alert the Home Secretary to it.

MATHER: Though you can always look at it this way: the hair stops growing *eventually*. That's not the same kettle of fish as an amputated foot.

McDAID: It's a fine-drawn distinction.

MATHER: It's a question of time-scale again. The hair is *potentially* dead – it's as good as dead.

McDAID: A donkey's potentially dead but you can still ride it. A woman's potentially dust and ashes but you can still take her to the pictures.

MATHER: That doesn't follow.

McDAID: A baby's a potential wife but I wouldn't walk one down the aisle.

MATHER: You can't take it to that extreme.

McDAID: (*Indicating* CONNOLLY *eating his food*) Would you not eat that breakfast because it's potentially shit?

MATHER: The act of execution extends forwards in time to encompass all of its future effects.

McDAID: So we're still shooting him two years later? We should put in for overtime.

MATHER: It's an ongoing process. The executed corpses in the prison cemetery are still in a certain sense living out their sentences.

McDAID: So they could come up for parole?

MATHER: Not for good conduct; they don't have sufficient conduct to be assessed. But strictly speaking you could exhume a man's sideburns and grant them a posthumous pardon.

McDAID: That's prejudicial to the clean-shaven.

MATHER: To execute a man is to grant him a stay of execution; there's a humanitarian component built into the act.

McDAID: An escape clause.

MATHER: Precisely.

McDAID: Death is not the end.

MATHER: Far from it. Life is a deferment of sentence and so is death.

McDAID: Nature abhors a vacuum.

MATHER: Things only happen once they're over; that's when the sausage hits the pan.

McDAID: That's when you have to run for cover.

MATHER: Life is lived backwards, causes construed from effects.
(*Pause.*)

McDAID: Were you around when old Damian Flannery was banged up in here?

MATHER: I was not.

McDAID: He was in for twelve years – robbery with violence. But he didn't have a sound limb on his body; gangrene in the lot of them. You could smell him at a hundred paces. So they amputated his right arm and Flannery asked them to send it to his old Ma as a sort of momento. Kind of a little bit of him to be going on with.

MATHER: It's not in the regulations.

McDAID: Well they did it anyway: humanitarian grounds. His old mother was dying.

MATHER: What of?

McDAID: Gangrene; it's genetic. Then old Flannery's left arm starts flaking to ribbons and they had to amputate that too. So he asked them to send that to his mother as well.

MATHER: And they did?

McDAID: They did so; there seemed no harm in it. Polished it up a bit and popped it in a parcel. Suspicion didn't set in until his left leg went on the blink.

MATHER: Did they send that off too?

McDAID: They did not; they'd finally got wise to him. The Governor goes to Flannery and says, 'Alright, Damian, we've rumbled your little game: you're trying to escape.'

MATHER: And was he?

McDAID: You bet he was. Couple more operations and the crafty sod would have been out.

(CONNOLLY *gives a loud groan and tosses violently.*)

McDAID: (*Coming over to him*) Histrionics will get you nowhere.

CONNOLLY: What time is it?

McDAID: It'd be a wise man could solve *that* little conundrum between taking a leak and buttoning up his trousers.

CONNOLLY: What day is it?

MATHER: Do you have any last requests?

CONNOLLY: What kind of requests?

MATHER: There are a number of possibilities.

CONNOLLY: I'd like to see my wife.

MATHER: You're allowed to cradle a new-born baby government issue in your arms for three minutes if you're that way inclined.

CONNOLLY: I've got a fever.

MATHER: Or you can choose between a quick blast of Beethoven's 'Pastoral', a short recitation from *The Eighteenth Brumaire of Louis Bonaparte* or a reading from any part of the Old Testament excluding the salacious bits of Leviticus. (*Pause.*) No?

McDAID: We can join you in a brief *pasa doblé* around the cell. Or my colleague here is prepared to perform rebel songs, 'The Croppy Boy' and 'My Old Fenian Gun' a speciality. He's even prepared to dance the cancan if you ask him nicely. If that doesn't suit you, we're willing to listen to any last whinings and bellyachings with averted yet compassionate countenances, recount amusing anecdotes, endure a few balls-aching childhood reminiscences or engage you in a spot of non-genital tickling.

MATHER: How about a view of an ineffectually executed charcoal drawing which might just possibly be your old Ma? (*Pause.*) He's not entranced.

McDAID: You are allowed two minutes wearing an item selected from a wardrobe we have outside the door containing an array of bizarre, alluring and otherwise unconventional garments including a stove-pipe hat, an illuminated revolving dickey bow, a cut-away suede leather jock-strap and a First Communion dress.

MATHER: Or for those of a more Proustian sensibility we have a range of bottled smells comprising ozone, boot polish, the fragrant whiff of fresh print, a waft of Glaswegian dogshite and the honest sweat of a Bulgarian bricklayer's armpit.

McDAID: Recorded sounds are also to hand, ranging from the whine of distant bagpipes, the grunt and slither of sexual intercourse, to the voice of Lord Alfred Tennyson reciting what could either be 'Maud' or 'The Charge of the Light Brigade'. Alternatively, my colleague and I are prepared to imitate the sound of sea-gulls, Herbert Asquith, the voices of any of your children or a swing plough being bumped softly across a field in Connemara, if you require something of a less mechanical nature.

MATHER: We are also permitted to engage in simulated sexual intercourse or lay on Holy Communion.

CONNOLLY: Would you hand me my rosary beads?

McDAID: We will not, for reasons which will become clear later in the proceedings.

MATHER: How about a quick foxtrot?

CONNOLLY: Can I ask about the execution?

MATHER: Technically or physiologically but not morally or politically.

CONNOLLY: What do you mean?

McDAID: You're not allowed to pass comments like 'I'm a victim of British imperialism' or 'This is a grotesque travesty of justice'.

CONNOLLY: Why not?

McDAID: Why not? Because they're *clichés*, that's why not.

MATHER: You don't want to die with a cliché stuck in your gob. Now is the time to think creatively.

McDAID: Now is the time to die to the old man and rise to new life. That way you'll escape the firing squad, since it's the old man we're shooting.

MATHER: You're permitted to ask the prison philosopher any questions concerning the meaning of life, if it isn't already transparently clear to you.

McDAID: Do you mind if I ask *you* a question?

CONNOLLY: What is it?

McDAID: This little rising of yours – was it *intended* to be a balls-up? (*Pause.*) I mean, did you set out deliberately to make the most almighty fucking cock-up of the whole affair? Was that part of a considered strategy?

CONNOLLY: It remains to be seen.

McDAID: You got the wrong day, didn't you? Supposed to be Easter Sunday and it happened on the Monday. Jesus, you lot'd be late for your own resurrections. Can you imagine Christ over-sleeping in the tomb? Wakes up, looks at his watch, panic, 'Oh Jesus it's Monday, I was supposed to nip up and see me old father yesterday.' Does that have the authentic scriptural resonance?

MATHER: They were late for their own revolution. 'Sorry, comrade, my bicycle broke down on the way, just warm them up with a bit of patter and I'll be there when they dish out the Minis-tries.' Wankers.

McDAID: Though they say they might have blundered.

MATHER: Who?

McDAID: The women – the ones who came to the tomb. They didn't find Jesus, they found this young feller there instead. So they asked him where Jesus was and he said 'He is not here.' From which they drew a highly tenuous conclusion.

MATHER: How do you mean?

McDAID: Your man didn't mean 'He's gone to heaven' – he meant 'He's in the *next* tomb. This is my tomb, he's one along.' It was dark, you see; they couldn't read the directions properly. A lot of things might have turned out different if they'd had a torch.

CONNOLLY: (*In a low voice*) I don't know whether anything happened or not.

MATHER: Jesus, he volunteered an entire sentence.

McDAID: You mean the resurrection?

CONNOLLY: There was a cart, jerking along with one wheel buckled. A youg girl shouting something, a boy selling newspapers, the post office steps gleaming in the rain. A few catcalls, a per-functory burst of applause. I lay with my nose squashed against the kerb and my ankle exploding in flame.

MATHER: He's hallucinating again.

CONNOLLY: Was it me lying there? Did it happen some other time? How can I know whether anything happened or not?

MATHER: There's no easy answer to that.

McDAID: How do we ever know?

MATHER: Maybe you'll know retrospectively – when it's all over. But of course then you'll be dead, so you won't. So as far as you're concerned, Jim, nothing happened; nothing will ever have happened.

McDAID: You're still looking for meaning. Why don't you knock it off?

MATHER: Why don't you just let go? If you could let go of that, you'd be free.

McDAID: It was a carnival, Jimmy; a circus, a theatre, a five-day orgy. There was humping in Grafton Street and the slums were awash with whiskey. It was the moment will live for ever, not its effects; isn't that enough for you?

CONNOLLY: I have to know what happened.

MATHER: It was a thing in itself; there was no rhyme or reason. Stop looking for a story for it to belong to.

McDAID: It's raining outside, Jim; do you think that's trying to tell us something? Oh, maybe it was different in the old days. In the old days the world was story-shaped, there was a plot to it all. The meeting at the crossroads, the leer of a beggar, the sudden swoop of an eagle: none of it was accidental. Everything was luminous and legible, everything was a sign of something else. It all slotted exquisitely together. That was a long time ago, Jim; there's no grand narrative any more. Just a cart, and the steps, and a girl shouting in the rain.

MATHER: Accept that and you'll be free. Accept that and they'll have no power over you.

McDAID: You did something magnificent, Jimmy: you hoisted yourselves out of history. You shot at the clocks and blasted yourselves out of time. Why fumble for a future? Think of the future and the whole meaning of it goes down the shoot.

MATHER: The whole meaningless meaning of it.

CONNOLLY: Have they shot Pearse yet?

MATHER: You were free for a moment; don't lose grip of it now. Don't thin it all down with meaning; don't look for a story to bury it in.

McDAID: It's a natural impulse of the mind.

MATHER: Natural? Of course it's natural. The mind revolts at brute events, it can't do anything with them. We need our fictions of order, even if they're tales of chaos.

McDAID: So it reads a connection in. It was yourselves you were reading, not Mother Ireland.

MATHER: You stared in the mirror of history and fired at your own faces.

McDAID: You're just sleep-walking – dreaming your way into death. Don't try to wake up now.

MATHER: Don't try to peer over death's shoulder; there's no future, you just killed it.

McDAID: It was just a hiccup in history; a pimple on the face of time.

MATHER: It was magnificent; it was a work of art.

CONNOLLY: Are you British Intelligence?

McDAID: That's a contradiction in terms.

MATHER: We're just trying to help you make some non-meaning out of this.

McDAID: Eternity's not the future, Jim; think of the fruits of action and you're sunk. Eternity's this cell, you and us, here and now. Bite that to the core if you can; forget about cause and effect.

MATHER: Don't turn yourself into a chapter of history; history's a bitch. You launched yourself out of all that in the post office; don't try to re-enter. Just keep yourself suspended in space.

McDAID: And don't look to death to make it all real; death's the last thing you experience.

MATHER: We won't feel it, and neither will you; so it won't happen to anybody.

McDAID: Which means it won't happen at all. There now, isn't that a little ray of sunshine for you?

MATHER: Not one door closes but another shuts.

(*The door opens and someone throws in a small parcel, shouting 'Mail!' The three stand staring at the parcel.*)

McDAID: (*To* CONNOLLY) Well? What are you waiting for?

MATHER: Go fetch it, Jim.

CONNOLLY: I can't move.

McDAID: You need the exercise; it's good for the gangrene. There might be one from your wife.

(CONNOLLY *heaves himself with difficulty from the bed and crawls towards the parcel, dragging his wounded foot.* MATHER *follows him and snatches the parcel as* CONNOLLY *is about to pick it up.*)

MATHER: Prison regulation 737, prisoners not permitted to open their own mail. (*Pats* CONNOLLY *on head.*) Well done, good boy, back to bed with you now.

(CONNOLLY *makes his way laboriously back to bed;* MATHER *picks up parcel and looks through the letters.*)

Alright, let's see what we've got here. Income tax return, you won't be needing that (*throws it aside*), Scottish Widows Insurance Fund, that might interest your wife; 'On the Point of Retiring?', I suppose you are but not in the way they have in mind (*throws aside*). Let's see, what's this (*opens letter, scans it*), somebody writing in from Ballydehob about a particularly thorny point in dialectical materialism (*throws aside, opens some more*), retired Brigadier from Swiss Cottage offering himself for the firing squad; young woman from Cork offering you a death-cell marriage, says she doesn't want to be tied down; obscene abuse from the Very Reverend Joseph A. Feeney of St Aidan's, Waterford, accompanied by sexually explicit sketches. Hello, what's this, a telegram from Moscow. (*Reads.*) 'Dear Comrade Connolly, I have often remarked that whoever dreams of a pure revolution will never live to see one. But dammit man, there *are* limits.' Signed V. I. Lenin, ever heard of him? Another telegram, this time from Italy, aren't you the popular lad? Know anyone called William Yeats? (*Reads.*) 'My dear Mr Connolly, I must protest at the way your uprising interrupted rehearsals at the Abbey Theatre of a play of mine concerning the regeneration of the Irish race. I am also dismayed that you commenced a revolution in Ireland without consulting me first. I am, I think, not unknown among the common people of this nation, and I am always pleased to bestow my patronage on any heroic undertaking which might restore them to their former greatness. If you wish to use my name on your letter-head or require a marching song or two, then I am your servant for a small fee. I can be contacted at The Tower, 37 Coole Park Cuttings, Gort, County Galway, under my mystical name Wilhelmus Lunaticus.

'As one who fathered this event in the dim womb of time, I feel a burden of responsibility for what may become of it. I have paced the great boards of my solitary chamber, those boards carved from an ancient oak Columba once blessed which echo still to the shouts of fighting men, the raillery of fools and the sighs of moonstruck girls with skins of alabaster, and asked myself in the great turmoil of my mind whether it was some work of mine, some gesture careless as a bird, which gave birth to this unmannerly clamour. Is it I, William Yeats, offspring of no huckster's loin, chip off no beggarly block, who am symbol of the coming times? Or will there be no place for me in the new republic because I am a pseudo-aristocratic Protestant with an effete hair-style and a purple cravat?

'I am persuaded by my researches into Bow-Legged Hennigan, the Great Ork of Kildoon and the Tibetan Book of the Dead that what Ireland has need of in these times is not the heart's bitter enmity nor the squabblings of shopkeepers but some great and simple wisdom, some antique joy as keen as a peasant's bright glance. Should you concur with these sentiments I am ready to take the next boat to Dublin and accept any humble place in your great venture you see fit to afford me, whether as President, *Führer*, Official Bard or Minister of Theosophy. Yours in Mad O'Brady of the Nine Tinctures, William Yeats.' That must have cost him a packet.

McDAID: Tampering with His Majesty's mail.

MATHER: Who?

McDAID: (*Indicating* CONNOLLY) His lot. That's what gets my goat.

MATHER: I understand your feeling.

McDAID: How can a man sleep easy in his bed when somebody's buggering up the post office?

MATHER: Post office! They couldn't knock off a frigging sweet-shop.

McDAID: You can't go meddling with the mail; letters are the life-blood of society. Show me a misaddressed missive and I'll show you a moral monstrosity.

MATHER: Huh?

McDAID: I receive your gas bill, you receive mine; I end up paying your rent, you find yourself footing the bill for my children's piano lessons. It strikes at the root of private property. Carry that to its logical conclusion and I end up sleeping with your wife.

MATHER: It's a reasonable hypothesis.

McDAID: It's an ineluctable fatality.

MATHER: I resent the implications of that remark.

McDAID: It was harmlessly intended.

MATHER: Are you suggesting that sleeping with my wife is not an action you would freely choose?

McDAID: I was illustrating a point in social theory.

MATHER: Was there some small hint in that comment that to be on sexually intimate terms with Mrs Mather is analogous in your own mind to being struck down with bubonic plague?

McDAID: You're reading that in.

MATHER: Was there just a faint suggestion that you wouldn't touch my old woman even if I turned down the blanket for you? Even if I sat there smoking a fag and gloating?

McDAID: Certainly not.

MATHER: Not even if I waved a twenty-pound note under your snout?

McDAID: You're straying beyond the bounds of propriety.

MATHER: I don't give a roasted fart for propriety; you keep your mitts off my wife.

McDAID: That's exactly my point. One misplaced mail-bag and you've got an outbreak of adultery on your hands.

MATHER: It doesn't follow.

McDAID: Let's say you write her love-letters and they get delivered to me. It subverts the natural bonds of society.

MATHER: It doesn't worry me unduly.

McDAID: The Post Office is a miracle of human reciprocity. It's the fundamental unit of social life. You pull the wrong lever in that particular works and what do you get? Chaos, cacophony: letters on the loose, metaphors with no fixed abode, improperly addressed polemics. Meanings wandering homeless in the street, beggarly postscripts, promiscuous paragraphs. Everyone taking in each other's dirty postcards. It's the thin end of the Bolshevik terror.

MATHER: It's a point of view.

McDAID: It's the end of personal identity as we know it. Let's say I get six letters a week addressed to some female. After a while I might begin to wonder whether some joker out there isn't casting aspersions.

MATHER: I'd have it out with him; I wouldn't take that lying down.

McDAID: You can't: they're anonymous. You can't know where a message is coming from.

MATHER: You can't tell whether something is meant or not.

(*Sudden blood-curdling scream off-stage.*)

CONNOLLY: What in the name of God was that?

McDAID: What?

CONNOLLY: Who was that, for Christ's sake?

MATHER: It's just routine.

CONNOLLY: Are they murdering somebody out there or what?

McDAID: (*To* MATHER) Who would you say that was?

MATHER: It's not a simple matter.

McDAID: Judging from pitch and duration I'd say it was MacBride.

MATHER: It's not the correct timbre.

McDAID: No, timbre's a different matter. When it comes to vocal texture I'd put my money on MacDonagh.

MATHER: He sounds a bit overwrought; they must have mentioned Cromwell to him by mistake.

CONNOLLY: Are you bastards torturing them out there?

McDAID: Why don't you take a look?

CONNOLLY: What?

McDAID: The cell door's open; go and look for yourself.

MATHER: Take your time over it; we wouldn't expect you back.

McDAID: That'd be a laugh.

MATHER: We'll carry the can; we'll say you overpowered us. You've got formidable biceps.

McDAID: We're giving you a break, Seamus. Look: we're turning our backs. (*Both turn their backs.*) We don't expect you to be here when we turn round.

CONNOLLY: I've heard that one before.

MATHER: We'll close our eyes and count to a hundred. Then it's coming-ready-or-not.

CONNOLLY: (*Lying back*) Why don't you leave off?

McDAID: (*Takes rifle from table, comes over to* CONNOLLY *and holds it to his head*) Well if you won't consent to escape, you leave us no choice but coercion. Up off the bed. Come on, man, shake a stump, shift your arse out of there.

CONNOLLY: Are you out of your mind?

McDAID: You've got fifty seconds to escape; that's a warning.

CONNOLLY: (*Turning over*) Well you'll have a long wait.

(McDAID *lays aside rifle; he and* MATHER *suddenly swoop on* CONNOLLY *and drag him to his feet.* MATHER *holds him up in an arm-lock,* McDAID *holds the rifle to his face.*)

McDAID: Now listen to me, you insubordinate scum: you're being ordered to escape. It's regulations, you can be shot for disobedience. Prisoner shot while attempting not to escape. Go on, get down on your knees, you tartan turd, you murdering piece of shite. (*They thrust* CONNOLLY *down on his knees;* McDAID *trains the rifle at his head.*) Now crawl. Come on, you useless streak of piss, get your thighs moving. (CONNOLLY *begins to crawl towards the door.*) That's the way, keep it moving. (*Prods him with rifle.*)

(CONNOLLY *starts to drip blood as he goes.*)

MATHER: (*Opening the door*) Look, the slimy bastard's leaving a trail.

CONNOLLY: I can't move . . . my leg . . .

(*He collapses.*)

McDAID: (*Yanking him up by the hair*) Come on, you Scotch shit-house, get out of it. Go and nose your way to freedom. (CONNOLLY *collapses again.*) He's a moral cripple.

MATHER: He's an ultra-leftist deviationist.

McDAID: He can't.

MATHER: (*Closing door*) He won't.

McDAID: He doesn't have it in him.

MATHER: Call yourself a dialectical materialist.

McDAID: We extended the hand of friendship and he spat in our face.

MATHER: He couldn't escape from a one-legged tortoise.

McDAID: Get him in the chair. (*They pull* CONNOLLY *up and carry him, moaning, to a chair.*) That's the way, easy does it. Now I want to know why you didn't take advantage of our generosity.

CONNOLLY: (*Head averted*) Leave me alone.

McDAID: That doesn't count as an answer.

CONNOLLY: Leave me be, you bastards.

McDAID: Should I tell you what you're afraid of, Jim? Being shot. And do you know what you're even more afraid of? Not being shot. (*Laughs uproariously.*) That's a good one. You're all the same, you lot; you're all in love with death. (*Prods him with rifle muzzle.*) You'd like me to stick my muzzle in your gob and jerk it around; you want the sweet rip of my bullet in the back of your throat. You'd like to wrap your great blubbery lips around my hard stem, you neo-Hegelian pervert. You want death to part its buttocks and let you disappear up its funnel for ever.

MATHER: It subverts the natural order of things.

McDAID: They marched out on Sackville Street: six minor poets, three asthmatic classicists, a couple of rubber daggers and a spavined republican tomcat. It wasn't spectacular, it wasn't sublime, it wasn't even bloody *tragic*. It was just embarrassing. And when the dust cleared, there was a solitary plaque on the wall: 'On this day, in Dublin 1916, Commandant-General James Connolly shot himself in the foot.'

MATHER: What happened to the paste?

McDAID: The paste?

MATHER: They had no paste. They had a cartful of posters proclaiming the revolution and nothing to stick them up with. Don't tell me that wasn't unconsciously intended; don't tell me that's how Augustus Caesar ran his Ministry of Works.

CONNOLLY: My foot's bleeding.

MATHER: Shake out your trousers.

McDAID: The show was fantastic, the script was brilliant if a trifle overblown; there was just no bleeding audience. Just rows of empty stalls like stacks of false teeth. Do you think *they* cared? Why didn't they just strangle each other behind the Gents lavatory and save the State some trouble?

MATHER: It was intended as symbolic.

McDAID: Symbols! They ought to slap a government health warning on that stuff in this country. Did you know that ten thousand people in Ireland died of symbolism last year? Symbolism of the liver, rhetoric of the lower bowel, allegory of the anus.

MATHER: Some revolutions are short on poetry; this one mislaid the bloody prose.

McDAID: They wanted to freeze time in mid-stride and twist it to their own image. But they faltered at the fatal moment; they turned and looked back.

MATHER: Looked back?

McDAID: Like Lot's wife. They couldn't resist a quick peek over their shoulder at the future; they were seduced by the life to come. So it was they who got frozen to stone, not history; they're trapped in a time-warp and history's just rumbling on.

MATHER: There's too much of it to destroy.

McDAID: Too much to control. You can't even control your own blood sugar; you can't pre-programme the effects of a fart.

MATHER: Oh, we can see how you're reckoning it, Jim. First the executions, then popular outcry, then the republic. It's a lot to stake on a single body; you're frail, you're feverish, you're only five foot four. There's many a slip in that little game.

McDAID: You brought yourselves to a standstill so you could put the skids under time. Well what if it sheers off in the wrong direction? Have you reckoned that into the equation?

MATHER: It's we who hold the future in our hands, not you. One nudge and we can alter the lot. It all unravels back to this cell, to what we do here and now. What if we lose that martyr's bullet – vanish it up our sleeve?

McDAID: If we don't kill you, then we kill the future; one false move with the forceps and it'll never get delivered. Just think how easy that would be; we could cut your throat and call it suicide. One minor adjustment in the here and now, one twiddle of the knob, and we wipe out the Irish language.

MATHER: Which would be as difficult as pulling the plug on a paraplegic.

McDAID: Just think of it, Jimmy: no presidential Paddy. No green
　　mailboxes for ever and ever. We can blow the future's brains
　　out with one lost bullet; now there's a power to envy.

MATHER: That's worth more than your Tones and O'Connells.

McDAID: And what if *you* twiddle the wrong knob? What if this time
　　machine of yours never takes off? It's a tricky operation:
　　catapulting yourself into the future, then turning round and
　　looking at how the planet will be in a century's time. What if
　　you just vanish for ever into thin air?

MATHER: What if you just land yourself back here for all eternity?

McDAID: Death's a dodgy launching pad. You think that if only we
　　bury you deep enough you can tunnel all the way through and
　　come out somewhere on the other side. Well maybe there
　　isn't another side; maybe you'll just hit rock-bottom.

MATHER: He's trapped; he can't escape.

McDAID: He's buggered if he does and he's buggered if he doesn't.

MATHER: It's a metaphysical dilemma.

McDAID: If you don't take yourself off, the thing will never have
　　meaning. But if you do, you won't be there to see it – so you'll
　　never know whether it was worth taking off in the first place.

CONNOLLY: It's a matter of faith.

MATHER: Prison regulations specifically prohibit blaspheming.

CONNOLLY: If you can forget about the future then it'll come. You
　　have to go into it empty-handed.

MATHER: Nobody can do that. *You* can't do it.

CONNOLLY: I can't know whether I'm doing it or not.

MATHER: But you're still hoping, aren't you? Looking for the flash of
　　light when you're up against the wall.

McDAID: The place where it all adds up. Except you won't be there to
　　do the adding.

MATHER: Nobody will be there. So it *does* add up – but not for anyone
　　in particular.

CONNOLLY: I think I'm going to keel over.

McDAID: Keel over? Why didn't you say so? Here, let's get him back
　　on the bed. (*They hoist him up.*) Just get your arm around my
　　shoulder, old pal. (*They carry him to the bed.*) That's the way,
　　easy does it. Oops-a-daisy. (*They lie him on the bed.*) Where's
　　the pillow? Oh sorry, there isn't one. Mather, get this man a
　　pillow.

MATHER: Can we fetch you some water? Brandy? Champagne?

McDAID: You've been a silly boy, Jim; you've tried to tough it out. If you're feeling a bit rough, just tell us for Jesus' sake, to hell with the old stiff upper lip.

MATHER: It's understandable.

McDAID: Understandable? It's bloody heroic. Here he is, leg hanging off, confronted with his own imminent demise, kicked around the place by a couple of sadistic bastards, and what does he say?

MATHER: Nothing.

McDAID: Meek as a little lamb. You have to hand it to him.

MATHER: It's unbelievable; I've never seen such resilience.

McDAID: I'd be begging for mercy; personally I'd be shitting myself. Just look at the dignity of the fellow. The cryptic composure of the Buddha.

MATHER: It restores your trust in human nature. It makes you think there might be something in what he says.

McDAID: How do you mean?

MATHER: You know: republicanism, all that.

McDAID: Something in it? Sweet Jesus, have you taken leave of your senses?

MATHER: It's just a hypothesis.

McDAID: You must be out of your skull, man. Of course there's something in it! There's a bloody sight more in it than the bleeding rule-book.

MATHER: Which, let's face it, represents the unacceptable face of colonialism. I mean, when all's said and done.

McDAID: Do you want to know what colonialism is? (*Dramatic pause.*) Colonialism is skunks like you and me, doing the imperialists' dirty work for them. Do you have the slightest cognizance of what we're engaged in here? We're engaged in the official murder of the greatest champion of our own people since Red Hugh O'Donnell. Now you just mull that one over and see if you can still look me in the eyes.

MATHER: We're just running dogs of imperialism. We'd execute St Patrick himself if they gave us time and a half.

McDAID: It's a miracle we can bear to look at ourselves. Is this what our nation has been reduced to? Have we really been brought so low?

MATHER: That's the true triumph of the conqueror, you see. Not the Penal Laws, not the suppression of our manufactures, not the gagging of our native tongue. It's the power to bring us to hate our own selves. Hate ourselves so much that we'd contemplate wielding the blood-stained axe of Britannia against one of our own kind.

MᴄDᴀɪᴅ: Because she's too bloody hypocritical to wield it herself.

Mᴀᴛʜᴇʀ: History will never forgive us for this.

MᴄDᴀɪᴅ: We make Judas Iscariot look like Baden-Powell.

Mᴀᴛʜᴇʀ: There'll be no Brownie points for us in the judgement of posterity.

MᴄDᴀɪᴅ: And do you know what the source of it all is? Do you know where it all stems from? Too much swanning around the Big House.

Mᴀᴛʜᴇʀ: Is that so?

MᴄDᴀɪᴅ: It was the cause of my own undoing. The hours I've frittered away in those accursed places, reclining on some antique *chaise longue* beneath the oil-paintings of horses, guzzling pheasant sandwiches from the hand of some delicate creature with eyes of aquamarine. The soft thud of croquet-balls amid the plashing of the fountains. And the talk – the endless talk into the small hours of Da Vinci and Madame Blavatsky, Homer and the price of a sack of horse manure. The young master of the house swaggering in from hounds, bronzed, flaxen, strangely chinless. And the old Earl himself in his snuff-stained waistcoat, one gouty foot up on a silver-tasselled pouffe, one gnarled hand at rest on the skull of a golden retriever. Culture was an impalpable taste on the air, the careless crook of a finger or curve of a waist. They evicted my father, they left the whole sixteen of us standing outside a burning cabin with only one pair of brogues between the lot of us, but by God the bastards had style.

Mᴀᴛʜᴇʀ: So you sold your soul for all that.

MᴄDᴀɪᴅ: I can't deny it; I have to confess I let it bedazzle me. It was those eyes of aquamarine that did for me entirely.

Mᴀᴛʜᴇʀ: And now look where we are.

MᴄDᴀɪᴅ: Screwed.

Mᴀᴛʜᴇʀ: About to top a man as spotless as Achilles.

MᴄDᴀɪᴅ: For thirty pieces of Britannia's coin.

Mᴀᴛʜᴇʀ: Are they paying you that much?

MᴄDᴀɪᴅ: I was speaking metaphorically.

Mᴀᴛʜᴇʀ: And what was his crime? To stand up for his country. To stand up there on the post office steps on his one good leg and summon Cuchulain to his side.

MᴄDᴀɪᴅ: You mean Pearse?

Mᴀᴛʜᴇʀ: Don't talk to me about that Nancy boy.

MCDAID: To stand there with the gore gushing from his trouser leg and proclaim the only enduring lesson that history has ever taught. Isn't it a curious thought now, that through all the varieties of human culture, through all the mutations and conflagrations and peregrinations of civilization, history has never ceased to whisper the one identical lesson into ears receptive enough to receive it?

MATHER: Which is?

MCDAID: Stick to your own kind. Stick to your own kind and you won't go far wrong.

MATHER: And for pronouncing that one simple truth they struck him down like our first martyr St Stephen. Who proclaimed the good news of our Blessed Saviour and got a gobful of rocks for his pains.

MCDAID: It isn't too late to turn back.

MATHER: You think not?

MCDAID: If there was grace for Mary Magdalen there'll be some juice in the bottom of the tank for us. Why don't we just tell the Governor to shove it? Why don't we tell him we won't serve?

MATHER: We've been slaves too long. Now is the time to stand up like men – like post-colonial subjects.
(*Three sudden beats at the cell door.* MATHER *and* MCDAID *move instantly into action.*)

MCDAID: That's it; look sharp now, it's time. (*Picks up rifle from table and goes over to* CONNOLLY.) Alright, Jim, rise and shine, time to be shot.

MATHER: Time for the old heart of the earth to be warmed with the red wine of the battlefield.

CONNOLLY: Is it night or day?

MCDAID: That's an academic question. Come on, Jock, on your feet.

CONNOLLY: Is this it?

MATHER: This is it.

CONNOLLY: (*Trying to get up*) I can't stand up.

MCDAID: No more play-acting.

CONNOLLY: I can't move I tell you.

MCDAID: Don't take your execution lying down.

MATHER: Have you any last requests?

CONNOLLY: No.

MATHER: Nobody you'd care to marry?

CONNOLLY: I'm married already.

MATHER: A spot of death-cell bigamy would probably pass unnoticed. And of course we won't offer you a cigarette because . . .

McDaid: We know you're trying to give them up. (*Short laugh.*)

Connolly: You'll have to help me.

McDaid: Have done with your bellyaching.

Connolly: Just let me lean on you.

Mather: It's not in the regulations but we'll stretch a point. (connolly *drapes his arms round their shoulders; they lift him from the bed.*)

McDaid: It's most irregular. (*They half drag him across the stage to the prison yard, and stand three in line facing the wall.*)

Mather: Alright now, we made it. (*Pause.*) What do we do next?

McDaid: Stand him against the wall.

Mather: He can't stand by himself.

Connolly: Have you got my rosary beads?

McDaid: No rosary beads, Jim; there are a lot of tricks a condemned man might get up to with a pair of rosary beads, none of them strictly kosher.

Connolly: Like what?

McDaid: You might try strangling yourself.

Mather: Or us.

McDaid: Or you might try to swallow them, or melt them down into a noxious liquid and either quaff it off or dash it in our faces in a last reckless gesture.

Connolly: I request a blindfold.

McDaid: What's the matter, don't you like my face?

Connolly: It's customary.

McDaid: So is tax evasion.

Mather: I'd advise you not to make any trouble; it won't look good on your record. (*To* mcdaid) OK, let's get him up against the wall. I'll hold him up and you do the firing.

McDaid: (*To* connolly) You can shout something if you want.

Connolly: What do you mean?

McDaid: You know, slogans; pregnant last words. 'Up the Republic', 'I didn't do it', 'Open up dem pearly gates', that class of thing. No? (*Raises rifle.*) All set?

Mather: (*Holding up* connolly) Just a minute.

McDaid: What is it?

Mather: I think there's a flaw in this arrangement.

McDaid: What are you talking about?

Mather: I think I'm going to stop a bullet.

McDaid: Don't be a fool, man, we can't execute you; it'd be invalid.

Mather: Do you have a steady hand?

McDaid: So-so. I wouldn't back myself against Billy the Kid.

Mather: Why don't you hold him up and I'll do the shooting?

McDaid: It's not material.

Mather: Well if it's not material why don't we try it?
(*Pause.*)

McDaid: I've got an idea; why don't we both hold him up?

Mather: Who's going to do the firing?

McDaid: (*Coming over, taking other side of* Connolly) Look: we can both support him like this, then I can manoeuvre the rifle like this. (*Tries ineffectually to point rifle inwards at* Connolly.) Nah, it's no use.

Mather: Could we authorize him to shoot himself?

McDaid: What, suicide? It's a violation of every divine and human edict.

Mather: Then it strikes me we're shafted.
(*Pause.*)

McDaid: His legs.

Mather: What about them?

McDaid: Why doesn't one of us crouch down and hold him up by the legs?

Mather: Which one?

McDaid: Both his legs.

Mather: No, I mean which one of us?

McDaid: It's immaterial.

Mather: Not to me it isn't. Why don't you do it? It was your suggestion.

McDaid: I did the head work, you do the physical bit; an equitable division of mental and manual labour.

Mather: Alright; but be sure to shoot over my head now.

McDaid: Consider it done. (Mather *crouches down and tries to support* Connolly *by the legs;* McDaid *prepares to fire.*) All ready?

Mather: Fire away.

McDaid: (*Lowering rifle and examining it*) There's something wrong here.

Mather: What's the problem?

McDaid: I think the trigger's jammed.

Mather: Let's have a look. (McDaid *brings rifle over to* Mather.) Do you know anything about firearms?

McDaid: Not much.

Mather: Neither do I.

McDAID: Here, Jim, you know about guns, take a look at this. (*Makes to give him the gun.*)

MATHER: Don't give it to him, you eejit!

McDAID: (*Fumbling with rifle*) I think it's working now. The safety catch was still on. (*Steps back, takes aim.*) Alright, here we go. (CONNOLLY *keels over and falls in a heap on top of* MATHER.) Oh, shit.

MATHER: (*Muffled voice*) Will you get yourself off me, you great Scotch git?

McDAID: (*Putting down rifle and coming over*) What are you playing at? (*Pulls* CONNOLLY *off* MATHER.) What are you trying to do, flatten the life out of him? He hasn't done you any harm. (MATHER *gets to his feet; they both hold up* CONNOLLY. *An electric bell rings suddenly.*) That's the end of the shift. Get him back into the cell. (*They carry* CONNOLLY *back to the bed.*) There we go, that's the way. (*Lower him on to the bed, then stand over him panting.*) Well, that was a close one, Jim; you came within sniffing distance of the old fire and brimstone there.

MATHER: We'll have another go tomorrow; try and keep yourself in a sort of facing-your-Maker frame of mind till then.

McDAID: (*Shouldering rifle*) See you in a bit, then. Connor and Kearney should be along any minute; they'll be giving you a body search, just routine.

MATHER: Just in case you manage to fashion or procure a weapon in between us going out and them coming in. Bye now.
(MCDAID *and* MATHER *exit. After a few moments* MCDAID's *voice can be heard outside the door. Re-enter* MCDAID *and* MATHER.)

McDAID: (*Chuckling as he comes in*) . . . so he says to me, you can douse it in banana juice till the end of the epicycle but you won't combat Confucianism with a bent scaroid!

MATHER: (*Chuckling*) Stupid bastard. Had he had a skinful?
(*They see* CONNOLLY *and halt in their tracks.*)

McDAID: Hello there, how's it going? No need to get up, I can see you're not too nippy on your pins.

MATHER: (*Settling into a chair and producing an apple and knife*) Looks like we're in for a long evening. (*To* CONNOLLY) How about a game of truth-or-consequences?
(CONNOLLY *looks slowly from one to the other; they smile at him benignly.*)

CURTAIN

ACT TWO

The cell again; CONNOLLY *lying on the bed,* MCDAID *and* MATHER *seated,* MCDAID *strumming a banjo or guitar. Back-projection: 'The A to Z of Erin'.*

(McDAID) (*Singing*)
        Oh A is for absentee landlords
        Who thrived while our forefathers pined
        And B's for Boru and his whole gallant crew
        Who doused the poor Danes in the brine.

        C is for colonization
        The source of our suffering and woe
        But also for mighty Cuchulain
        Whom no foreign power could bring low.

        D is for Davis and Davitt
        Young Ireland and bold IRB
        And E's for evictions they fought to oppose
        From Dingle to Donaghadee.

        F's for our Fenian martyrs
        And Edward Fitzgerald the brave
        And G's for those fine Gaelic Leaguers
        And the language they struggled to save.

        H is the terrible hunger
        Britannia neglected and scorned
        And I's for imperialism
        That held our whole people in pawn.

        J's for our Jacobin comrades
        Who granted us succour and aid
        And K's for Kilkenny's grim statutes
        By cowards enforced and made.

        L is for Larkin and Land League
        Who fought to set free the oppressed

And M is for our manufactures
By England destroyed and suppressed.

N's for a free Irish nation
United and fearless and strong
And O's for O'Neill and O'Connell
Who thundered against Erin's wrong.

P stands for Pearse our redeemer
And also for mighty Parnell
And Q's for the quislings who sold out our cause
Please God they're now baking in hell.

R's for that evil rack-renting
The Ribbonmen fought to set right
And S is for brave Patrick Scarsfield
Who sought to repair Erin's plight.

T stands for Tone our young leader
His seat is assured 'midst the great
and U's for his United Irishmen
Who struck for us in '98.

V's for the battle of Vinegar Hill
Where the Wexford boys fought to the end
And W's the Whiteboys who guarded our soil
The peasant's true champion and friend.

X Y and Z is the future
Which lies in our power to create
A land fit for Tone, Pearse and Parnell
That knows no division or hate.

McDAID: (*Laying down instrument*) Ah, it's a darlin' song. (*Pause.*)
    Lot of bollocks, of course.
MATHER: That's your considered opinion?
McDAID: Not a word of truth in the whole ditty. It's about as histori-
    cally accurate as 'Little Bo Peep'.
MATHER: That's for sure. You can weave a plot out of being pissed on
    just like anything else. It makes Cinderella look scientifically
    reputable.
McDAID: It makes the Koran read like the racing results. Terrible
    hunger!
MATHER: You take a different view?

McDAID: Famine? Spot of food shortage. It was all got up by the peasants. The cunning bastards poisoned their own potatoes and blamed it on the Brits.

MATHER: I never heard that one before.

McDAID: You haven't been keeping abreast of the latest historical research.

MATHER: But there was surely a lot of hardship?

McDAID: Hardship? The British rushed in enough food supplies to sink the whole bloody island. Robert Peel took the food out of his own children's mouths – there were five of the little beggars died of rickets within the month.

MATHER: D'you know, I never knew that.

McDAID: The place was awash with grub: enough rashers and sides of ham to keep every belly in the country stuffed to bursting for five years. And do you know what the bastard Fenians did? Flogged the whole lot off for guns and ammunition.

MATHER: Is that the truth?

McDAID: They filled every workhouse in the land with their own men got up as famished peasants. Paid them good money to go staggering along the roads howling and bawling and clutching their bellies whenever some English liberal with a bad conscience was in the vicinity.

MATHER: But there was fever? Typhoid and that?

McDAID: Oh, there was fever right enough. But who *introduced* the fever, that's what I'd like to know. That's what the history books don't tell you.

MATHER: It comes from starving, doesn't it?

McDAID: It came from a Fenian laboratory in south Boston and that's the God's honest truth.

MATHER: You're not telling me they sunk to that?

McDAID: They cultivated the virus in Boston and shipped it over here in steel canisters. Those fellers would stop at nothing.

MATHER: It's enough to make you revise your most deep-seated convictions.

McDAID: That's the reality behind the myth, my son; those are the cold facts behind all the glamorous talk of famine. Myth is just history speaking out of the back of its neck.

MATHER: The British landlords were a bad bunch, though; there's no arguing against that.

McDAID: British landlords! Sure they were about as British as Pontius Pilate himself. The landlords were as Irish as St Patrick.

MATHER: St Patrick wasn't Irish.

McDAID: Another myth bites the dust. They just *looked* different, you see; all satin pantaloons and lah-di-dah accents. So your thick peasants took them for foreigners. They couldn't have told an Englishman from a fifth-century Athenian.

MATHER: A case of mistaken identity?

McDAID: Identity! They couldn't have identified their own mothers at ten paces without a name tag.

MATHER: But the Normans came over? That's beyond dispute?

McDAID: They came over, yes. Stayed for a couple of months, threw up a few towers, then buggered off back to Britain. There was nothing here for them, you see – no fancy wines, no troubadours, no cunningly embroidered tapestries. What in the name of God would a civilized class of men like the Normans be doing in a God-forsaken place like this?

MATHER: So the old Celtic civilization lived on?

McDAID: Civilization, my arse. You know what those fellers were? Cannibals.

MATHER: You're not telling me that.

McDAID: Cannibals, sheep-shaggers and penis-worshippers. Every second female infant roasted on a spit; that's your golden age for you. They ran around stark bollock naked, not a pair of trousers between the lot of them.

MATHER: And they talk of Celtic culture.

McDAID: Culture! Where were your Celtic Mozarts, your Dantes, your Longfellows? The only culture those laddos knew anything about was playing football with the heads of their own children. The only music they ever made came from a pointed stick up the backside.

MATHER: I was never taken in by our friend Charles Stewart; I never had much time for that boyo.

McDAID: Parnell! The only man in Ireland who could speak up for virginity in the morning and free love in the afternoon. That gobshite had so many faces it took him five hours to shave.

MATHER: He'd preach atheistic materialism out of one side of his mouth and say the Angelus out of the other.

McDAID: He thought sincerity was a town in New York State. There were more false promises in that bowsie than a back-street astrologer.

MATHER: There were more forks in that feller's tongue than a tray of cutlery. He'd persuade you that Cleopatra was a celibate.

McDAID: He'd persuade you that the Pope was a celibate.

MATHER: The biggest bullshitter since Baron von Munchhausen. He'd convince you that your belly button was for unscrewing your arse.

McDAID: He'd have your braces off while slapping you on the back.

MATHER: Talk about enigmatic! He made the Sphinx look like the Blarney stone.

McDAID: He made a Trappist monk sound like Dan O'Connell.

MATHER: The only man in Ireland who could crawl backwards with his head between his legs and make it look like a war-dance. A martyr for old Ireland! The only thing that prowling tomcat was ever a martyr to was his own prick.

McDAID: Do you know what true freedom is in this country? Freedom's being able to have a quiet wank without the clergy breaking down your bedroom door. That's the Irish disease if you want one: not colonial paralysis or imperial arthritis but wanker's wrist. A whole nation stiff in the arm joint.

MATHER: And as for that loud-mouthed scut O'Connell –

McDAID: I've heard there never was an O'Connell.

MATHER: Is that so?

McDAID: Another Fenian invention, or so it now appears. In fact the latest school of geography is beginning to cast doubt on the existence of the whole island. I believe they only use the term Ireland these days in quotation marks.

MATHER: I never had much time for this Patrick Pearse.

McDAID: Pearse! – a spoilt priest. Giving him a rifle is like giving a saxophone to a gorilla. He thinks murder's alright as long as you do it to organ music.

MATHER: He'd slit you from gizzard to belly button while singing the Ave Maria.

McDAID: There are more wet dreams in that bumboy than the collected works of Freud. He's about as much use as a soldier as a one-legged Mother Superior with pacifist leanings.

MATHER: That boyo is to war what Attila the Hun is to peace.

McDAID: There's more hot air in him than the Bay of Biscay. He thinks vice is eating too much sago pudding.

MATHER: Talk about idealism! He makes Plato look like Lloyd George.

McDAID: He makes George Washington look like a bent bookie.

MATHER: I'll tell you what: if I dropped my hat standing next to that ageing choirboy I wouldn't bend over and pick it up.

McDAID: I'd kick it all the way to the door.

MATHER: I wouldn't put my nippers in *his* school, I can tell you; too much prancing around in the shower baths for my taste. Still, I suppose his heart's in the right place. (*Sudden violent rattle of gun-fire off-stage.*) Was.

CONNOLLY: (*Starting up*) What's that?

MATHER: It's alright, Jim, we're only practising; just so we'll be word-perfect on the night.

McDAID: Speaking of which, how about a spot of exercise? – get yourself in trim for the big event. We don't want your foot dropping off at an inconvenient moment.

MATHER: (*Coming over to the bed*) Let's take a look at it. (*Pulls back the bandages a little, expression of disgust.*) Jesus.

McDAID: What's the matter?

MATHER: It's disgusting; it's a miracle he's still alive.

McDAID: (*Taking a look*) Well his foot's certainly a patriot if the colour's anything to go by. (*Puts hand on* CONNOLLY's *leg.*) Can you feel anything there?

CONNOLLY: No.

McDAID: We've got to head it off before it gets to his heart; it's a race against time.

MATHER: We can't let him croak; it'd make a mockery of justice.

McDAID: It'd make a mockery of our future in the prison service, more to the point. (*Examines leg again.*) Can you feel that?

CONNOLLY: I can't feel anything.

MATHER: We ought to get him a doctor.

McDAID: That's not a simple matter.

MATHER: There's one on the premises.

McDAID: It's a tricky juridical point. If we get him a doctor, then we're in a certain sense reversing the course of justice. We're supposed to be killing him, not keeping him alive.

MATHER: We can't do one without the other.

McDAID: That's a fair point; it's a logician we need here, not a physician.

MATHER: I see what you mean, though. Seen in a certain light, medical treatment would be tantamount to contempt of court.

McDAID: Precisely. I mean, how far do you go? If he had a coronary here and now, would we give him six hours of open-heart surgery?

MATHER: I wouldn't fancy explaining that to the taxpayer.

McDAID: We'd be conspiring to pervert the course of justice. Any
doctor who laid a scalpel on him might be criminally liable.

MATHER: (*Peering at the foot*) It doesn't look too good, though. There
are humanitarian considerations.

McDAID: He ought to have thought of that when he was mowing
down young kids from Birmingham just because they were
wearing berets. (*Puts arm around* CONNOLLY's *shoulder*.) Come
on, Seamus, let's take a wee trot around the cell. You can't
lie there introspecting all the time, it's morbid. (McDAID *and*
MATHER *help him up off the bed*.) Up you come, that's the style.

MATHER: You just stick hold of uncle Frank and you won't go far
wrong.

(*They begin to half walk, half carry him around the cell*.)

MATHER: (*Stumbling a little*) Just a minute, we're geting out of step
here.

McDAID: So what? It's not the twelfth of July. We're not the bleeding
Highland Light Infantry.

MATHER: (*Trying to mark time*) One – two – three – four . . .

McDAID: Come on, Jim, keep it up, nice and easy now.

MATHER: That's it, good man yourself, keep with the rhythm. One –
two – three – four . . . (*They are swaying in unison to* MATHER's
beat; MATHER *starts to hum 'The Lambeth Walk' as they go
round and round, and gradually finds voice. They totter together like a crippled music-hall troupe*.)

MATHER: (*Singing softly*)

> Any evening, any day
> If you go down Lambeth way
> You'll find 'em all
> Doin' the Lambeth walk, Oh!

(*He makes one or two little twirling motions with hands and
feet*.)

McDAID: Alright, that'll do, that'll do for that. Let's have a little
dignity here; let's recall we're in the service of the Crown.
Here you are, sit him in the chair. (*They lower* CONNOLLY *into
a chair*.) That's the way. Now then, that got the old animal
spirits stirring, eh?

MATHER: (*Peering into* CONNOLLY's *face*) There's a visible improve-
ment; he's got more colour in him.

McDAID: It was a humane act.

MATHER: It was more than he'd bloody well do for us.

McDAID: There's truth to that; he wouldn't have waltzed us around the post office if our legs had been in jeopardy.

MATHER: He'd have pulled them off and hit us with the soggy end.

McDAID: What was the point of it all, Jim? This botched little charade of yours in Sackville Street? What was the motive?

CONNOLLY: Just let me rest, will you.

McDAID: Was it love of country, existential *Angst*, instructions from Lenin, the upward social mobility of a colonial petty bourgeoisie, or was it just that the boozers were shut? Did you want to restore Ireland to its proper place among the nations, or did you just want to get your name in the newspapers?

MATHER: The whole incident is still too shrouded in mythology to allow for judgement. We must await the disinterested verdict of posterity.

McDAID: Ah yes, posterity – that's what you were out to manufacture. But you got it the wrong way round, you see: they'll manufacture *you*. You thought you were making history; you're just an effect of it.

MATHER: A character in your own narrative.

McDAID: A Frankenstein whose monstrous creature is already on the loose.

MATHER: There's a plot here somewhere, Jim, a proper penny dreadful, but you're not the author; you're not even the detective, you're just the corpse.

McDAID: Posterity will peer down the microscope of history and draw what they see. And do you know what they'll end up drawing? Their own eye.

MATHER: That's what you always draw.

McDAID: You've released your body to the undertakers of the future. They'll read into it anything they want, they'll write you into any narrative they choose. What if they turn the empty tomb into a mausoleum? They did it with Jesus; why are you so special?

MATHER: The future can mummify anything – including emptiness.

McDAID: Emptiness all the easier; they just twist one bit of non-meaning into another.

MATHER: You don't even grasp the meaning of it yourself – you can't. Only posterity can do that, and they're the last people who can do it. It's a slim basis on which to build.

CONNOLLY: There's no other basis. A corpse is the only sure foundation; there's always non-meaning at the root of meaning.

McDAID: They'll hang you on the wall and burn joss-sticks to cover the stink. You're giving birth to your own grave-diggers, Jim; when we shoot you, you'll just vanish into mythology.

MATHER: He's dwindling already; he's evaporating by the minute. Look, you can see through his ribs; you can see the slime in his lungs.

McDAID: You'll be a bad smell, a whiff of the drains, a bit of faded newsreel. The future can sniff you already and it's heaving. You'll be the original sin of the Irish state, the primordial cock-up, the trespass at the twinkling of time. You'll scatter the debris of this down the generations, they'll never do anything properly again. They'll scrub the soil and plant their bungalows over you, but you'll come seeping up through the floor-boards.

MATHER: You think you can fashion the future? It's remaking you as you sit here.

McDAID: It was a cosmetic job. They manned the barricades and round the corner they went on drinking in the pubs. Nothing got transfigured; everyday life carried on.

MATHER: Politics is like religion: it's when it starts interfering with your daily life that it's time to give it up.

McDAID: Just a bunch of overeducated clerks looking for desk jobs in Dublin Castle.

MATHER: One overeducated clerk is a tragedy; two is sociology.

McDAID: (*Going to table and picking up a tea mug*) Look: here's a tea mug. How are you going to revolutionize that? Remake its molecular structure in the image of eternity? Can you see the face of God staring out of this? Because that's the only revolution that'll make a difference.

MATHER: The only rising is the transfiguration of the flesh. And yours, old son, is going down the plug-hole at an alarming rate of knots.

McDAID: They're all the same, these immigrants – coming over here, trying to muscle in on our revolution.

MATHER: Flocking over here, taking our insurrectionary jobs; there aren't enough of them for our own people.

McDAID: Why don't you bugger off back to Scotland?

MATHER: Too bloody tight to pay the boat fare. He wouldn't give you the snot from his nose to stick your thumb back on.

McDAID: You can tell he's a Jock (*indicates table*), he's got a fork in the sugar bowl.

MATHER: He wouldn't give you the steam off his piss.

McDAID: He uses both sides of the lavatory paper.

MATHER: You're a blow-in, Connolly, a carpet-bagger. We've got our own revolutionaries, good decent God-fearing Irish ones; we don't need any of your outside agitators.

McDAID: There's nothing wrong with our revolution, it's in perfect shape; you keep your Scotch mitts off it.

CONNOLLY: Can I lie on the bed?

McDAID: Should we let him lie on the bed?

MATHER: It might be a ploy. They're canny, these Jocks, they'd have the wax out of your ears while patting you on the head.

McDAID: Why do you want to lie down?

CONNOLLY: What else can I do?

McDAID: There's plenty to do. We could read to you from the Acts of the Apostles. Or from one of your own works, perhaps; how about *Labour in Irish History*?

MATHER: Or the *Arabian Nights* – it's the same kind of stuff.

CONNOLLY: I can't sit here any more, I'm going to faint.

McDAID: Alright, you can lie on the bed, then. But you'll have to crawl; we're fed up of carting you around.

MATHER: We need a bloody sedan-chair for this job.

(CONNOLLY *crawls towards the bed.*)

McDAID: I think you'd better stay put till the final call. If you lose any more blood you'll be flapping like a mail sack.

MATHER: It doesn't present an easy target.

McDAID: This is what comes of fanaticism.

MATHER: It springs from an excess of conviction. That's where the British have the edge over us.

McDAID: You believe so?

MATHER: No question of it. You don't catch the British marauding around post offices waving their willies at an army twenty times their size. They've got more sense. If they had an uprising they'd do it gradually – a little bit at a time.

McDAID: Take over one Ministry every six months.

MATHER: Easy does it: that's the British style. I read in the paper they were thinking of changing over to driving on the right, but they're going to do it in stages. Try it all at once and you just get disruption.

McDAID: You see, that's the kind of spirit we lack over here. We go at things too bull-headed, we're all piss and wind and up-and-at-'em. Whereas with the Brits it's a litle bit of this, then a little bit of that; knock off Jamaica over here, then Malaya over there. Nothing too immoderate.

MATHER: It comes from centuries of breeding – a kind of natural reticence and obliquity.

McDAID: Huh?

MATHER: It's not a style you can pick up like a dose of the clap. It has to be bred in the bone.

McDAID: Whereas the trouble with this place is that there are too many *ideas* knocking around. Every poxy estate agent's clerk has to have his little clutch of metaphysical notions. The British never bothered themselves with all that; they assembled the greatest empire known to man and they've never had a bloody idea in their heads.

MATHER: It was all just an oversight; they never asked to rule the seas, it just fell into their lap.

McDAID: So they just got on with it; they didn't ask any questions. They didn't start blathering about freedom and the rights of man and the death of the language.

MATHER: Was their language on the blink as well?

McDAID: Well they don't speak like Geoffrey Chaucer any more, do they? But they didn't make a big song and dance about it; they didn't go around forcing their school kids to speak like the Wife of Bath. You can get a job in the British Civil Service without having to talk like the bleeding *Canterbury Tales*.

MATHER: There's too much belief in this country altogether; that's where the British beat us hands down. Too many dogmas, creeds, too much partisanship. Why can't we all just get together – see each other's point of view? I've never had a conviction in my life and it's never held me back. We're all human, aren't we? – all part of the same great family. Why has there always got to be division? Put two Irishmen on a desert island and before the week is out they'll be running rival coconut factories. (*Gathering slowly to a passionate crescendo.*) Does it *have* to be like that? Are there no good ordinary decent people left? Am I the only one left standing in the middle? I didn't ask to be normal – it's a positive liability. I can see everybody's point of view but my own. I express some viewpoint and somebody only has to say bollocks or I suspect there's an excluded middle in your syllogism or why don't you step outside and I'm agreeing with them straight off. I'm just constitutionally consensual; I don't see why it always has to be one side against the other. Why can't we have a little bit of everything? Why is everyone else such a FUCKING FREAK?

(*Back-projection: 'Song of the Liberal'.*)

(Mather): (*Sings*)

    Some say the poor are starving
    While the rich do as they please
    But I always think as I teeter on the brink
    It's a question of priorities.
    Between murder, boys, and freedom
    You must get the balance right
    And as I always say the truth it lies half-way
    Between sort of black and sort of white.

    On the one hand there is bacon
    On the other there is eggs
    In the top half we have arms, friends
    And in the bottom, legs.
    If there's such a thing as winter
    There's also a thing called spring
    And if you're keen to know just what I mean
    Well it doesn't mean a bloody thing.

    I believe in the individual
    And I can't stand violence
    And I always feel that all human strife might heal
    With a little bit of common sense.
    For there's none of us stop learning
    There are two sides to every coin
    And to prove I'm not benighted I reply 'Quite delighted'
    When they say 'Can we kick you in the groin?'

    Now I'm very highly conscious
    You may find my conclusions lame
    But I always think it would be a funny world
    If everybody felt the same
    I don't like labels and isms
    And if you want to know my creed

It's getting rather merry on non-racialistic sherry
And following the argument wherever it may lead.

Now I'm sure this raises more questions than it
    answers
I'm sure it's probably wrong
It's a very partial tentative exploratory initial
Introduction to a prolegomenon.
Don't take what I say as gospel
'Cos my case could easily fall
So what I'm trying to say in my self-effacing way
Is in short I've said sod all.

(*Two loud raps at the door.*)

MATHER: Who's that?

McDAID: It's probably the neighbours complaining about the noise. (*Goes to door, opens it, a few muttered words with someone invisible; back on stage.*) It's ready.

MATHER: What, is it time for him? (*Indicating* CONNOLLY)

McDAID: No, no. (*Looks towards* CONNOLLY *and lowers voice.*) The surprise. It's arrived.

MATHER: It's here already?

McDAID: Delivered outside the door.

MATHER: Why don't we bring it in?

McDAID: We'd better tell him first; we don't want to spring it on him too suddenly.

MATHER: Do you think he's going to like it?

McDAID: I should hope so; there's a lot of planning gone into this.

MATHER: Maybe you should tell him; I feel a bit . . .

McDAID: What?

MATHER: I dunno; sort of . . . shy.

McDAID: I understand how you feel. The affair has a certain – poignancy.

MATHER: Treat it lightly – don't lay it on too thick. We don't want him blubbering.

McDAID: There'll be no fear of that. (*Coming over to* CONNOLLY.) Jim, we've got a little surprise for you outside the door.

CONNOLLY: Is it Lillie? Is it my wife?

McDAID: It's a present – from the two of us. From Mr Mather here and myself.

CONNOLLY: A present?

McDAID: Well we know it's not your birthday, in fact it's exactly the opposite, but we wanted you to have some trifling token of our regard. You've been a model prisoner, Jim, apart from the gangrene and all the lugging around and the odd republican outburst.

CONNOLLY: I don't need any presents.

McDAID: You shouldn't prejudge the issue; I think you'll find it to your taste. Close your eyes.

CONNOLLY: What?

McDAID: Close your eyes and swear not to peep.

CONNOLLY: Oh, for God's sake. (*Lies back again and closes eyes.*)

McDAID: (*Crossing to door, to* MATHER) You'd better help me with it, it's a hefty thing to lift. (*They disappear momentarily outside the door and reappear carrying a large object wrapped in sacking.*) There we go, have you got your end now?

MATHER: I've got a grip on it, steady as you go. (*They deposit the object centre-stage.*) That's fine, just about here, that'll do.

McDAID: You can open your eyes now, Jim. (CONNOLLY *lies motionless.*) Come on, old son, don't be a spoil-sport; why don't you take a peek?

CONNOLLY: (*Lifting his head perfunctorily*) What is it?

MATHER: (*To* McDAID) Ready? After three. (*They both count.*) One two – three . . .

(*They whisk away the sack to reveal a tiny wizened man with a fixed, inane grin, dressed like a caricature of an Irish peasant.*)

McDAID: There now. I bet you weren't expecting that.

CONNOLLY: Who is he?

McDAID: Who is he? He's the incarnation of everything you've been fighting for, that's who he is. Government issue, name of Liam. Say hello to the company, Liam.

LIAM: (*Mechanical recitation in exaggerated 'culchie' accent*) God's blessing on Your Honours and peace be to this house.

CONNOLLY: What's he doing here?

McDAID: You're looking at a sliver of the purest Gaelic stock to be found throughout the length and breadth of Connemara. The only man in the country who learnt English by Linguaphone.

MATHER: He's so racy of the soil he smells like the inside of a badger's bum. (*To* LIAM, *who is standing to attention*) It's alright, you can relax, stroll round a bit, you're not awaiting inspection from Field Marshall Haig.

McDAID: Liam took an active part in the rebellion of '48. He remembers being taken as a boy by his father to Clontarf to hear O'Connell speak.

MATHER: O'Connell cancelled Clontarf, didn't he?

McDAID: It was the bitterest blow of Liam's young life. His earliest memories are of Gratton denouncing the Act of Union, his Ribbonman father bludgeoning the landlord's bailiff to death with a two-foot piece of lead piping and Father Murphy riding o'er the hill like a mighty wave. Isn't that right, Liam? (*No response from* LIAM; *warningly*) Li-am!

LIAM: (*Starting to life*) God's blessing on Your Honours and peace be to this house.

MATHER: Liam narrowly survived the Famine by holding up an Ascendancy dining club at pistol point and later refused a landlord's bribe to emigrate. He acted as Parnell's personal interpreter in the Land League, and would probably be in the next cell to yourself right now if he hadn't been at the races during the Rising.

McDAID: Liam has three sisters who are Mother Superiors and his ambition is to visit the King's palace in London and gob on the sentries. His motto is 'Stick to your own kind and make mine a Bushmills', and for recreation he enjoys winter sports, karate, the later fiction of Emile Zola and roasting landlords' bailiffs over a small turf fire.

MATHER: When asked how he viewed the future of civilization, Liam gave one of his characteristically enigmatic smiles and replied that he thought it would be an excellent idea. Didn't you, Liam? (*Nudgingly*) Li-am!

LIAM: (*As if reciting from memory*) Sure 'tis a cold dark place you're after bringing me to here Michael McDaid with no more lepping and soft laughter than the black crags of Maamturk when the mist is on them and I'm thinking it would shake the fat of a man's heart to be lying here lonesome with only a bare plank for his head and a sup of straw and nothing to put in his belly but a bit of stinking fish and him keening and pining for . . . (*Hesitates.*)

McDAID: (*Low voice*) Go on; go on, man, you're doing fine.

LIAM: . . . and him keening and pining for the sight of a heron in the harsh skies and the sweet talk of a woman and wouldn't he be giving a mountainy ram and a load of dung to be squatting by

his own hearth with sheep on the back hills and the stir of
laying hens, the way he could stretch half the day with his
belly to the wide heavens and feel the taste of freedom on his
lips like a mouthful of fine wine.

McDAID: Good man yourself.

LIAM: And isn't it a pitiful thing surely that yourself James Connolly
(*Turns to address* MATHER) –

McDAID: (*Hissing*) Not him, you eejit; that's Connolly on the bed.

LIAM: (*Turns to bed*) – that yourself James Connolly should be lying
here with only a poor bit of a shirt for your back and a few
wet sticks for your fire scalding your heart for your loved ones
when your only sin under heaven was to love your country
dearer than your own life? And isn't it only a small while now
you'll be lost in the great wind that blows from beyond time
and us destroyed and heart-sore with the fearfulness of it and
it'll be weeping there'll be on the black rocks of Aran and
under the cold stones of Ballincree and we'll be praying there
for your soul James Connolly and it going up in glory to the
souls of God.

(LIAM *gives a slight bow;* MCDAID *and* MATHER *applaud discreetly.*)

McDAID: Well spoken, Liam lad. Edmund Burke couldn't have done
better if he'd rehearsed it for a month.

MATHER: Exquisitely composed and tunefully rendered. You won't
find sentiments like that on the North Circular Road.

McDAID: Are we your last customers today, Liam?

LIAM: You are, an' please Your Honour.

McDAID: (*To* CONNOLLY) He's in great demand, we were lucky to get
him. Had to book him a month in advance, non-returnable
deposit.

MATHER: Do you have any requests for him, Jim? Bit of keening,
perhaps? – it's one of his specialities.

McDAID: Or he can recite in various languages: Irish of course,
English both standard and pidgin, Old Norse, Estonian . . .

MATHER: Or maybe you'd just like to feast your eyes on him. Go
ahead, he's not self-conscious.

(*Pause.*)

McDAID: He's disappointed with his present; you can tell by his face.

MATHER: It's better than six pairs of socks.

McDAID: Which he wouldn't have much use for anyway. Ah
well. Well done, Liam, God bless you, I think that'll be all for
today.

MATHER: (*Holding open the door*) Thanks for coming, Liam; you've done more good work here today than you can know.

LIAM: (*Working-class Dublin accent, low voice*) You'll settle up with me outside? I'm a bit short of change at the moment, you know how it is.

MATHER: We'll see you right, don't worry your head about it.

(*Exit* LIAM.)

McDAID: Well there you are, Jim, that was a bit of a send-off for you, wasn't it?

MATHER: You see, I have this theory that what a man hears at the moment of death somehow stays with him. So you'll be off up to heaven with the sound of that voice ringing in your ears for all eternity.

McDAID: We can't do better than that. If ever you're tempted to forget what you're fighting for, just call to mind that wise and simple visage.

(*Pause.*)

MATHER: He still doesn't look happy.

McDAID: Well I give up, I really do. (*To* CONNOLLY) What more do you want, in God's name? We permitted you five minutes with your wife three weeks ago, we gave you as faithful as possible an imitation of your new-born child, don't blame us that you won't be clapping eyes on it, we've scrupulously avoided all casual allusions to feet, legs, socks and putrefaction, we've offered on several occasions to engage in convincingly simulated sexual intercourse, distasteful though the notion is to men of our strong heterosexual persuasion, but you seem a mite depleted in that department. (*To* MATHER) We've offered him all this and what does he say?

MATHER: Nothing. He just lies there like the Sphinx with laryngitis.

McDAID: And this is the man they say can incite a mob in six different languages simultaneously.

MATHER: He couldn't incite a bishop into a brothel.

McDAID: You know what it is, don't you? Intellectual snobbery. As far as he's concerned we're just a couple of dozy Micks fit to change his bandage and empty his shit. They're all elitists, these Marxists – spout about the working man and couldn't tell a spanner from schistosomiasis.

MATHER: What's schistosomiasis?

McDAID: As the name should make abundantly clear, it's a disease of the pelvic region caused by a tropical flatworm of the genus

Bilharzia. Don't parade your ignorance, it'll just confirm his prejudices. (*Squaring up to* CONNOLLY) You want to fight it out? You want to take me on? What's it going to be: a quick plot summary of the *Divine Comedy*? Choose your ground, Jock, and I'm your man; come off your bed arguing and I'll land you a rhetorical swipe in the gob before you've got time to get your prolegomenon together.

MATHER: We come of a cultivated race, Connolly. Our theologians were running the Vatican back in St Peter's day. We had ontology and cosmology while you lot were still trying to figure out what your willies were for.

McDAID: We kept the light of the intellect burning throughout the Dark Ages; we had philosophers could make Socrates sound like a retarded wombat. This island was stiff with saints – contemplating, levitating, bilocating, you name it. And what did the Scots ever invent? A musical instrument that sounds like one prolonged fart and a game called tossing the cabor specially designed for those who can't get it up.

MATHER: So what do you say to that? (*Pause.*) Come on, man, why don't you say something? It's not against regulations. You can be as inflammatory as you like, we can take it.

CONNOLLY: What do you want me to say?

MATHER: Just speak. Feel free. Break the silence.

(*Pause.*)

CONNOLLY: I heard a sound once that broke the silence. It was in the countryside, in Donegal; I was just standing there in the darkness. The hills stunned, holding their breath, attending to their own stillness. And then suddenly, imprinting the silence like the quick press of a bird's claw, a sound: eerie, unblemished, utterly inhuman. A momentary wailing, like the bleat of some fabulous beast, so pure and unfractured that the blood stood still. I knew then that I'd strive to imitate that sound – cup the words in my palms and let it resonate through them. But it's all a poor sort of ventriloquism. The noise of your life gets in the way, all that garbled blood and breathing. To utter that sound we'd have to pare away all *this* (*indicates around him*), and that's not easy. Our language drags all this in its wake like a ball and chain.

McDAID: There's no such sound, Jimmy; you were hallucinating again.

CONNOLLY: Oh yes – there's a sound way beyond the present. But we can only speak of it in the tongue we have.

McDAID: Which is why it can never come.

CONNOLLY: It can come. You just have to use language as a kind of trampoline, to bounce yourself beyond it. Either that, or bear witness to that sound by keeping silent.

McDAID: If you speak with their tongue then you fight with their weapons. That means you're complicit.

CONNOLLY: There's no other tongue to speak. You just have to inflect it differently – find a way of speaking it which will get you beyond it.

McDAID: You're playing their game; that's why you can't win. That's how you've undone yourself.

CONNOLLY: To be ourselves, we have to risk turning into the image of them. Some time, a long time ago, we fell into meaning – into history. A fall up, of course, not down. And there's no way back now. The other animals are mute; that's why they can't torture each other. They have no words, so they can be neither Catholic nor Protestant. It's speech that's our undoing, but we have to plough on with it – go all the way through it and come out somewhere on the other side.

McDAID: You can't pre-calculate where you'll come out. What if you fall off the edge?

CONNOLLY: It's a matter of faith. Faith that there's something beyond the human which isn't against the human.

McDAID: That sound you heard – that was animal, Jim, inhuman. There's violence in that sound.

CONNOLLY: No: violence is all too human. That's why we have to get rid of it. It was the murmuring of a world where we might speak otherwise; that's bound to seem inhuman to us now.

McDAID: You can't be sure of that.

CONNOLLY: No, I can't be sure. I can't know for certain whether that sound's pregnant with meaning or just a cypher. I've just staked my life on it – that's why I'm here.

McDAID: It was a cry from the past – the death rattle of some prehistoric beast. You're not the first puff, you're the fag end.

CONNOLLY: There's no clear distinction; that's a risk I've got to take. I'm dead already: there's no blood left in me. But when I look at you, it's the past I'm staring at. It's like gazing at the stars, forgetting they're already dead. It's you that's the living dead,

not me. You backed the wrong horse, McDaid; your masters
are packing their suitcases and they won't be taking you with
them, they have enough obedient lackeys over the water.
When the dust of all this settles I'll have disappeared – but so
will you.

McDAID: You tried to blow a hole in the present; well the future will
just get sucked through that vacuum into the past. It'll just be
the past with a different address – a different letter-head. It'll
all just come back again.

CONNOLLY: That's not my responsibility. You said it yourself, I can't
control what comes after. I'm just trying to take myself off –
clear a space in which it can happen.

McDAID: You're walking backwards into the future with your eyes
fixed on the past. You can easily trip up that way.

CONNOLLY: It's the only way to move. It's not dreams of liberated
grandchildren which stir men and women to revolt, but
memories of enslaved ancestors.

McDAID: And when you get where you're going, you'll find it's all
strangely familiar. You'll have dragged the past with you.

CONNOLLY: If that happens, then I've failed; that's beyond my power.

McDAID: What is it you want, Connolly?

CONNOLLY: I want to go on sleep-walking into death, so I won't be
thinking of the fruits of action. That way it'll bear fruit.

McDAID: You want the moment of truth – you're leching after it.

CONNOLLY: No: I want to bear witness to the truth by keeping quiet
about it. I've said too much already.

(McDAID *turns from* CONNOLLY *and takes* MATHER *aside.*)

McDAID: We've got to get him to the wall.

MATHER: What's the rush?

McDAID: (*Insistently*) He's got to be put down.

MATHER: It's what he wants.

McDAID: That can't be helped.

MATHER: Why hand it him on a plate? Why not make him sweat for
it?

McDAID: It's got to be done now.

MATHER: It doesn't do to be too co-operative. He'll think the law's just
a big softie, catering to his every whim. The law can't fall over
itself to top him any time he clicks his fingers, it's undignified.

McDAID: I don't like his frame of mind.

MATHER: Neither do I; make him hang around a bit and he'll have
more respect.

McDAID: It's worrying – disturbing.

MATHER: He's quiet enough; that makes life easier for us.

McDAID: He's quiet because he's lost his fear of death. That's a dangerous situation; it's contaminating.

MATHER: Contaminating?

McDAID: I've seen the non-fear of death run through a prison like a dose of salts. It's demoralizing – it loosens the social bond. Fear of death lies at the root of all propriety; get rid of that and anything's permitted.

MATHER: You mean we've got a loose cannon on our hands?

McDAID: He's glimpsed the emperor without his clothes. He's seen that the grim reaper is just another poor old bollix like you or me. So he's free – that's why we've got to keep him locked up. He'd wreak havoc otherwise.

MATHER: It's not the kind of power one can have on the loose.

McDAID: We've got no hold over him any more; we're just playing gooseberry between him and death. We've got to dispatch him before it becomes too monstrous – too indecent.

MATHER: If death loses its authority, what else is sacred?

McDAID: We've got to send him on his way before he slips through our fingers entirely. We're holding on to him by a hair as it is.

MATHER: If you live backwards from death there's no power can resist you.

McDAID: He's invulnerable; he's *using* his death, weighing it in the palm of his hand. Some people would use anything.

MATHER: Some people would squeeze a meaning from the fluff between their toes. You hunt them down, you trap them in a corner, you strip them of everything, and what do they do? They turn on you at the last moment and run up a symbol from the poor bit of biology that's left to them.

McDAID: Were you around when William O'Brien was banged up in here?

MATHER: The big Fenian? I heard he withdrew co-operation.

McDAID: He withdrew more than that; he went on constipation strike.

MATHER: Is there no end to human deviousness?

McDAID: He had perfect control over his bowels – a maestro of his own motions. The stubborn bastard wouldn't even give us the smell of his shit.

MATHER: Well at least he was saved the bother of slopping out.

(*Pause.*)

McDAID: (*Looking over to* CONNOLLY) My vote's for doing it now.

MATHER: I see your point. We can't let him make a mockery of the law.

McDAID: (*Coming over to* CONNOLLY) OK, Jim, this is it; this time it's for real. (*Takes rifle.*) Get yourself up – get yourself off the bed.

(MCDAID *and* MATHER *hook* CONNOLLY's *arms around them and drag him over to the wall.*)

MATHER: This time there'll be no mistake.

(*The three stand facing the wall.*)

McDAID: How are we going to manage it?

MATHER: I don't know. It takes an orderly mind.

McDAID: We could try lying him on the ground.

MATHER: You can't kill a man when he's down.

McDAID: We could drive a nail into the wall and peg his collar to it.

MATHER: We might hang him by mistake; that'd invalidate the execution.

(*Pause.*)

McDAID: Is there another side to this wall?

MATHER: Extrapolating from my general experience of walls I'd say the answer lay in the affirmative.

McDAID: No, I mean is there some way of getting at it?

MATHER: What's so grand about the other side? It's his leg that's knackered, not the wall.

McDAID: (*Exploring the edge of the wall*) Just a minute – I could get round here.

MATHER: Are you thinking of holding him up *through* the wall?

McDAID: Hang on a minute.

(*Disappears round the wall.*)

MATHER: (*Holding up* CONNOLLY) We'll sort this one out somehow – don't you worry your head about it. You just relax and leave the logistics to us.

(MCDAID *appears suddenly above the top of the wall from behind.*)

McDAID: How about this, then?

MATHER: (*To* CONNOLLY) I beg your pardon?

McDAID: Look – up here.

MATHER: (*Looking up*) What in Jesus name are you doing up there?

McDAID: I climbed up the other side – there are some footholds here.

MATHER: We're supposed to be carrying out an execution, not compiling a surveyor's report.

McDAID: (*Bending precariously over wall*) Look, you see: I can bend down like this and dangle him by the arms. Here y'are, give me his arms.

MATHER: (*To* CONNOLLY) Put your arms up – just stretch them up now. (CONNOLLY *raises his arms.*) That's the way.

McDAID: (*Bending down further to grab them*) I can't reach them . . . Can you not stretch them up a bit further? (*There is a ludicrously evident gap between the two men.*) I tell you what, if someone could just cling on to my legs round here I could reach down a bit further . . . (*Pause.*) It's not going to work, is it?

MATHER: (*Coldly*) Why not just blow his brains out from where you're standing? Even you couldn't make a balls-up of that. (*Pause.*)

McDAID: I think I'd better get down; I'm not much use to anybody up here.

MATHER: (*To* CONNOLLY) He was always a realist. (McDAID *disappears.*) I'm very sorry for all this, Jim; we're usually much more streamlined. Less short-staffed as well.

McDAID: (*Emerging*) I had another idea on the way down.

MATHER: Couldn't you have put up some resistance?

McDAID: Why not just sit him in a chair?

MATHER: A chair? You can't shoot a man sitting down.

McDAID: Why not?

MATHER: It's too casual – too undignified. We have to preserve the formalities; there has to be a bit of ceremony here.

McDAID: Well I can't think of any other way.

MATHER: (*After slight pause*) OK. I'll hold him up and you fetch a chair. (McDAID *goes back into cell to fetch a chair.*)

MATHER: (*Arm around* CONNOLLY) It's just like having your photograph taken really.

McDAID: (*Bringing up chair*) Here we are, how about this?

MATHER: That's grand. You shove it under him and I'll lower him on to it. (*Lowering* CONNOLLY *on to chair.*) There you are, Jim, you'll have a grandstand view of your own execution.

McDAID: (*Aiming rifle*) Here we go; all ready, Jim?

CONNOLLY: I'm ready. Make sure your aim is good – I don't want *this* job botched.

McDAID: It'll be as clean as a whistle. After three, then? One – two – three . . .

(MCDAID *fires; smoke, semi-black-out. Lights slowly up again;* CONNOLLY's *chair is empty.* MCDAID *and* MATHER *stand for a while staring bemusedly at it.*)

McDAID: The bastard got away.

MATHER: Look under the chair, he might be hiding.

McDAID: Don't be so bloody daft.

(*Pause.*)

MATHER: He gave us the slip.

McDAID: We left it too late; there wasn't enough blood in him to kill him.

MATHER: He was dead already; you can't kill a dead man.

McDAID: It's contrary to regulations.

MATHER: Now you see him, now you don't.

(*Pause.*)

McDAID: Well, that's it, then.

MATHER: Looks like it.

McDAID: Who have we got left?

MATHER: (*Pulling notebook from pocket*) Let's see: we've done Pearse, Clarke, Plunkett, Ceannt and MacBride. That leaves MacDermott next on the list.

McDAID: Is he sound in wind and limb?

MATHER: Perfect in every part; a model of anatomical correctness.

McDAID: Well, that's a blessing. Alright, let's go.

MATHER: Yes, let's go.

(*They do not move.*)

CURTAIN

———————◆———————

Disappearances

To be produced at the Salisbury Playhouse in 1997.

CHARACTERS

KAMAN, aged 50–5, sloppily dressed
DAVID MANN, bespectacled, neatly dressed American in his mid-twenties
SALAH, middle-aged or elderly man, dressed as a servant
RICHARD RYAN, younger than Kaman, with a trace of a northern English accent
RAAN, around 40, snappily dressed, with an educated English accent
YANA, Kaman's daughter, 20 years old, dressed as a student
MARA, Kaman's wife, about 40
JEREMY BLACKWELL, upper-class Englishman, same age as Kaman
ROSSITER, a professor of anthropology
A woman

The setting is a compromise between an apartment or expensive hotel room in London and some more abstract space without formal entrances.

Time: the present.

To be produced at the Salisbury Playhouse in 1997.

ACT ONE

The stage is in darkness. A huge video screen at the back of the set springs to life, showing KAMAN *performing at a poetry reading. He is wearing national dress with a neat multi-coloured hat, sweating beneath arc lamps. A brilliant performer, rhetorical and expressive. Sounds of an enormous appreciative audience.*

As he reads on screen (see Appendix *for his poems), we hear a gradual stirring and groaning at the front of the stage. The real* KAMAN *is awakening from a drunken torpor. We can discern him dimly, first flat on his belly, then flailing, moaning, moving. He pulls himself to an armchair, clumsily switches on a lamp, and starts to hunt around for the whiskey bottle.*

KAMAN: (*Peering under armchair*) OK, baby, we know you're in there. Come out with your hands up.
> (*He searches on hands and knees around the armchair, occasionally shouting out broken phrases of his own poetry picked up from the video screen. Finally locates a half-empty whiskey bottle under the armchair cushion, along with a glass.*)

Well fancy that. Extraordinary thing.
> (*He hoists himself laboriously into the armchair, fills the glass full of whiskey and drinks deeply. Lies back, becomes aware of the video and raises his glass vaguely towards it in semi-greeting.*)
> (*Listening to his own performance as he drinks*) Right on, baby ... Damn fine image that ... I'll second that ... Eat your heart out, Heaney ... You disgusting little genius. ... Encore, encore ... Watch your back, Pasternak ... What a groovy little mover ... Come on, man, do your Mick Jagger mouth ... Give us your Sammy Davis dead-eye ...
> (*The film finally flickers to an end, as* KAMAN *finishes a poem amidst stormy applause. The real* KAMAN *carries on drinking, muttering to himself, raising his glass unsteadily to the empty screen, sunk deep in the armchair. Lapses into silence, long pause. Then, suddenly, a voice from the darkness opposite* KAMAN, *earnest, American.*)

MANN: Sir?

KAMAN: (*Starting violently from armchair, half falling on floor*) Jesus! What ... Who the hell ... ?

MANN: Excuse me, sir.

KAMAN: Christ. Am I hallucinating again?

(MANN *switches on the lamp next to his armchair opposite* KAMAN's. *A young blazered, moon-faced, bespectacled American, with a notepad on his knee. Smiles a little uneasily.*)

KAMAN: Who the hell are you?

MANN: Mann, sir.

KAMAN: I can see that, you fuckwit.

MANN: No Mann, sir – David Mann. That's my name.

KAMAN: Who let you in?

MANN: You did, Mr Kaman.

KAMAN: I did? Now why should I do a thing like that?

MANN: I was interviewing you, sir. You kinda . . . took a rest as we were talking.

KAMAN: You mean I fell into a drunken torpor?

MANN: I guess you were kinda tired.

KAMAN: Or maybe your questions were of a peculiarly mind-numbing nature. (*Takes the bottle and lurches towards* MANN.) It's alright, I'm only teasing. You look very clever in those glasses. Here, have a drink.

MANN: Thank you.

KAMAN: Is that an English yes or an American no?

MANN: No thanks.

KAMAN: Where do you come from again?

MANN: I'm a graduate student at Princeton.

KAMAN: I thought as much. Don't drink, don't smoke, don't screw. Do you still take the odd piss?

MANN: It's a bit early for me.

KAMAN: What, for the odd piss? I don't know, you Yanks – why don't you just wrap yourselves in silver foil and climb into the icebox? Hey?

MANN: I'm not much of a drinker, sir.

KAMAN: Life is unhygienic, sonny. Why don't you just douse yourself in carrot juice and jump into a plastic bag? You're still going to die, you know. That's the only thing Uncle Sam haven't been able to colonize yet.

MANN: We were talking about literature before you . . .

KAMAN: Fell into a drunken torpor. I take the odd drink myself, you know. It's in my publisher's contract.

MANN: Sir?

KAMAN: You've got to be a drunk if you want to be a great poet. It's something my agent insists on. I just do what I'm told. I assure you I take very little pleasure in it. In fact (*drinking noisily*) the stuff positively nauseates me. But one has to observe the forms. Keep up appearances, that sort of thing.

MANN: (*Faint laugh*) Well, I guess that's true enough where I come from. I mean, Lowell, Berryman, Bishop . . .

KAMAN: That's not because they were poets, it's because they were Americans. It's a condition only alcohol can relieve.

MANN: Well, I'm not surprised you're critical of the States. I mean, seen from a Third World perspective . . .

KAMAN: Oh, it's not political. Just personal. I just don't like shallow pretentious flashy loud-mouthed fuckwits. Politics doesn't come into it. Are you getting all this down?

MANN: (*Consulting notes*) I think we were discussing marginality.

KAMAN: Ah yes, marginality.

MANN: I mean, would it be true to say that your poetry kinda deconstructs the opposition between margins and centre? Like in one sense the Third World margins have shifted to the metropolitan centre but in another sense like the centre has moved to the margins?
(*Pause.*)

KAMAN: Are you unusually well hung?

MANN: Excuse me?

KAMAN: Sorry, I didn't mean to intrude. Nothing personal. Do forgive me.

MANN: No, that's OK.

KAMAN: It just sort of flashed through my mind. (*Comes over to* MANN.) Forget it, it's of no importance. Please don't feel constrained to reply.

MANN: No, really, that's fine.

KAMAN: I just ask people sometimes. It's a kind of hobby. (*Lays hand on* MANN's *arm*.) I hope you didn't take it personally.

MANN: No, not at all.

KAMAN: (*Crouching beside him*) I mean I hope you didn't take it as a . . . you know . . .

MANN: Sir?

KAMAN: A . . . come-on. I'm not gay, you know.

MANN: Er . . . no, I didn't think you were. I mean, I haven't read that you were.

KAMAN: Well it wouldn't say so on the dust-jacket, you know. 'Mr Kaman is a leading Third World poet and a bit of a shirtlifter.' They don't tend to write that kind of thing. But no, as a matter of fact I'm not. I have enough minority problems to be going on with.

MANN: Maybe we could talk about how you feel about . . .

KAMAN: I mean you have to draw the line somewhere. I don't go the whole hog. Is that your English expression?

MANN: (*Confused*) Well, I agree with that.

KAMAN: Ah: a man of moderation. That's what I like to see. I don't even go the whole hog as far as the Third World is concerned.

MANN: How do you mean?

KAMAN: Well, I'm coloured, but I'm not *badly* coloured. I mean if you squinted at me through a damaged eye in a darkened room I might just pass for Paul McCartney. Wouldn't you say?

MANN: Maybe we could get back to how the ethnic issue affects your view of poetry.

KAMAN: Well, as I see it, we're all members of one big family. All brothers and sisters under the skin. It's just that some of us have a touch more leprosy on top of it. (*Drinks.*) I'm not, by the way.

MANN: Not what?

KAMAN: Unusually well hung. Just between you and me; there's no need to write that down. When I was in prison, they suggested at one point driving a bamboo cane up the end of it. Don't worry, they didn't; it was only a suggestion. I didn't fancy the idea at all.

MANN: Your poetry changed when you came out of prison.

KAMAN: Did it? I suppose it did.

MANN: I mean it was more political before then. More – committed.

KAMAN: All poetry is political. Poetry is just language turning its backside on history. That's political alright.

MANN: So you still see your work as committed?

KAMAN: Did you know that there's no taste or smell left in the West any more? It's all been commodifed out of existence. Poetry is the taste of words on the tongue. That's a kind of politics.

MANN: So you see your art as trying to change things?

KAMAN: Of course not. There's nothing more useless than poetry, except perhaps for the Pentagon. That's why it's so subversive.

MANN: I'm sorry, I don't get it.

KAMAN: Art exists for its own sake, and so should we – if only United Fruit would let us. It reminds us of a world where things might manage to rhyme – like us, for instance.

MANN: How do you mean?

KAMAN: Well, Mann and Kaman. That's *almost* a rhyme.

> (SALAH *enters, dressed in a servant's short jacket and neat black trousers. He bows briefly, first to* KAMAN *and then to* MANN.)

SALAH: (*Speaking to* KAMAN *in what sounds vaguely like rhymed verse*)
Tala daleesh mahir quaro tali wetan mara daro, Shoshomi lumba reto kakari mensi leto.

KAMAN: Taleesh hiri lumbrini kikiro.

> (SALAH *bows and exits.*)

KAMAN: What do you think he said?

MANN: I've no idea. I'm afraid I don't –

KAMAN: What did it sound like?

MANN: What did it sound like?

KAMAN: That's what I asked.

MANN: I dunno. I guess . . . I guess it sounded kinda like . . . like verse.

KAMAN: That's what it was.

MANN: Oh really?

KAMAN: Really. In fact it was a soppy little nursery rhyme. Sort of our equivalent to 'Little Bo Peep'.

MANN: Really?

KAMAN: Oh come on, man, for Christ's sake, don't be so bloody *polite*. I mean don't you feel the least twinge of curiosity about why my servant should come wandering in here to recite a stupid nursery rhyme?

MANN: Well, I guess it is kind of strange.

KAMAN: Jesus. (*Long pause.*) Go on, man, ask me!

MANN: Er – why did he do it?

KAMAN: Good lad, well done. You finally asked a coherent question. He came in and said that so that I could tell you that what he said was 'There's an urgent phone call for you from Washington'. So then I could throw you out.

MANN: (*Rising*) Hey, I'm sorry, I didn't realize you –

KAMAN: No no, sit down, take it easy. I'm not throwing you out – it's just that he gave me the chance to if I wanted. But as a matter of fact I don't. And do you know why I don't?

MANN: No, sir.

KAMAN: Because I think you're *fun*. Because I think you're a bit of a riot.

MANN: Thanks very much.

KAMAN: You see, I have to protect myself. Some interviewers can be a real pain.

MANN: I can believe that.

KAMAN: Oh, you wouldn't believe the types I get in here. Earnest young bespectacled idiots full of portentous jargon and wet behind the ears.

MANN: (*Knowing laugh*) Sure, I know the type.

KAMAN: (*Approaching him*) Whereas you – you're . . . different from the others somehow. (*Crouches down beside him.*) Did anyone ever tell you how . . . fascinating . . . you are? (*Lays hand on arm.*)

MANN: (*Embarrassedly consulting notebook*) Er, well, I don't recall . . .

KAMAN: (*Bringing his face close to* MANN, *low voice*) I'd like to gobble you up.

MANN: (*Peering into notebook*) Could I ask you a question, Mr Kaman?

KAMAN: (*Theatrically*) Ask me *anything*.

MANN: Why didn't he just say it straight?

KAMAN: Who?

MANN: Your – er – butler.

KAMAN: You mean my valet?

MANN: Why didn't he just say there was a call from Washington?

KAMAN: Ah. Another devastatingly perceptive question. Why not indeed? (*Returns to armchair.*) Well, Rupert . . . I can call you Rupert, can I?

MANN: Well my name's David actually. . . .

KAMAN: Really? What a pity. Well David, the reason why he didn't say it straight is because we are not on the whole a straight kind of people. In fact, not to put too fine a point on it, we're the most crooked crew of shifty shaggers in the so-called developing world. Which means you probably shouldn't believe a word of that either. In me it takes the form of poetry; in my valet it's called lying through your teeth.

MANN: (*Writing furiously*) I'll just get some of this down if you don't mind . . .

KAMAN: Language, Mr Mann, is all that is left to a colonized people. Not their *own* language, of course. You don't catch me writing poems in that God-forsaken argot now, do you?

MANN: You used to.

KAMAN: So I did. But I rather enjoy being read by more than seventeen people, most of them my close relatives.

MANN: You don't see language as being about truth?

KAMAN: Oh, anything but. Language is how the oppressed conceal their thoughts from their masters. My valet recited a nursery rhyme because he enjoyed the momentary thrill of fooling you. A minor piece of post-colonial malice.

MANN: I think your poems are so brilliant exactly because English isn't your first language.

KAMAN: That's right. When I first came to England I saw a road sign saying 'Loose Chippings' and thought it was a village.

MANN: Do you feel the West is your home now?

KAMAN: Oh, I can be homeless absolutely anywhere. You show me a nice comfy little niche and I'll be homeless in it right away. My home is in language, Mr Mann. The English language, of course; you were good enough to rent it out to me. I don't live in my own tongue any more: it's too ramshackle. Art is the third world I inhabit.

(SALAH *enters*.)

SALAH: Urgent phone call from Paris, sir.

KAMAN: (*To* MANN) Do you think he's telling the truth?

MANN: I . . . I dunno . . .

KAMAN: If he speaks to me in English it's the truth. It's only his own language he associates with lying. Don't you find him strangely enigmatic?

MANN: I wouldn't say so.

KAMAN: He does everything for me but vomit and write my poems, don't you Salah? Not that there's a deal of difference these days.

(RICHARD RYAN *enters*.)

RICHARD: There's a phone call from Washington for you.

KAMAN: It's alright; he's heard that one already. But there's a real one from Paris, I believe.

RICHARD: Oh really?

KAMAN: Yes, Salah took it. (*To* SALAH) Tell them I'm out.

SALAH: They say very urgent, sir.

KAMAN: Tell them I'm looking for a rhyme for scissors. (SALAH *bows and exits*.) Mr Mann, my agent and hired companion Richard Ryan. Richard acts for me: he's my wife's lover.

RICHARD: Fuck off, Kaman.

KAMAN: We have a free-and-easy relationship, as you can see. Rupert Mann, a professor from Cornell.

MANN: It's Princeton, actually. (*Shakes hands with* RICHARD.) How do you do, sir.

RICHARD: Are you really a professor?

MANN: No no, I'm just a grad student. I'm writing my Ph.D. on Mr Kaman's work.

RICHARD: I know, I spoke to you on the phone. I just wondered whether you told Mr Kaman you were a professor.

KAMAN: No, he didn't. He didn't tell me what he thought of my poetry either.

MANN: I think you're the greatest poet of the English language.

RICHARD: That's a coincidence; so does he.

KAMAN: How about the Wordsworth of the Third World? The Tennyson of Tonga? The Lord Byron of Borneo? (*Claps* MANN *on back and leads him to door.*) Well, don't forget, Rupert: there's a third world inside us all. There's a fine phrase for your thesis now.

MANN: (*Producing his notebook*) If I can just get that down . . .

KAMAN: Oh for Christ's sake, Rupert, don't be such a twerp. It doesn't *mean* anything, it just sounds good. That's poetry for you. Poetry's just a technique, don't you see? It's just a question of flicking words in the air and making sure you don't drop any.

MANN: Well, you've sure given me a lot to think about, Mr Kaman. I really appreciate it. (*Shakes hands.*) Goodbye, sir. Thanks a million. (*To* RICHARD) Bye, sir.
(*Exit.*)

RICHARD: You gave him almost two hours. That's too much.

KAMAN: I fell asleep in the middle.

RICHARD: And shooting your mouth off.

KAMAN: It's a thesis. Who reads a thesis? (RICHARD *produces some papers.*) So what's the schedule?

RICHARD: There's a school in Birmingham wants you to judge their poetry competition.

KAMAN: (*Casually*) Are you crazy?

RICHARD: There are lots of Asian kids – it'll look bad if you turn them down. I'll go through the stuff and pull out a few good ones for you. Then there's Cambridge on Tuesday.

KAMAN: On Tuesday? How the hell do I get to Cambridge by Tuesday?

RICHARD: Cambridge *England*. There's a university there, they're giving you an honorary degree, remember?

KAMAN: Ah yes, I believe I was a student there some years ago. Or was it that other place with the punts and the pointy roofs?

RICHARD: You have lunch in Trinity with the Master and Vice-

Chancellor, then process to the Senate House. There'll be some stuff in Latin. You'll need to rehearse your speech a bit, so don't get legless.

KAMAN: I'll be fine down to the knees; beyond that I can't promise. What's after Cambridge?

RICHARD: Lots of media stuff you can forget about for now. And a gig at the South Bank with Heaney and Walcott.

KAMAN: I refuse to consort with cheap rhymsters.

RICHARD: The fee's two grand.

KAMAN: I'll stretch a point; they're promising young lads. When do I get to see Yana?

RICHARD: Do you think that's a good idea?

KAMAN: I have a right to see my own daughter after five years. I have a right to a free day.

RICHARD: Free day? There isn't a free ten minutes. By the way, what the hell were you playing at, calling me your wife's lover?

KAMAN: You mean you're not?

RICHARD: You don't want to hear the answer to that. You're afraid of it.

KAMAN: Afraid to hear you're sleeping with Mara?

RICHARD: Afraid to hear I'm not. Then you might have to start feeling sorry for her, left on her own.

KAMAN: (*Drinking*) You know Richard, discovering I couldn't manage it any more was the most liberating moment of my life. Like shucking off a terminal illness. Or (*gestures to groin*) amputating a diseased limb. 'Course it left the groupies a bit miffed. Ah, groupies: they only want me for my mind. It's so degrading. I wish someone would desire me for my stomach muscles.

RICHARD: I suppose you need a touch of failure in your life. It reminds you of home.

KAMAN: Failure's the only condition that's real. That's what the West can't understand.

RICHARD: Which is why you're picking up two thousand nicker on the South Bank.

KAMAN: I wouldn't be too sniffy about it, old fruit; you get ten per cent.

RICHARD: You weren't a failure back home, Kaman. Your old man ruled the roost and you went to a school that makes Harrow look like Borstal. My dad was a fitter in Warrington and I lived beside a river not even canned fish could survive in.

KAMAN: Well, welcome to marginality.

RICHARD: You're piqued because you're a toff in your own country and an alien over here. So every time they give you a prize you sink a crate of whiskey – just to show them you're not dependent. Display your contempt for them by puking all over your trousers.

KAMAN: You fashioned us in your own image, so I deface the image.

RICHARD: Either beat us or join us, friend; there's no third way. Third World is just a fancy name for screwing yourself up. (*Pulls out a script.*) Here's your Cambridge speech. We'd better try a run-through. (*Hands script to* KAMAN.)

KAMAN: (*Glancing at it*) I thought it was in Latin.

RICHARD: No, their speech about you is in Latin. You reply in English.

KAMAN: So how do we know what to say?

RICHARD: Because they sent me a translation of what *they're* going to say.

KAMAN: And what do they say?

RICHARD: Usual shit. Just like our reply.

KAMAN: Did you know a guy at Cambridge called Blackwell?

RICHARD: I wasn't at Cambridge.

KAMAN: Sorry, I forgot: you lived in an old fish can at the bottom of a river and your dad was an epileptic.

RICHARD: A *fitter*. That's a job, not an illness.

KAMAN: I'll never get the hang of this sodding language. Do you know, when I first came to England I –

RICHARD: Saw a road sign saying 'Loose Chippings' and thought it was a village.

KAMAN: No, I saw a road sign saying 'Beware of Sheep' and wondered what had become of the spirit of Dunkirk. I thought you told me you knew Blackwell.

RICHARD: Blackwell of the F.O.? Yes, sort of; we live in the same village.

KAMAN: He's not Foreign Office, he's MI6. He was in my year – recruited by my Tutor. My Tutor pimped for MI6 and next door there was a Marxist economist who touted for the KGB. I suppose they compared notes over lunch.

RICHARD: But he never tried it on with you?

KAMAN: Oh no: wogs and proles were strictly off-bounds. Though I must confess I felt a bit peeved at not being approached, especially after the labour I'd put into acquiring this absurd

accent. There was a curious quality about young Blackwell –
something that made you want to slug him very hard in the
stomach.

RICHARD: OK, let's try the speech.

KAMAN: (*Reading*) Mr Vice-Challenger, Ladies and –

RICHARD: Chancellor.

KAMAN: Mr Vice-Chancellor, Ladies and Gentlemen. It is with genuine humility – (*Aside to* RICHARD) humility! – that I accept today
this Honorary Doctorate of Letters from the University of
Cambridge. When I first came to this ancient university,
many years ago, as an undergraduate from overseas, I came
as one for whom London was no more than a populous
labyrinth portrayed by Dickens, the Lake District a haunting
presence in the pages of Wordsworth, and (*swerving from
script*) Queen Victoria a raddled old floozie who was humping
her groom. (*Back to script.*) It was Cambridge, with its spires
and cloisters, its shaded courts and cobbled alley-ways,
which first incarnated for me the spirit of England; and if I
remember it today with affection, it is above all for (*swerves
from script*) its felicitous oversight in failing to recruit me into
British Intelligence and winding up in a back alley in Belfast
with my guts round my kneecaps. (*Back to script.*) Since that
time, I have made my living by the language of Milton and
Shakespeare; (*throwing aside script and breaking into stand-
up comedian routine*) and isn't it amazing how you get to
meet the US President just because you can think up a rhyme
for rhubarb? I mean, how gullible can you lot get? A nifty way
with *terza rima* and you get to stay in the Ritz. A couple of
allusions to Dante and before you know where you are you're
dancing tit to tit with Madonna. Which isn't bad if like me
you come from the arse-end of nowhere. As the man said
about the dog walking on hind legs, it's not done too well but
it's surprising it's done at all, so give him a bone and a big
hand folks. You think I'm cynical? You should meet my
family. In fact if you're not a nice audience we'll come and
live next door to you. We're not all that different, you know.
We didn't have a pet baboon, my old man didn't park a rhino
in the drive. I was born in a leafy suburb that could have been
Boston or Birmingham – it's just that down the road people
were selling their seven-year-old daughters for five bob an
hour to tourists who looked just like your uncle Albert. And

we have our own culture too – mostly of the oral kind, it's
safer. We don't have publishers, we send our stuff by smoke
signal. Epics are a bit hard on the old arm muscles, so we
tend to keep our poems to a few slim puffs.

And despite all this, you took me in. Furnished only with
Paradise Lost and a penis sheath. You pulled out of our bit of
the globe some years back, leaving us with navy knickers, 'All
in the April Evening' and an economy as lopsided as Long
John Silver. But you still can't leave us alone. Because the
truth is that the West is so screwed up that it can't bear to
look at itself, so it drools over anything different. One inva-
sion from Venus will be alarming; two, and they'll be hiring
them in the cultural studies departments. But don't forget,
folks: as the wise man said, it's better to be rich and happy
rather than poor and miserable.

*A lighting change indicates that the real ceremony is now under
way. Two men and a woman, formally dressed and holding
cocktails, gather round and hand a glass to* RICHARD. KAMAN
assumes a formal public tone and re-consults his script.

In conclusion, Mr Vice-Chancellor, I wish to thank you and
the Master of Trinity for your most generous hospitality, and
the Public Orator for his witty and gracious compliments.
The Latin speech in which his remarks were couched was
once the shared idiom of the world; today, it is the language
of Shakespeare and Milton, of Bunyan and the Authorized
Version, which holds sway from Kerry to Kuala Lumpur. It
has been wisely said that to share a language is to share a
form of life; and nothing could persuade me more of my own
place within your community than the high honour you have
conferred upon me today.

(*Applause from the bystanders;* KAMAN *goes over and takes a
tumbler full of whiskey from* RICHARD, *knocking most of it back.
The bystanders gather round him; lighting change: a cocktail
party.*)

WOMAN: (*To* KAMAN) I thought your speech was splendid, Mr Kaman.
KAMAN: Oh, just a modest attempt to promote harmony among the
    nations. I do it all the time. Just think of me as a kind of
    spiritual Secretary-General.
WOMAN: Have you ever lectured in West Africa?
KAMAN: Not recently. But a friend of mine – English woman – has
    just come back from teaching in Lagos. In fact there's rather

an amusing story attached to that. (*The others cease chatting among themselves and gather round him.*) You see, she'd been there once before a few years ago, when there were some marvellous peacocks on the university lawn. But this time the peacocks weren't there. So she buttonholes the Vice-Chancellor at a sherry party, and being a bit waggish says to him: 'Whatever happened to the peacocks? I hope you didn't eat them!' Whereupon the Vice-Chancellor gazes at her sombrely and replies: 'Dr and Mrs Peacock returned to London last year.'

(*A silence; then a few embarrassed perfunctory chuckles from the company.* KAMAN *downs more drink.*)

Don't you think that's funny? Forgive me, perhaps I'm not telling it well. Maybe you don't get the point. You see, she was implying that they were cannibals. (*Roars with laughter and drinks. To* WOMAN): Don't you think that's hilarious?

WOMAN: Not very, no.

KAMAN: Perhaps you think it's racist.

WOMAN: Yes, I'm afraid I do.

KAMAN: But it's funny as well, though?

WOMAN: I don't find racism amusing.

KAMAN: I didn't say it was.

RICHARD: (*Low tones*) Come on, man, back off, will you.

KAMAN: (*Now thoroughly drunk, to* WOMAN) This is my agent. And my wife's lover.

(WOMAN *moves away.*)

RICHARD: Finish the drink and we'll be off, OK?

MAN: Mr Kaman, my name's Bob Rossiter, I'm in the Anthropology Faculty.

KAMAN: You want to measure my skull?

ROSSITER: (*Embarrassed laugh*) I think we got beyond that a while back. It's just that I read somewhere that you were interested in song. That's one of my own areas.

KAMAN: (*Loudly*) The man wants a song!

RICHARD: Let's split, Kaman.

KAMAN: I'll give you a song if you want, sonny. Now this, ladies and gentlemen, is the first song I ever learnt as a child. We used to sing it everywhere. We chanted it on the beaches and on the roof-tops, it was heard in the pubs and in the cafés. We whammed out a verse before breakfast and a chorus after cocoa, and we were still crooning it in our sleep. And I think you'll agree that it speaks more profoundly of my native culture than – with all due respect – Shakespeare ever spoke for England. It condenses our history, it distils our soul. And it goes something – like – this:

> Maybe it's because I'm a Londoner
> That I love London so
> Maybe it's because I'm a Londoner
> That I think of her wherever I go
> I gets a funny feelin' inside of me
> When I'm walkin' up and down
> Maybe it's because I'm a Londoner
> That I love London town.

(KAMAN *sings the verse in a passable Cockney accent and accompanies it with a little dancing and arch hand-twirling. The company greet the song with embarrassed silence.*)

KAMAN: Well, talk about playing the Glasgow Palais on a wet Wednesday.
(*Black-out. Lights slowly up again on* KAMAN *standing looking out to the audience, and* RAAN *standing behind him.*)

KAMAN: (*Meditatively, as if to himself*) They cart me from hotel room to dinner party like a sack of spuds. There are times I'm not even sure what hemisphere I'm in. Not that it matters much: anywhere is everywhere these days.

RAAN: Then come home. Stop running. Come to us.

KAMAN: It's the way I keep faith. Its my emptiness that binds me to what I walked out on. My home's an airport, theirs is a shack. They're both transitory.

RAAN: You can't feel the rain through an airport roof.

KAMAN: I stay on the hoof: that way I can be true to the impermanence you call home.

RAAN: You're everything out here, and nothing. Back home you have a meaning.

KAMAN: That's what I'm afraid of. If I go back I'll forget I'm nobody. Here they rub my nose in it every time they applaud.

RAAN: We're going to be someone again. We're going to have a history of our own.

KAMAN: Only the victors have that. You're breaking faith with failure.

RAAN: So what do you suggest? That the children go on dying?

KAMAN: That you stop peddling illusions. Every five-year plan you unfold is a lie to the people. At least they know the truth; you'd even strip them of that. It's a useless sort of truth, like art; but it's better than your revolutionary fictions.

RAAN: So you're abandoning them to the death squads. That's honest, at least.

KAMAN: I've turned into the image of those I despise. That's what'll happen to you too, if you overthrow Janda. You'll be shaving yourself at his gold-plated sink and showing Princess Anne round the palace.

RAAN: The Yanks want Janda out of the way.

KAMAN: That's funny – they put him there in the first place.

RAAN: He's out of control – sucking up to the Japs, sounding off against the US bases. The States wants free elections.

KAMAN: They blocked them for thirty years. They sent the Company in to screw them up. You know that, Raan.

RAAN: That was history; this is the future.

KAMAN: So you've got Uncle Sam behind your revolution? Washington gold?

RAAN: You're crazy, Kaman. They may be pissed off with Janda but they're not exactly looking for a socialist alternative.

KAMAN: And the last time there was a *coup* they shipped in 23,000 troops and left a dozen death squads behind them. The White House called it stability.

RAAN: But they could justify all that with the Communists. Now they've lost their bogeyman. So Janda is on the cover of *Time* magazine with big bloodshot eyes crunching up little kids. Eighteen months ago he was guardian of democracy, now he's a paranoid pornographer. And the people are still eating off garbage dumps.

KAMAN: In the good old days there was a formula for beating hunger, spreading happiness and getting the Yanks off your back. It was called revolution. Now it's known as heroin.

RAAN: So what are you going to do about it?

KAMAN: What are *you* going to do about it?

RAAN: We're ready to move. We have units in the countryside, we've got whole squadrons of the Army. And the students are straining at the leash.

KAMAN: So you oust Janda. Then what? Expropriate foreign capital?

RAAN: And have the Marines in in a week? Come on, Kaman, you know the score. We have to move one step at a time. We can't survive outside the world market.

KAMAN: You can't survive inside it either. So what changes? The new President wears a collar and tie rather than looking like something out of *Star Wars*?

RAAN: We see off a gang of thugs who bleed the people dry.

KAMAN: And substitute a bunch of Cambridge graduates who'll bleed them white.

RAAN: We run the economy for the benefit of the people.

KAMAN: Ah, the economy. I was wondering if we still had one of those. And what are the multinationals going to say? You going to take them over?

RAAN: We've got to start from where we are. We're talking about 78 per cent illiteracy, Kaman. We're talking about three-quarters of a million people living in quarries after the earthquake.

KAMAN: You can't skin a tiger claw by claw. You'll take over and you'll fuck up; what about the debt, for God's sake? It's a toss-up which will happen first, paying off the IMF or the sun running out of steam. They'll stuff you with military bases, and just because you've got a photograph of yourself with Prince Charles on your mantelpiece and that dreary little ditty that goes by the name of the National Anthem, you'll be swishing up to the UN in your stretch limos imagining you're independent. And then another bunch of Cambridge graduates looking for cushy jobs in Government House will come knocking on the door.

RANN: I hear you call yourself an exile these days.

KAMAN: So I am: a self-exile. I beat the hell out of myself a long time ago. I'm a running dog of Faber and Faber and the only authentic thing about me is that I know it. I sign my books for head-bangers and dole out prizes for pretentious tossers and that, you see, is my private anti-colonial campaign. Because if they're stupid enough to wet their pants over a wanker like me, then everything we've ever said about them is true.

RAAN: They don't see you as a wanker back home. Have you any idea of how they venerate you? They have your picture in every other house; they put candles under it, they lay it on the sick to cure them. You're bigger than Jesus back there, Kaman; you're almost as big as Clint Eastwood.

KAMAN: They admire me because I acted out their fantasies. I took the first plane out.

RAAN: We could use that devotion, Kaman. We need your support.

KAMAN: You need a Poet Laureate?

RAAN: We need you to speak out against Janda. When the right moment comes. That'll help in the West, and it'll help back home.

KAMAN: Look, Raan: there's one place left where we can still play a little, and it's called art. It's a thin margin, but it's all we've got. Do you want to know how I live? I take a vowel, I roll it on my tongue like a piece of sherbert, savour its musty flavour and salvage it from the wreckage. My job is to redeem words from history, so we can still have a currency of sorts.

RAAN: You know what real politics is about. You were tortured back there.

KAMAN: Torture's like art – it's a world apart. Its rules don't relate to this one.

RAAN: We need your voice, Kaman. There's a state of emergency.

KAMAN: There's always a state of emergency.

RAAN: I want to go home, Kaman. I want you to help me go home.

KAMAN: It was never anybody's home. You think I feel guilty about getting out? Guilt's a private luxury, like perfume. You can't drink a coffee without screwing a Brazlian worker; you can't tie your shoe-laces without getting involved with the World Bank.

RAAN: So you're going to sit here nursing your freedom?

KAMAN: I'm going to sit here nursing my refusal. That's the one thing they can't take away from me.

RAAN: So you've handed in your membership card?

KAMAN: I'm not sure I was ever issued with one.

RAAN: You're going to die, Kaman.

KAMAN: Oh, I know. It's the ultimate disengagement. The World Bank can't take that away from me either.

RAAN: You're letting them destroy you.

KAMAN: We were dead already, Raan; we never had a chance.

RAAN: You're letting them win.

KAMAN: No, no. Power thrives on opposition. I'm just lying quiet so that power can have no hold over me. Don't try to act, Raan: it'll only suck you in.

RAAN: You know I can't do that, Kaman.

KAMAN: Of course I do. I just thought I ought to let you know.

(RAAN *goes out. During the latter part of this scene, two men and a woman, dressed as stereotypical 'Third World' peasants, have come one by one on-stage and stand round listening to the*

dialogue, occasionally whispering together and gesturing.
KAMAN *sits in his armchair and begins to drink, gradually falling*
asleep. The CHORUS *begins to chant, sometimes singly, some-*
times together.)

(Chorus)
    The great Kaman has crossed the ocean
    The ocean we have never seen
    He has music in his mouth
    And our hope creased in his fist
    He will pitch his tent among the mighty
    And pluck this sorrow from us like an old cloak

    He will pitch his tent among the mighty
    And when they are dull with sleep smite them in our name
    He will ensnare them with his soft words
    And bind them fast in the coils of his speech
    Then he will stride to our barred door
    And release us like angry birds

    For our land is empty as a beggar's belly
    And dark as a gouged eye
    Silence stalks the suburbs
    And the city withers at the root
    The jackal squats in his palace
    Gnawing an infant's bone

    But the panthers crouch on the hillside
    Awaiting great Kaman's call
    Strong is his magic, steadfast his power
    And his music moves in us like the wind
    He will rise from the sea to deliver us
    Wrapped in the cloak of his ancestors

    Cracked are the village cisterns
    And the babies suck bloody tears
    Our young men vanish like clouds
    And only the grave-diggers profit
    The people drift like dry leaves
    And scatter like a spent wave

    But the forests crane their tousled heads
    To glimpse the great Kaman's return
    He will sail into our stone harbour

Armed only in his song
He will rip the heart from the jackal
And feed it to his sleek wives

For justice shines on his brow
And mercy lives in his mouth
And his ship cuts the foaming current
Like a lover in haste to his bride
Heap the valleys with tender petals
Strew rushes beneath his strong feet

For his voice is thunderous in the valleys
And lightning plays on his brow
And his words are bread to our children
And wine to our sturdy warriors
With his lute he makes whole the leper
His tongue restores the dying

The great Kaman has crossed the ocean
The ocean we have never seen
There is music in his mouth
And our hope creased in his fist
He will pitch his tent among the mighty
And pluck this sorrow from us like an old cloak.

(CHORUS *exit. A pause, then* KAMAN *wakes with a cry in a surreal light.*)

KAMAN: I was holding Yana. They put her on my knee and her flesh was rough and dry and as light as cork. I looked down and I could see right through her, there was nothing inside her at all. And I looked past her to my own limbs and they were fading, dwindling, just curved beaks, and the light was pouring through them so that I was just a cavity on the air and my chest a scooped bloody crater with a great mess of plucked veins where my heart had been. I bent forward to gather Yana up, and nothing happened, I couldn't bend down because there was nothing of me left, it was just the ghost of an action, the emptiness was weaving me through and through so that she slipped through my fingers like a trickle of blood leaving only a smear of herself on my thumb. And there was just a mouth hovering on the air, hers, mine maybe, the lips swollen like a puckered wound.

Lights suddenly up. YANA *is standing looking at* KAMAN. *He moves slowly, stumblingly towards her.*

KAMAN: So. So it's Yana.

YANA: Yes. It's me.

KAMAN: I can't believe you're real.

YANA: Don't say it.

KAMAN: What?

YANA: Don't tell me I've got big.

KAMAN: (*Laughs*) Well, no, I wasn't going to say that. Don't tell me I've got old.

YANA: You haven't. You're just as I remember you.

KAMAN: You can't remember much.

YANA: I remember everything. I was thirteen, you know; that wasn't so long ago.

KAMAN: So what do you remember?

YANA: I remember looking at you through the glass. Your hair was shaved and there was blood on your shirt, where they'd beaten you. I put my finger against the glass and you put your finger against mine and wiggled it around.

KAMAN: You were holding a blue and white carrier bag, and you had a pigtail.

YANA: Pony-tail.

KAMAN: Alright, pony-tail. (*Pause.*) How's your mother?

YANA: She's alright. Tell me why you wouldn't see me.

KAMAN: You know why. Your mother told you why.

YANA: I want to hear it from you.

KAMAN: Because of your mother. Because she got out and brought you over here, and then when I got out of prison and came over I pestered her, I was drunk, violent, I didn't know what I was doing. So she convinced the courts I was trying to kidnap you and they prevented me from seeing you until now.

YANA: You could have seen me anyway.

KAMAN: It wasn't safe; my status here wasn't secure, they could have deported me. Then I grew big and famous and well-behaved and they lifted the court order.

YANA: You wanted me to forget you.

KAMAN: If I'd wanted that I wouldn't have written to you. But I wanted a new life for you, yes. The old one was a bit too dramatic.

YANA: I don't want a new life; I want the old one back.

KAMAN: Well, Yana, I'm not the father you visited in prison.

YANA: You are to me.

KAMAN: A lot of things have changed since then.

YANA: No they haven't. I haven't changed; things at home haven't changed.

KAMAN: No, that's true; that's why England is your home now.

YANA: This isn't my home.

> (*Pause.*)

KAMAN: How's student life treating you?

YANA: I don't find it very real. I spend most of my time in politics.

KAMAN: Politics?

YANA: I'm in the Revolutionary Socialist League. We do a lot of work in the East End – anti-racism, hospital campaigns, that kind of thing.

KAMAN: Well, it must be genetic. Does your mother approve?

YANA: Not much; I think it reminds her of you. (*Pause.*) You're very famous now, aren't you? The only way I've kept in touch with you is through the telly. Oh, and I've been at some of your poetry readings.

KAMAN: Oh really? I didn't see you.

YANA: I kept my head down – didn't want to get you into trouble with the law.

KAMAN: Well, that's very law-abiding for a revolutionary. I'm sure nobody would have minded. Is it a problem for you, my being famous?

YANA: Of course not – except that everyone expects me to write fantastic poetry. It's not a problem, I'm very proud of you.

KAMAN: But it's the prison you remember most.

YANA: Well, that's the last time I saw you.

KAMAN: You've seen me since.

YANA: I don't count that. I want to go back and fight against Janda.

KAMAN: I'm not sure that would be very wise.

YANA: Why not? Why haven't you been speaking out against him? People admire you, you could have some influence.

KAMAN: Well, that's a long story. I'll tell you about it some day.

YANA: Tell me now.

KAMAN: I'm not sure you'd entirely understand.

YANA: I understand politics; I understand about oppression. I think sometimes that's about all I understand.

KAMAN: Well, there are other things.

YANA: Not for me there aren't.

> (*Pause.*)

KAMAN: Are you happy?

YANA: Of course I'm not happy. I've got a dreadful mother and I want to be back home with you fighting the regime. And I should have taken Political Science rather than English. I don't like English Literature, I'm just good at it.

KAMAN: I hope you don't have to study me.

YANA: They don't do Third World literature.

KAMAN: That's because it doesn't exist. The Third World is an imaginary construct of the West, like Purgatory.

YANA: I know, I was born there. (*Pause.*) I'm very glad to see you.

KAMAN: (*Stretching out his hand to her*) It's my happiest moment since getting out of the nick. (*Takes her in his arms.*) My darling girl. (YANA *starts to cry uncontrollably.*) There now. There now, my precious, my little one. It's alright, it really is.

YANA: (*Sobbing*) No it's not. It's horrible.

KAMAN: (*Stroking her hair*) Well, well, it's not so horrible. It's not all horrible, dearest. We can be together now, that's the main thing.

YANA: Can we go home now?

KAMAN: Well, we'll just have to see. We'll have to see. I'm not sure the *mater* would be too keen on that.

YANA: I don't give a shit what my mother thinks. She took me away from you.

KAMAN: Ah well, you mustn't be too hard on her – she thought I was a danger to you. She had a hard time, hitched to an old bastard like me. (YANA *laughs a little through her tears;* KAMAN *follows up his advantage.*) You know what a silly old sod you've got for a father, don't you?

YANA: No I don't.

KAMAN: I couldn't even change a bloody light bulb.

YANA: Who cares about that? Who cares when you're the best writer in the world?

KAMAN: Well, I think your mother might have preferred the best chef.

YANA: That just shows how stupid she is. She didn't deserve to be married to a revolutionary.

KAMAN: Well, she stood by me when I was in prison. They gave her a hard time, you know.

YANA: Yes, I know. I feel sorry for her sometimes, but you can't let emotions get in the way of the struggle. You didn't.

KAMAN: No, I certainly didn't.

(*Pause.*)

YANA: I'd better be going. I've got a cell meeting.

KAMAN: Sounds a bit monastic. Should I give you a ring?

YANA: No, I'll ring you.

KAMAN: It's alright – I'm not going to run out on you, you know.

YANA: I know. I'd just feel better if I could ring you any time.

KAMAN: Any time of the day or night. Leave a message if I'm not in.
(*Kisses her.*) Goodbye, sweetheart. Take care, see you soon.

YANA: Bye.
(*Exits.* RICHARD *enters.*)

RICHARD: Be careful, Kaman. Don't let her get too close. Let her be
the one woman you didn't ruin. Leave her with her illusions.
OK?

CURTAIN

———————◆———————

ACT TWO

KAMAN, RAAN, RICHARD *and* SALAH *are watching the video screen, which shows an elderly General reading a script to camera in what sounds like* KAMAN's *language. We can hardly hear his words for the sounds of gun-fire, which may or may not be coming from the screen. The General finishes his speech and the screen goes blank.*

RICHARD: What was he saying?

RAAN: He's making no concessions. Two more students dead from their injuries. That brings the body count to seven.

RICHARD: Did *he* say that?

RAAN: (*Withering look*) Of course not. I had it from home this morning.

KAMAN: You set up those students, Raan.

RAAN: We set up nobody; it's nothing to do with us. They were trying to turn all the economics courses into the pure milk of the free market and the students wouldn't buy it. Singing a hymn to Janda every morning is one thing, having your studies dictated by Coca-Cola is another.

KAMAN: They must be out of their minds. Two thousand half-starved students against two hundred tanks.

RAAN: Yes, it's adventurism.

KAMAN: I thought there'd be a word in your revolutionary lexicon for it.

RAAN: And of course the soldiers are just peasants, so they love to get their hands on middle-class intellectuals.

KAMAN: So what are you lot up to?

RAAN: I don't know, the news coming through is pretty confused. The units in the capital are holding back for the moment. It's a matter of which way the Army jumps.

KAMAN: Well that's reassuring: you're the next Prime Minister, you're thousands of miles away and you don't know what the fuck's going on.

RAAN: I'm not the next Prime Minister. And they need me here in the West. Not to speak of the fact that I'd be shot the moment I stepped off the plane.

KAMAN: So you'll arrive back just when they're dishing out the Ministries. What do you think of all this, Salah?

SALAH: (*Nodding vigorously*) Very good, sir. Everything very good.

KAMAN: Well, there speaks the revolutionary voice of the people. Go and get me some more booze, there's a good fellow.

SALAH: Very good, sir.

(*Bows and exits.*)

RAAN: It's looking bad.

KAMAN: It's under control. He's contained the situation, the students have backed off, there'll be no more trouble.

RICHARD: So you don't think the Americans will go in?

KAMAN: The *Americans*? Over seven dead students?

RICHARD: Well, they're backing Janda, aren't they?

KAMAN: Not any more.

RICHARD: I thought they set him up.

RAAN: So they did. The Yanks adored Janda, he did everything they asked him to. Slashed welfare programmes, smashed the labour unions, disappeared a few ornery priests and community activists. Trickle-down economics.

RICHARD: What's that?

KAMAN: That means you help the rich get richer and they piss on the poor.

RAAN: He's got security forces trained by the Israeli Secret Service and the SAS. He started off a bit wet behind the ears about electrodes, but they soon put him right on that. Oh yes, he did all the right things.

RICHARD: What sort of things?

RAAN: Cut farm subsidies, halted land reform, brown-nosed the IMF. You've heard of the IMF?

RICHARD: Yes.

KAMAN: Indescribably Miserable Future.

RAAN: Death squads, vigilantes, disappearances. Radical nuns found decapitated in ditches.

RICHARD: I don't believe it.

RAAN: And a dab hand in drug trafficking, with a spot of support from the Company.

RICHARD: What company?

RAAN: The CIA. Except that then he started to stash away too much of the loot.

RICHARD: You're telling me the CIA are into drug trafficking?

KAMAN: My dear Richard, where *have* you been hiding? So are some of the big American finance corporations.

RICHARD: Where do you get all this from?

KAMAN: Well not from the *Guildford Advertiser*.

RAAN: Then there's the organ trade.

RICHARD: Organ? What kind of organs?

KAMAN: Well not the sort they play in Canterbury Cathedral.

RAAN: Trade in children's organs. They run baby farms, kill the kids, strip them of a few select organs they might be needing in Boston and ship them over.

RICHARD: That's incredible. That's a myth.

RAAN: It was brought up in the European Parliament. Happens in Honduras, happens with us.

KAMAN: The European Parliament? Oh well that's alright then. For a moment I thought they might be getting away with it.

RICHARD: It can't be as bad as that. I mean, I've no brief for the CIA, but this is Loch Ness monster stuff.

KAMAN: Janda lives in a fantasy world, Richard; he's sick, he's paranoid, he destroys for the hell of it. That's what happens when nobody tells you the truth. He just wants to stuff the whole world inside himself. What do you think we're giving you, Communist propaganda? Well there aren't any Communists any more. Which means that we've moved up a notch. I mean, when Eastern Europe was still on the go, they were the Second World and we were the Third. So now they've collapsed we get promotion. There's progress for you.

RAAN: Or they're moving down; it comes to the same thing.

KAMAN: Then there's the environment. Did you know that the US satellite passing over our place reports no possibility of human life? Maybe we should try waving. Or get the whole population to lie down in a big HELP sign.

RICHARD: But what about aid? The West puts in a lot of aid. Alright, I know it doesn't always get to the right places but –

KAMAN: Oh, we get plenty of aid back home; how else do you think Janda gets to run three palaces?

RAAN: At the moment there are two political parties to choose between, one run by a General and the other by a Colonel. They're brothers.

RICHARD: What about this guy – what's his name – that politician Janda put in prison?

KAMAN: Well, that covers about five thousand people. Which one are you thinking of?

RICHARD: You know, the socialist. The bald one with the beard.

RAAN: Malek?

RICHARD: That's him.

RAAN: Malek was a violin candidate.

RICHARD: What does that mean?

RAAN: Put up by the Left and played by the Right.

RICHARD: Was, you say?

RAAN: Yes, the Company had him stabilized.

RICHARD: Stabilized?

RAAN: Shot through the head.

KAMAN: Anyway, pretty soon Janda won't be able to get a government together; he's running out of relatives. It's either going to mean going outside the family or a six-year-old Minister of Justice.

RAAN: There was an opposition leader back in 1961, when we still had that sort of thing, who thought up a brilliant way to power. He had the whole Cabinet assassinated. He thought that by the Constitution he'd be invited to form a government.

RICHARD: What happened?

RAAN: They hanged him. You see there wasn't a Constitution.

(*Enter* SALAH *in some haste.*)

SALAH: You are wanted, Mr Raan. Very urgent.

RAAN: See you later.

(*Exits with* SALAH).

KAMAN: Good old Raan. He'd be arguing about peasants' co-operatives while Janda was setting fire to the shanty towns.

RICHARD: How does all this affect you?

KAMAN: It doesn't affect me at all.

RICHARD: People are going to pressurize you.

KAMAN: So what? Oh, there might be a change of government back there, but so what else is new? Leaders back home are like babies' nappies: they need to be changed regularly, and for much the same reasons. In the bad old days before independence we were just cheap labour, raw materials and a market. But we've stood all that on its head. Now we're a market, raw materials and cheap labour.

RICHARD: I note you're taking it all with your usual sloppy emotionalism.

KAMAN: Feelings are for poetry, Richard; I can't afford them in real life. Getting angry about injustice implies you believe in justice. I abandoned that fiction a long time ago. (RAAN *enters, grim-faced.*) So what's the latest?

RAAN: Get me a drink, will you.

KAMAN: (*Getting him a drink*) What's the old maniac up to now? Appointing an orang-utang Vice-President?

RAAN: (*Rounding furiously on him*) Can't you be serious just for once in your bleeding useless existence?

KAMAN: (*Quietly*) What is it?

RAAN: (*Pointing to video screen, voice shaking*) While he was speaking – at the very moment he was speaking – saying that he had the situation under control – his goons were rounding up the students and herding them into the football stadium. They left them there for a couple of hours and some of the students got bored and began chanting slogans. So they opened fire.

RICHARD: The soldiers?

RAAN: Sprayed them with machine-guns. For about three minutes, non-stop. Something like three hundred dead, hundreds wounded. A massacre.

(*Long pause.*)

RICHARD: Jesus Christ.

RAAN: And there's more. He's let loose the death squads in the villages – the villages the student leaders come from. They're carting off the people – something Janda calls 'collective responsibility'. There are reports of kids bayoneted, old women. Rapes.

(*Pause.* KAMAN *goes to pour himself a drink.*)

RICHARD: He's mad.

RAAN: He's out of control.

(SALAH *enters, stricken-faced.*)

SALAH: Mr Kaman . . . Mr Kaman, . . . please sir . . . please sir . . .

(KAMAN *goes over and puts his arms round him.*)

KAMAN: I know, Salah, I know. It'll be alright now. Don't you worry.

SALAH: Mr Kaman, you help us. You do something, sir. You great man. You help us, sir?

KAMAN: (*Still holding him*) It'll be alright, Salah. Don't you worry now. It'll all be OK.

Black-out. Sounds of gun-fire, shouting, screaming. Lights gradually up on KAMAN *standing at a lectern, delivering a lecture.*

KAMAN: Shelley called poets the unacknowledged legislators of the world. Auden remarked that that sounded more like the secret police. And of course he was right: it is the secret police, not the poets, who can determine in the end whether we shall live or die. It is they, not the poets, who sound the depths of our soul, in that ceremonial ritual known as torture. The poets can only envy the fineness of their perceptions, the subtlety of their discourse. The professional inquisitor, unlike the poet, is an artist who makes things happen. Whereas the poet knows himself to be the most craven and retarded of God's creatures, one who is terrified of relinquishing the breast and sucks instead at the mighty dug of speech. It is language which the poet will bully and cajole, force or seduce into his service, with all the devotion with which the torturer works on the bodies of his victims. The poet's concern is with words, not flesh, and the torturer deals in flesh with all the clinical precision with which the poet arranges his sentences. But the torturer will always succeed, where the poet is doomed to fail. For there is nobody on earth who can withstand the modern technology of torture, an apparatus which, like the Almightly himself, is utterly perfect and will always achieve its end. There will always come that mysterious moment, in the ceremonious ritual between inquisitor and victim, when the soul of the victim is written on his body for all to see – when the inmost secret of a man or woman is inscribed on their flesh in letters of blood. The torturer is the supreme example of the success ethic, the business executive writ large. Whereas the poet remains wedded to failure, aware that the moment of truth is always missed, that it arrives, like happiness, too soon or too late to be of service. The poet strives for the impossible, to render the world in words; and though there is the occasional miracle, he knows it to be as illusory as pulling a rabbit from a hat. It is this eternal non-coincidence between words and things which is the source of the poet's infinite sorrow; but since, were these to coincide, all human life would cease, his failure is also the source of his power. It is in this way, then, that the poet preserves a pact with that suffering which is the only spot from which new life might spring.

Black-out. Then lights up on KAMAN *flanked by* RAAN *and* RICHARD. RAAN *with a portable telephone.*

RAAN: (*To* KAMAN) You're the biggest thing we've got. Our greatest national asset. You've got to use it.

KAMAN: You overestimate the power of art.

RAAN: It's nothing to do with bloody poetry, it's to do with fame. Fame makes you mythical, unkillable: it's like sitting in a tank. We could do with some of that.

KAMAN: Myths don't prevent massacres; they're usually responsible for them.

RAAN: They can slaughter the people, but they can't lay a glove on you. The West has made a hero out of you; now's your chance to turn it to advantage.

KAMAN: What do you say, Richard? Do you fancy me as Che Guevara?

RICHARD: I don't believe you should get caught up in violence.

RAAN: Children go hungry, twelve-year-olds are deflowered in brothels; you don't call that violence? You're caught up in violence every time you change a five-pound note.

RICHARD: It has to be resolved democratically. Otherwise you're just perpetuating the same old system.

KAMAN: (*To* RAAN) I think he may be worrying about the Nobel prize.

RICHARD: So what if I am? I'm your agent, remember. The committee aren't going to look too kindly on a supporter of terrorism.

KAMAN: And you wouldn't look too kindly on losing your ten per cent of a million bucks.

RICHARD: Oh, it's easy enough, isn't it – issue a statement and see your words turn into bullets for those back home. I suppose one angry sentence could mow down a few demonstrators.

RAAN: He can't evade his responsibility.

KAMAN: Why should a poet be any more responsible than a plumber? Why should I have any more authority than a trapeze artist? I have a way with words, Raan, that's all; there's nothing *moral* about it. Who do you think I am, the Dalai Lama?

RAAN: I told you, it's nothing to do with poetry. We made you, Kaman, we set you up; we have a right to ask for something back. The West's turned you into its pet savage – you're the image of all those they've messed up back home. Now you can put your failure at their disposal.

KAMAN: So what are you asking me to do?

RAAN: (*Glancing at* RICHARD) We can talk about that later.

RICHARD: Don't try to be authentic, Kaman. It wouldn't be authentic.

RAAN: I'm not asking you to be anybody. I'm asking you to identify with a nation of non-persons. You don't have to get off your back; you just have to change the meaning of it.
(*Pause.*)

KAMAN: (*Meditatively, to himself*) You see, ever since I came out of prison I've only known one feeling, and that's refusal. Like a permanent clenched fist in my guts. I walked out into the sunlight and took a look around and turned in my membership card. It seemed the only decent thing to do. Because I don't accept that suffering will ever be redeemed, and I don't accept a world in which it won't be. If I dance to their tune, it's because not doing so would be a way of caring; and that would mean getting involved. And getting involved with this world would be a betrayal of those it crucifies. So what I can't decide – what I can't get straight – is whether speaking out would be a form of involvement or a form of refusal.

During this speech RICHARD *moves back into the darkness out of sight.*

RAAN: It's not about your conscience, Kaman; forget about your precious conscience. It's about the people.

KAMAN: So what if I do make a statement? What difference would that make?

RAAN: Not a lot. That's not what we're after.

KAMAN: What do you want, Raan?

RAAN: We want you to be President.

KAMAN: (*After a pause*) I think an orang-utang might be a bit more suitable.

RAAN: The people worship you, Kaman. They'd strike against Janda for *you*; for us, well, we can't be sure.

KAMAN: Do I really have that kind of power?

RAAN: Yes, you really do. They haven't forgotten the prison years.

KAMAN: It disgusts me. It makes me sick.

RAAN: That's immaterial.

KAMAN: President of the nation, eh? Well, I suppose if a senile crook could be President of the United States, an alcoholic nihilist wouldn't be out of place back home.

RAAN: It wouldn't involve you in much. It's the idea of it that matters.

KAMAN: The last time a writer became president of his country it almost instantly broke up.

RAAN: We aren't Czechoslovakia.

KAMAN: And you think the people would respond?

RAAN: Sure they would. Some of them read your stuff – the early nationalist stuff – and they love it. The rest of them just like the idea of you.

KAMAN: So do the groupies. It's the reality they find a bit hard to stomach.

RANN: We can't dispense with mythology, Kaman.

KAMAN: So that's to be my contribution? To supply your revolution

with its odour of sanctity? A kind of cross between Zapata
and Vaclav Havel?

RAAN: That's right. We need a founding father.

KAMAN: My final consecration as a non-person. Well, there's certainly some logic to it.

RAAN: You might as well put your uselessness to some use. Over here
you're everything and nothing; over there you have a meaning. It doesn't have to be *your* meaning. You just have to let
yourself be lugged around like you are now. The only difference is that you'll be helping to save your country from a
murderous megalomaniac.

KAMAN: It sounds like a commitment. That doesn't sound like me.

RAAN: It's no commitment. The President's so far above politics that
he might as well be an orang-utang. We've had one or two
who weren't far off. You could drink yourself to death in the
presidential palace for all we care. Not too soon, of course;
you'd need to show your face a bit at first. It's all a matter of
symbolism – what better job for a poet?

KAMAN: You can't possibly imagine I'll accept. Though I admit it's
insane enough to be tempting.

RAAN: You have no choice, Kaman. It's those kids with glaucoma or
a slow death in the Savoy. (*Pause.*) Sorry, old comrade, but
I'm afraid you have absolutely no choice.

Black-out. Lights up on KAMAN *and* MARA.

KAMAN: You're looking good.

MARA: Isn't that your old joke?

KAMAN: What?

MARA: You know – the three ages of man: youth, middle age, and
you're looking good.

KAMAN: I'd forgotten.

MARA: You're looking older.

KAMAN: Yes, I've grown since you saw me last. Sideways, I mean.

MARA: How are you?

KAMAN: Alright. No, not alright – but it's alright. Why did you want
to see me?

MARA: Oh – just because.

KAMAN: Because of what's happening at home?

MARA: I suppose so, in a way. It made me think of you – us – again.
What's going to happen?

KAMAN: I don't know. The Yanks are dithering over Janda.

MARA: Are we going to get socialism?

KAMAN: Well, it's hardly the flavour of the month.

MARA: I don't suppose you're involved.

KAMAN: You'd be astonished.

MARA: So you *are* involved?

KAMAN: I don't know whether I am or not.

MARA: Yana says I should have sent her to a public school because they teach you how to use a rifle.

KAMAN: It must be a full-time job, having Joan of Arc for a daughter.

MARA: She can't get over seeing you. She's been talking about nothing else ever since.

KAMAN: Is that why you wanted to see me?

MARA: How do you mean?

KAMAN: I don't know: first I see her, then you. I'm not sure I can cope with this sudden rush of domesticity.

MARA: Do you mean that?

KAMAN: No. It's very good to see you.

MARA: I'm sorry I kept her from you. It's just that I had to protect her.

KAMAN: I was never a threat to her.

MARA: Well, turning up at her school with two one-way air tickets to Malaga . . .

KAMAN: I was too legless to cross the playground, let alone climb on to a Boeing. Anyway, the boys in white jackets scooped me up before I freaked her out.

MARA: She's your child, not mine – you can see that. But you're still a danger to her, you know.

KAMAN: Is that what you came to tell me?

MARA: Yes, partly. Now that you're seeing her again. She idealizes you so much, you see – it's her way of clinging on to the past. Yana only likes the past and future; she can't live in the present.

KAMAN: I'm not too keen on any of them myself.

MARA: She still thinks of you as a hero. And so you were. But it's hard enough for me, living with someone with so much faith.

KAMAN: You're afraid I might infect her?

MARA: She'd find it corrosive; I don't think she could take that. I'm hanging on to her by a hair as it is. She remembers you as you were; I'd like to keep it that way.

KAMAN: And you? How do you remember me?

MARA: I didn't just come to talk about Yana. I came to ask for your forgiveness.

KAMAN: For what?

MARA: For helping to make you what you are. For trying to make you into something different from what you were. I could see that politics weren't right for you, that you were denaturing yourself. But I thought I could replace it. I don't think any woman could – not even Yana. You never really wanted women, you can't take love, it's lethal for you. You can't let anyone inside you because you're afraid they'll find there's nothing there.

KAMAN: Afraid they'll find I disappeared a long time ago.

MARA: Yes. And so you wouldn't be able to take Yana either; you'd end up damaging her too.

KAMAN: You used to tell me I didn't know what I wanted.

MARA: That's right. There's just this gaping hole in you where what you want ought to be. You just fill it with booze, or words, or applause, they're the same kind of thing.

KAMAN: Well, I'm lying low.

MARA: I helped to bring you down, and I'm frightened that'll bring down Yana too.

KAMAN: I'll keep my head down. I won't harm her.

MARA: You mustn't think it's your fault. You didn't have a chance, baby.

KAMAN: I know.

MARA: When you got out of prison I just had to stand by and watch you slipping away bit by bit.

KAMAN: Well, there's a piece of me still left.

MARA: There's a lot of you still left, my love. You turned yourself into words, and that's sad, but they're wonderful words, and they're what will survive you. You'll have left your mark. It's just a pity it had to happen that way.

Black-out. Lights up on KAMAN *and* BLACKWELL.

BLACKWELL: Yes, that's it. You lived in New Court in the third year and I lived in Great Court. Then when we graduated –

KAMAN: You disappeared into the Foreign Office and were never seen again. Rose without trace, as it were.

BLACKWELL: Well, I went back for the gaudy some years ago. Didn't see you there though.

KAMAN: That's because I was in prison, Mr Blackwell. As I'm sure you're aware. They don't let you out for gaudy night.

BLACKWELL: Ah yes, so you were. Bad business back there at the moment.

KAMAN: Is that what you came to tell me?

BLACKWELL: Not really. I came to advise you to stay out of it.

KAMAN: Oh really?

BLACKWELL: I'd sit a bit loose to our friend Mr Raan if I were you. He comes up with some rather fanciful notions from time to time.

KAMAN: I take it you've been bugging the seat of his pants.

BLACKWELL: Mr Raan and my employers don't quite see eye to eye. We'd rather like to keep Janda afloat for a bit.

KAMAN: I thought the West wanted to see him off the premises.

BLACKWELL: The States, maybe. We're not their pet lap-dogs, you know.

KAMAN: You could have fooled me.

BLACKWELL: Though actually they're not too decided at the moment.

KAMAN: They don't like the colour of the alternative.

BLACKWELL: Precisely. And to tell you the truth, we don't like the sniff of it at all.

KAMAN: So what? There are no big British interests at stake.

BLACKWELL: Not there, no. But there are some rather important ones dotted around the region. We can't afford too much instability just at the moment, it might be contagious. A successful *coup* in your neck of the woods wouldn't set the best example.

KAMAN: So you're pimping for Janda.

BLACKWELL: Good Lord, no, the man's a monster. We're not a lot of Fascist beasts, you know. You mustn't think that anyone to the right of you is a reactionary hyena.

KAMAN: From what I know of MI6, no self-respecting hyena would give you the steam off his piss.

BLACKWELL: Look here, Kaman, you may not believe this, but we find old Janda every bit as distasteful as you do. What's going on out there is absolutely despicable. It's an affront to every democratic freedom you and I hold dear.

KAMAN: So is bugging Raan's phone. And mine.

BLACKWELL: But it's the wrong moment, you see.

KAMAN: The wrong moment for who? Janda's political prisoners?

BLACKWELL: Look, old Janda's days are numbered, that's clear enough. But if you move against him now the shock waves of it might turn out to be rather nasty.

KAMAN: Nasty for who?

BLACKWELL: (*Quietly, after a pause*) Well in the end, old chap, nasty for you, I'm afraid.

KAMAN: I take it that's what they call a threat.

BLACKWELL: You won't get anywhere by using violence.

KAMAN: I didn't know MI6 were pacifists.

BLACKWELL: It has to be done by democratic means.

KAMAN: There isn't any democracy. If we could do it by democratic means, there wouldn't be any need to do it.

BLACKWELL: I think you ought to consider very carefully your own part in all this.

KAMAN: I don't have a part in it.

BLACKWELL: Really? I thought you'd been offered rather a star role.

KAMAN: I suppose you could tell me what colour of underpants I'm wearing.

BLACKWELL: I could make an informed guess.

KAMAN: Well, OK, they did make me an offer, but my agent wasn't too keen on it. He thinks I'm destined for lower things.

BLACKWELL: That sounds eminently sensible advice. You see, Mr Kaman, we're very conscious of the extraordinarily high regard in which you're held back home, and to tell you the truth, we find that rather worrying.

KAMAN: Welcome to the club.

BLACKWELL: Or to put it another way, we think Mr Raan's calculations in that department are really rather shrewd. Not infallible by any means, but then there are no certainties in politics.

KAMAN: I'm sure he'd agree.

BLACKWELL: I mean, the idea sounds pretty wacky when you first think about it –

KAMAN: Thanks a lot.

BLACKWELL: – but I must confess it's really rather ingenious.

KAMAN: You ought to consider employing him; you could use a few bright ideas.

BLACKWELL: Well it's certainly a bold concept – but of course it might just work.

KAMAN: And you find that rather worrying.

BLACKWELL: Well, you see, the thing is that even if it doesn't work it's going to create a bit of a stir over there. And that's just what we'd rather not have. Not at the moment, anyway.

KAMAN: There's quite a stir over there already.

BLACKWELL: Well yes. But it's a long way short of toppling the old bastard at the moment. And that's the way we'd like to keep it for the moment, if at all possible.

KAMAN: Well I'm sorry to be a bit of a headache, old boy, but I really don't see there's a damn thing you can do about it. Short of bumping me off, of course, but I suppose that might create even more of a stir.

BLACKWELL: I suppose it would rather. I'm a great admirer of your poetry, you know.

KAMAN: And you wouldn't like to see it slither to an abrupt halt.

BLACKWELL: My dear fellow, perish the thought. We mustn't get this out of proportion, you know. I mean, Raan's little brainwave might not come off anyway, and even if it did it wouldn't be the end of the world. But all the same, too much heave-ho in that area at the moment might just pose a bit of a problem for some ideas of our own we have in hand. So I would appeal to you – I mean really appeal to you – to stick to the old poetry.

KAMAN: I'll give it serious consideration.

BLACKWELL: Well look, sorry to be awkward, but I'm afraid we'd rather like a little more than that. I mean we'd rather like your word on it.

KAMAN: You'd like my word that I won't interfere with whatever squalid schemes British Intelligence has in store for my part of the world.

BLACKWELL: We'd like your promise that you won't involve yourself in any way in the situation back home.

KAMAN: Well I appreciate your point of view, Mr Blackwell. And my considered response to your appeal is that you can stick your head up your ass. If that means you can't find your own way out, I'm sure my valet would be delighted to assist you.

BLACKWELL: Ah well. Worth a try, I suppose. (*Moves off.*) It was good of you to see me, Mr Kaman; I hope I haven't taken up too much of your time.

KAMAN: Not at all. It's been most intriguing – so to speak. Goodbye, Mr Blackwell.

BLACKWELL: Goodbye, Mr Kaman. Do give my best wishes to your daughter, by the way. How's she getting on these days?

KAMAN: (*After a pause*) My daughter?

BLACKWELL: Yes.

KAMAN: She's getting on just fine.

BLACKWELL: Delighed to hear it. I hope she's not wasting too much of her time with those silly little Trots – what do they call themselves, the Revolutionary Socialist League? Three men and a dog sort of outfit. Still, they can get themselves into trouble, you know. I mean some employers don't take too kindly to that sort of record – if they find out about it, of course.

KAMAN: I see relations between you lot and your colleagues in MI5 have improved of late.

BLACKWELL: And of course our American chums aren't too keen on that sort of thing either. I believe she's applied for a scholarship to work over there? I do hope all goes well with that. By the way, don't mention I was asking after her, will you? They have one or two rather well-known journalists in that little red army of theirs – we wouldn't like to read anything too embarrassing about ourselves.

KAMAN: (*Moving across to him*) You know, Blackwell, it's a funny thing, but I was talking about you to a friend of mine only the other day. Richard Ryan, I think you may know him? (*Pause;* BLACKWELL *is silent.*) I was reminiscing about the good old student days. And I remember saying to him – funny it should come back to me now – that every time I saw your loathsome-looking mug in Great Court I had an irresistible impulse to slug you in the stomach. (BLACKWELL *starts to back away.*) Now don't you think that's a bit of a coincidence?

BLACKWELL: Careful, Kaman.

(KAMAN *hits him hard in the stomach.* BLACKWELL *doubles up with a groan and falls to the ground.*)

KAMAN: (*Shouting*) Salah!

(SALAH *enters.*)

SALAH: Yes, sir?

KAMAN: Salah, this is Jeremy Blackwell. He's a British spy.

SALAH: Yes, sir.

KAMAN: I just hit him in the stomach.

SALAH: Very well done, Mr Kaman. I kick him, sir?

KAMAN: No, I wouldn't do that, Salah. It's not cricket.

Black-out. Lights up on KAMAN *and* RICHARD.

KAMAN: Tell me again.

RICHARD: You're crazy, Kaman, you're paranoid. I didn't even know Blackwell was in the bloody Secret Service till you told me.

KAMAN: That's the point. I told you – I gave you the idea.

RICHARD: You're off your head, man. I hardly know the guy – met him a few times in the village pub, that's all.

KAMAN: And ran to him to protect your ten per cent.

RICHARD: Look, Kaman, this is real science fiction stuff. I shop you to the British Secret Service because I want a lousy cut in a

Nobel prize you haven't even got. I mean this is seriously off
the wall. Anyway, what am I supposed to have told him? How
do I know what's been going on between you and Raan?

KAMAN: You've been hanging around.

RICHARD: They've probably got a bug in every milk jug in this place,
any place that Raan's around. They don't need me to tell
them.

KAMAN: Tell them what?

RICHARD: How the hell should I know? All I know is that Raan wants
you to make some sort of statement. I've told you what I think
about that, you know I don't approve, but that doesn't mean
I run squealing to MI6 or whatever Blackwell's supposed to
be.

KAMAN: It just seems a pretty hefty coincidence. I mention Blackwell
to you one day and he turns up on the doorstep the next. How
do you account for that?

RICHARD: I can't account for it. It doesn't need accounting for, it's a
coincidence.

KAMAN: Well I'll tell you what, Richard. That cunt – that chinless
dickhead straight out of P. G. Wodehouse – threatened my
daughter.

RICHARD: I know, you've told me.

KAMAN: He could screw up the rest of her life with a flick of his
fingers.

RICHARD: Well I'm sorry to hear that, and I've said so twice already.
But the idea that I was somehow behind it – well, that's
unworthy of you, Kaman.

KAMAN: I hope so; I hope so for your sake. Because if you set that
piece of shite on my daughter, I'll break your back.

RICHARD: And this is what they call trust between friends.

KAMAN: Whenever were you my friend, Richard? *Friend!* You don't
even call me by my first name.

RICHARD: Nobody calls you by your Christian name. Nobody even
knows your bloody Christian name.

KAMAN: What's Christian about it?

RICHARD: I tell you the truth about yourself; that's what you want,
that's why you hired me. You don't need a friend, Kaman, you
wouldn't know what to do with one. I've taken over Mara's
role with you.

KAMAN: Oh really? I thought you'd taken over my role with her.

RICHARD: My job is to clean up your puke and be the only one around who doesn't kiss your ass. You couldn't take that from a woman any longer, so you had to take it from me.

KAMAN: Well I don't need to take it from anyone any more.

RICHARD: Be careful, Kaman, don't push it too far. You need me. You need someone who'll be there but won't get too close. An agent's the best you can do by way of a lover.

KAMAN: You're full of shit, Richard.

RICHARD: You can't make out on your own and you can't make out with anyone else. So I'm the ideal compromise. Don't push me off, Kaman; don't indulge yourself.

KAMAN: Indulge myself!

RICHARD: Don't use me in your little drama of self-destruction. I stand outside all that, right? That's our agreement. Don't drag me into it – don't use me like the bottle.

KAMAN: You're talking a lot of crap.

RICHARD: Don't break our agreement, Kaman. You need me.

KAMAN: You set that dickhead on my daughter.

RICHARD: You're out of control, Kaman. You know that's not true, but you want to believe it so you can be rid of me – so you'll have nobody to stand between you and your fantasies. You can't do this to yourself, I won't let you.

KAMAN: I can do what I want. I can live as I please.

RICHARD: (*Slowly*) You know, you and this Janda guy: you're birds of a feather.

KAMAN: Get out of here, Richard.

RICHARD: Don't do it, Kaman.

KAMAN: Get out of my sight.

RICHARD: I'm warning you.

KAMAN: Get out of here and don't come back.

> (RICHARD *stares at him for a moment, then exits.*)
> *Black-out. Lights up on* KAMAN *and* YANA.

YANA: I want to go back.

KAMAN: You can't; there may be civil war.

YANA: That's why I want to go.

KAMAN: You're too young; you have to stay here and study. You'll go back one day; you'll be more use to them with some education.

YANA: Reading *Pride and Prejudice* while people are getting killed.

KAMAN: Well, if more people read *Pride and Prejudice* fewer people might get killed.

YANA: God, you sound just like our English professor. Do you really believe that?

KAMAN: I don't know. In a complicated sort of way, maybe.

YANA: Are you going back?

KAMAN: No.

YANA: Why not? You could, you're not banned, you're too big.

KAMAN: No, but it's not as simple as that.

YANA: Of course it's simple. That's what intellectuals don't understand. They're always going on about things being subtle and difficult and complicated and they're not, not basically. When you get down to it, we're right and the Fascists are wrong.

KAMAN: Well, I can't disagree with that.

YANA: So why aren't you going back? They can't arrest you, you're too famous.

KAMAN: You've got to be realistic.

YANA: Realism's a cop-out. Realism's just a fancy word for keeping things as they are.

KAMAN: I mean realistic about me. You've got to see me as I am; we can't have a good relationship without that.

YANA: I know who you are.

KAMAN: I'm not sure you do. You remember me from the prison; well that was a long time ago. I've changed since then, and you've stayed the same.

YANA: Of course I'm not the same; I was only thirteen then.

KAMAN: Yes, but in some ways you haven't changed. And that's very good – it's not a criticism. It's good to be an idealist, to dream of a world where people won't go hungry. But it's bad to idealize people – to put them on a pedestal. That's a form of exploitation. That's what people do to me all the time, and it's a kind of put-down.

YANA: So you think I see you like they do?

KAMAN: If you idealize people they'll only disappoint you, and then you'll get disillusioned. We can't live without ideals, but they can also be a kind of terrorism. They just rub people's noses in their failure.

YANA: You're not a failure.

KAMAN: Everyone's a failure. That's what we've got to start from. It's only by accepting that that we can succeed.

YANA: They put me on a pedestal too. When I was at school they used to call me princess and ask me whether people still ate each other back home.

KAMAN: Well there you are, that's just what I mean.

YANA: They used to ask me if I could handle a knife and fork, and whether I felt comfortable wearing shoes. And whether my parents were going to fix up a husband for me.

KAMAN: Well, they're very ignorant. It's not their fault. The most ignorant nation is the one with its gunboats in everyone else's country.

YANA: They look at me on the tube as though I've just dropped in from Mars. A man came up to me on Euston station and said he hoped I hadn't had my clitoris cut out because he'd be happy to oblige. I felt sick, but deep down I didn't mind; I could take it because I knew this wasn't really my home, I wasn't really here. I just sort of detached myself inside.

KAMAN: It runs in the family.

YANA: I've just been waiting – waiting for you to come back so we could go home again.

KAMAN: Yana, if you're really grown up you can see me as I am. You were just a little girl then.

YANA: I was never a little girl. I watched them drag you out of the house and put you in the jeep with mum crying and your shirt torn and I was a woman then. I've always been a woman because I'm your daughter.

KAMAN: As long as you need a hero then you're still a child. If you want a Third World hero get yourself a poster of Che Guevara.

YANA: I don't want a hero, I want a father. Aren't you even going to give a speech or something? You've got the words. Haven't you even signed a petition?

KAMAN: No, love, I haven't given a speech and I'm not going to sign any petitions.

YANA: Why not?

KAMAN: It's a complicated story.

YANA: Oh, fuck your complications. Tell me why not.

KAMAN: Listen, Yana, sometimes it's hard to know how to –

YANA: Tell me why not!

(*Pause.*)

KAMAN: I can't tell you why not.

YANA: It's because you don't care any more, isn't it? Because you've just disappeared into the West. You've let them take you over.

KAMAN: No, it's not that.

YANA: What else can it be? They give you a lot of praise and prizes and things and you don't want to upset them. People are getting killed back home and you spend your time chatting to a lot of wankers on *The Late Show*. You've let them buy you.

KAMAN: You won't understand this, but there are some things more precious to me than politics.

YANA: What's more precious? What's more important than people's lives? *Poetry?*

KAMAN: No, not poetry.

YANA: I reckon that's all you care about. Well you can't be a great poet if you don't care.

KAMAN: Yes, that's true.

YANA: Why did you do it? You could have kept fighting, you could have stood up for our people. You didn't have to go soft; you didn't have to sell out.
(*Pause.*)

KAMAN: Look, sweetheart, listen – it's not . . . I . . . I can't . . . I know . . . it's hard to . . . Please try to understand, my darling.
(*Pause.*)

YANA: I don't understand. I don't understand anything any more.

KAMAN: You and I have to stick together, you know.

YANA: I waited for you for seven years. I waited for a father and now I've got a cop-out.

KAMAN: Don't be too hard on me, my dear. Please don't be too hard on me.

YANA: What about me? Why are you doing this to me?

KAMAN: It's not my choice; it's not my fault. Let's just keep seeing each other and talking and then maybe you'll understand.

YANA: I don't think I want that any more.
(YANA *exits;* RAAN *enters.*)

RAAN: Well?

KAMAN: (*After a long pause, mastering his emotions*) No.

RAAN: You won't?

KAMAN: I won't.

RAAN: The big refusal?

KAMAN: The big refusal.
(*Pause.*)

RAAN: Then you have betrayed your people. You are no longer a countryman.
(RAAN *exits.*)
Black-out. Lights up on KAMAN.

KAMAN: (*To audience*) Well, what can you do? No, seriously, I'm asking you, what can you do? When it comes to your own kids, I mean. The sprogs, the bairns, the lambkins, the sweetie-pies. Threaten them and they've got you by the paternal short and curlies. Well, it's only nature, isn't it? What do you take me for, some kind of monster? Don't answer that question. I mean, what parent wouldn't leap into a white hot furnace to rescue their spotty glue-crazed adolescent? OK, so I can think of a few. But not me; no, sir. Because when you get down to it, that's what really matters: your own flesh and blood. Don't get me wrong: principles are all very fine in their place. But let's face it, what's a principle compared to your own family? Are you really telling me you wouldn't blow up a bus load of school-kids to save the life of your own child? I mean, who here wouldn't cheerfully roast a whole raft of babies over a fire just to win your own kid a bit of happiness? You wouldn't? Call yourself loving parents! Callous bastards. I mean, what's the point of trying to look after everyone else if you can't take care of your own? Come on, what are you asking me to do, ruin my own daughter? OK, so if I don't, then Janda will ruin someone else's. Is that my fault? I'm not Jesus Christ, and neither was he. To thine own self be true – which means, in a word, if you're a shit then for Christ's sake act like one. I may not be courageous but at least I'm consistent. So what I'm trying to say – the point I'm trying to make – what it all comes down to is: immorality begins at home.

Black-out. Lights slowly up on KAMAN *sitting in his armchair, drunk,* SALAH *standing opposite him.*

KAMAN: So you see, I used to imagine . . . I used to dream . . . of this word, this one word. This was a long time ago, in our country, when I was young. A shy sort of word, nestling between the lines of my writing like a tiny insect. Or like some frail ghost of a phrase hidden in the sentences of an old manuscript, that springs out at you as you turn the leaf. You know what I mean, Salah?

SALAH: Yes, Mr Kaman.

KAMAN: I could feel it on the tip of my tongue, I could taste it but not close my teeth round it. It was there hovering at the corner of my eye, but it vanished every time I looked at it straight. Oh, not one of those big words like God, state, selfhood. Just some stray hieroglyph, some humble little sound, that was utterly strange and yet as close to me as breathing. The word that would say it all, unlock the destiny of nations. How are we doing for booze?

SALAH: More bottles in the kitchen, sir.

KAMAN: Good man. (*Drinks.*) Some murmur of another world – something you could savour on your tongue like wine. I was young in those days, Salah. One hard push and we'd all be free. They were endless days, endless sunlight. Yana was only a baby. And Mara was still a student. We used to sit up all night with Laka talking about Fanon. (*Pause.*) Laka died in prison. Well, there's no such word, Salah; it's a phantom. But there's a hunger to find it – a terrible, remorseless hunger. And all we know of it again and again is our failure to pronounce it. But I don't know, Salah – sometimes I think I won't rest till it's settled on my tongue. Till it breaks upon us like a burst of sunlight. (*Pause, drinks.*) Well, I don't know. I don't have the words.

SALAH: (*Moving forward*) You have words, sir. You great man, Mr Kaman. You put music in our mouths. You take words and make them dance. You give us words to be free. We know your words, we sing them. (*Begins to recite.*) *Tala meno sushuri naji kam maka, nieto napala chi, Dhajuri saluti hai, kulamu hostoko na yati di benvoto-ko hai hiroti ya, serima-ma tikki palama-ti dai naya, jaal nokiti-yali rabuti.*
(*Long pause.*)

KAMAN: You learnt that?

SALAH: I learn back home, sir. You write poems of freedom. My family, we sing them together.

KAMAN: (*After a pause*) Well, maybe one day I'll write like that again. Maybe I will, one day.

CURTAIN

———————◆———————

APPENDIX: KAMAN'S POEMS

(i)

Do you know a land
whose people live more still, more forlorn
than a temple deep in the mountains,
the fourth hour past midnight,
a quiet dream?

Do you know of a land whose people live
with their words folded away, hung
on a rack beneath the clothes
worn for occasions?

Whose flesh is cheapest in the world.
A land where a dollar is more than enough
to buy two or three pretty young poppies,
and the heart
is never sold. Perhaps
pawned, but never sold, despite
two thousand years'
betrothal.

And with that pledge redeemed,
starting home, a land
that could live on kimchi,
rice,
and water,
ten thousand years
for another such pledge
to wait.

Where the sun
will return, eyes cast aside
like a remorseful lover –
Do you know of such a land?

(ii)

I listen, but the sea and I are the only ones here.
Above the countless waves drawn in and out
countless nights come and go,
the road always somewhere,
as the road finally is nowhere.

When was it? I bloomed as a single
peony. And one pretty maid who lived
beside me, the two of us
watching each other's faces.

One day after
the peony petals fell, dried
to ash, became one
with the earth.
Soon that maiden too,
she died and was buried
in that edge of the earth
where the rains poured down,
down on peony, ashes to earth,
washed away with the river
waters, the blood
of the maiden, stored
under the earth, flows
away with the river.

Ashes, peony ashes
in the river's water
turned into flesh
and blood of the fish,
and currents of the river
joined in their floe by the maiden's blood
surged near that fish,
that fish transported with joy
leaps from the waterfall at the edge
of the sky,
snatched up by a bird,
lifted up into the sunshine,
the maiden following too
into clouds under the bird's wing,
till the bird, struck by the hunter's arrow,
falls, though the cloud would hold it,
drawing the cloud down, the showers
pouring down into the yard
of the house
where the dead bird was carried.

That house, the man
and the woman at table
take and eat the flesh of that bird.
Soon, twin babies are born
to that house,

and the couple raise them,
while the shower that fell in the yard
soaks deep into the seed
of the peony that sprouts and climbs,
again climbing high on the stem of the flower.

This yard, this day the peony bloomed,
maiden and peony again gazing at each other,
and already the maiden
has entered the blossom and the blossom
of yesterday's peony
is what I became,
looking on.

From *Selected Poems of So Chongju*, trans. David R. McCann, Copyright ©
Columbia University Press, quoted by kind permission of the publisher.

God's Locusts

God's Locusts was first produced on BBC Radio 3 in October 1995. The cast was as follows:

HAMISH MCCLINTOCK	Roger Lloyd Pack
WILLIAM SMITH O'BRIEN	Ian McElhinney
JOHN MITCHEL	Colum Convey
GEORGE DAINTON	Dan Gordon
MOLLY BYRNE	Farrell Fleming
JANE ELGEE	Barbara Griffin
NIGEL CREIGHTON	Charlie Bonner
JAMES BRACKEN	Mario Rosenstock

Director   Pam Brighton

ACT ONE

An office in the Treasury in mid-Victorian London. A small part of the stage is symbolically cordoned off to represent the office of the Chief Under-Secretary; the rest of the stage forms a general office with working places for three officials and a slightly surreal portrait of the young Queen Victoria on the back wall.

The Chief Under-Secretary at the Treasury, HAMISH MCCLINTOCK, *dressed in Victorian style with frock-coat and side whiskers, is slumped face down across his desk in his office. The actor playing* BRACKEN, *dressed like a snappy modern-day young stockbroker, is prowling around the stage, hand cupped occasionally to ear, rehearsing his English accent.*

BRACKEN: (*Irish accent*) A decent man by Jaysus. (*English accent*) A decent man by Jesus. A decent man by Jesus. (*Irish accent*) I had a good laugh in the bath. (*English accent*) I had a good laugh in the bath. (*Repeats*) I had a good laugh in the bath. (*Irish accent*) I had a good fart in the park. (*English accent*) I had a good fart in the park. (*Irish accent*) Me ma was a Marxist artist. (*English accent*) My ma was a Marxist artist. (*English accent*) Three trees, three trees, tree trees. (*Irish accent*) Oh fuggit (*English accent*) Oh fuck it, oh fuck it. (*Irish accent*) Oi roide the choilde broide. (*English accent*) I ride the child bride. (*Pause. Irish accent*) What, the Munster Military Requisitions? (*English accent*) What, the Munster Military Requisitions? (*Repeats*) Right, got it.

(CREIGHTON *enters, also dressed like a stockbroker, clutching a sheaf of papers.*)

CREIGHTON: (*English accent*) I've got the MMRs.

BRACKEN: (*English accent*) What, the Munster Military Requisitions?

CREIGHTON: No, you stupid prat, the Monthly Mortality Returns.

BRACKEN: (*Whoop of glee*) Yaaah-hoooh! Alright, you old scumbag, let's see if we can have the braces off your back. (*Goes over to portrait of Queen Victoria and removes it from its frame, lying it down, revealing beneath a small blackboard with two columns of four chalked figures, each column with one of the two men's initials above it.*) There we go, petal, on your back. Oh man, I tell you, you are so dead, you are so fucking *dead*. (*Both men lay down four one-pound notes.*)

CREIGHTON: I'll blow you out of the water, you poxy little pillock.

BRACKEN: Alright, come on then, make with the figures. (*Looks at blackboard.*) What have we got first here? Ah yes, Wexford. (*Takes returns from* CREIGHTON *and shuffles through them.*) Let's see, where are we, here we are now – Wexford: 782 mortalities.

CREIGHTON: (*Scrutinizing board*) 782, eh? Tough shit, old sport, you guessed 612, I bet 824. There we go now, first blood to me. I think I'll be collaring one of those if you don't mind. (*Slides one of* BRACKEN's *pound notes to his own pile.*)

BRACKEN: (*Looking at board*) OK, let's take a look at Roscommon. How many snuffed it since the end of August?

CREIGHTON: (*Looking at board*) You say 403, I say 935. Ah, you're way off there, man – I mean *Roscommon* for Christ's sake, they're dropping like knickers in a whorehouse over there.

BRACKEN: (*Consulting paper*) Ah bollocks. 1137.

CREIGHTON: (*Whoop of triumph, taking a pound note*) There we go, what did I tell you? You see, old fruit, your trouble is you don't approach this thing *scientifically*. I mean you can't just pluck figures out of the air – you've got to weigh up the ecological factors, multiply by the regional variants, take away the number you first thought of and divide by the length of your willie.

BRACKEN: Which in your case would be a minus factor. OK, what's next in line here? (*Looks at board.*) Antrim. Where's that again?

CREIGHTON: Top right-hand corner. Frisky little place, Antrim, not too many stiffs around, keep themselves in the pink up there. What did I guess then?

BRACKEN: 19.

CREIGHTON: Christ, talk about optimism. What about you?

BRACKEN: 57. (*Consults papers.*) Antrim, let's see. Here we are: 48. Hey, that's one to me. (*Slides a pound note across.*)

CREIGHTON: Jammy sod. (*Looks at board.*) OK, hang on to your hat, here comes the big one. (*Imaginary roll of drums and blare of trumpet.*) MAYO! (*Staggers, clutches throat, falls theatrically to floor and thrashes around making death-rattle noises. Stage-Irish accent.*) Oh Jaysus Mary and Joseph sure 'tis the hard auld life we do be having here God love us and us with nothing to put in our shtomachs at all at all at all . . . (*Cranes up head.*) OK, come on then, how many croaked in Mayo?

BRACKEN: (*Consulting paper*) Phew. 2018. Mayo walks away with the jackpot again, folks.

CREIGHTON: (*Getting to his feet*) Really? I didn't know there were that many of them left. (*Looking at board*) Let's see, who's closest? Yessir, I do believe it's me by the slimmest of whiskers. (*Takes a pound note.*) 3 to 1 to me, old girl. That's five wins on the trot.

BRACKEN: (*Replacing Victoria's portrait*) There we are, ducks, back to bed with you now. What do you mean, five? August was a draw, remember?

CREIGHTON: Well, four then. You're outclassed, Bracken, you're way out of your depth, why don't you just crawl back under your stone? (*They sit at their desks, start to write. Pause.*) Which stone did you crawl out from, by the way?

BRACKEN: What?

CREIGHTON: Where were you brought up?

BRACKEN: I told you: the west country.

CREIGHTON: West of what?

BRACKEN: West of England, you nerd. Devon, actually.

CREIGHTON: (*Quizzical look*) Is that right?

BRACKEN: What's bugging you?

CREIGHTON: You got your report ready?

BRACKEN: Sure it's ready. It's the same as last week's anyway. Old Highland Mist'll never notice. (*Indicates* MCCLINTOCK; *they both listen.*) Do you think he's dead in there? You can usually hear him snuffling a bit.

CREIGHTON: Maybe he's slipped out the back to the knocking shop.

BRACKEN: Talking of knocking shops, how's your sister?

CREIGHTON: Who, slaggy Sammy? Oh, same as ever. She really is the most appalling little scumbag, is our Samantha.

BRACKEN: Is she still chasing that wanker in the Scots Guards?

CREIGHTON: What, Flash Harry? Nah, he's washed up, shafted, is old Henry Headbanger.

BRACKEN: So who's she throwing herself at now?

CREIGHTON: She's decided she's a dyke.

BRACKEN: You're kidding.

CREIGHTON: Cross my heart. She's trying to get her leg over some skinny little slut from Bermondsey.

BRACKEN: Get away!

CREIGHTON: She's a bit of a hoot though, I can't deny that. Did you hear what she said to Rupert?

BRACKEN: What, Rupert with the ears?

CREIGHTON: No no, Rupert from the Bank – you know, the demented dwarf.

BRACKEN: Oh, that Rupert.

CREIGHTON: He turned up at Amanda's party with the most unbelievable bunch of oiks. True-born tossers the lot, I mean your genuine prize pillocks. They were all at Rugby or some crummy joint like that. Anyway, they'd all come hot-foot from that new night-club, you know, what's-its-face, the place where the tarts dress up like matrons and feed you warmed-up school dinners and whack you on the bum if you don't lap it up.

BRACKEN: Fourth Formers.

CREIGHTON: That's it. So anyway they were all totally shit-faced, not that that mattered much because old Mandy was pretty out of it herself, but then this real vintage wally, stupid-looking prat with big floppy feet and a beard but no moustache –

BRACKEN: Uggh!

CREIGHTON: Yeah, don't you hate that? Well, this guy started puking into the tropical fish tank. I mean real classy fish, rare as hell.

BRACKEN: Get away.

CREIGHTON: And then Freddie Moser, you know, Jew boy, Freddie of the F.O., had been poking his ratty snout around Westminster and said something to Mandy about a new party, some breakaway Free Traders or something, and Mandy said 'A party, a party, why wasn't I invited?', and jumped through the conservatory roof. They were still picking the splinters out of her when I left. Mind you, she makes old Genevieve look like a nun.

BRACKEN: Quite a gal, old Genevieve.

CREIGHTON: I'll say. Can't think why I ever married her. How's that little scrubber of yours coming along?

BRACKEN: Don't like to boast, old boy, but which one of the troupe do you have in mind?

CREIGHTON: Oh, so there's more than one, is there?

BRACKEN: Well yes, but they're not interconscious.

CREIGHTON: What?

BRACKEN: They don't know about each other. I think Cordelia was the one you met. Big redhead with buck teeth?

CREIGHTON: That's the one. She's loaded, isn't she?

BRACKEN: Is the Pope a Catholic! Her old man owns half of Berkshire.

CREIGHTON: She'd need a rich daddy with teeth like that.

BRACKEN: So what did Amanda say to Rupert?

CREIGHTON: Rupert?

BRACKEN: You know, the demented dwarf.

CREIGHTON: (*Coldly*) How should I know what she said to Rupert?

(GEORGE DAINTON *enters, also dressed as a stockbroker, crosses silently to his work-place and starts to write.*)

CREIGHTON: Should we tell him the news?

BRACKEN: I dunno. Might knock him back a bit.

CREIGHTON: (*Strolling over to* DAINTON) George old fruit, the MMRs arrived while you were out. 'Fraid it doesn't look too chirpy. In fact – just brace yourself, old sport – it seems that the whole population of Ireland has collectively croaked. (*Strangulated sob.*) Well, all but three of them to be exact: a one-legged Kerryman, a syphilitic Mother Superior and a dipsomaniac donkey-shagger from Dundrum. It seems they're busy eating each other even as we speak.

BRACKEN: It's the greatest tragedy since *The Merry Wives of Windsor*.

CREIGHTON: Evidently the pigs have taken over and the economy's already on the up. By the way, did you hear the one about the Irishman who took shelter in a pigsty? The stink was unbearable.

BRACKEN: Yeah, we know, so the pig ran out. What's a Kerryman's foreplay?

CREIGHTON: Dunno.

BRACKEN: (*Guttural stage-Irish accent*) Turn over, Mary. (*Looking at* DAINTON) He doesn't seem too bothered.

CREIGHTON: Callous bastard. A clear-cut case of Famine fatigue.

BRACKEN: The whole bloody nation goes down the plug-hole and he doesn't twitch an eyelid. I've heard of Little Englandism but this is ridiculous.

DAINTON: Have you totalled the MMRs?

CREIGHTON: Oh, and I almost forgot, Little Janey dropped in while you were out.

DAINTON: Miss Elgee?

CREIGHTON: The very lass. Said it was destroyed she was to miss you begob and begorrah but would call back later wearing nothing but a sprig of shamrock if you fancied a bit of how's-your-father.

DAINTON: (*Quietly*) You really are such a prick, Creighton.

CREIGHTON:

> There was a young lass called Elgee
> Who urgently needed a pee
> So she stuck her ass over

The high cliffs of Moher
Crying I'm no cute Rose of Tralee.

DAINTON: (*Rising and collaring* CREIGHTON) Shut your slimy mouth,
   Creighton, or I'll stuff my fist down your –
McCILINTOCK: (*Raising his head with a loud wail*) Merciful Jesus!
   (DAINTON *and* CREIGHTON *disengage; all pause and listen.*)
BRACKEN: (*Low voice*) Hello, old Tam O'Shanter's surfaced.
   (*They listen intently again, then relax.*)
CREIGHTON: (*Lowish voice*) What's the problem, Dainton, you got no
   ear for poetry? Where's your soul, man?
DAINTON: You are such a craphouse, Creighton.
BRACKEN: Come on now, back off lads, or Rob Roy'll be banging your
   heads together. There we go, back to work, that's the style.
   Which naughty boy hasn't finished his report then? You'll get
   no sago pudding if you don't.
   (*They return to their desks and write in silence for a while.*)
CREIGHTON: How do you spell Tipperaray?
BRACKEN: Two ps, one r.
   (*Silence.*)
CREIGHTON: Where is it?
BRACKEN: Lower down than Carlow, higher up than Cork.
CREIGHTON: Fat lot of help that is.
   (*Silence.*)
BRACKEN: How do you spell oedema?
CREIGHTON: I dunno. Is that when your belly swells out or when your
   eyes pack up?
BRACKEN: Dunno. The Chief thought it was a village in Armagh.
   (*Silence.*)
CREIGHTON: (*Pushing his papers suddenly away*) This is such a pain in
   the bum.
BRACKEN: What?
CREIGHTON: This. (*Indicates office.*) All this. I mean, what's the *point*
   of it all?
BRACKEN: What are you on about, Creighton?
CREIGHTON: I mean can anyone tell me what we're doing trying to
   bail out a lot of bare-arsed bog-trotters?
BRACKEN: We're servants of the Crown, Nigel darling.
CREIGHTON: I mean it's not as though the chimps are even grateful.
      They don't even have any industry over there – too frigging lazy.
BRACKEN: They've got no raw materials, mate.

CREIGHTON: You can run an industry on peat, for Christ's sake. Lot of two-faced cringers all piss and wind and God save Your Honour and they'd have a pike in your guts and the Pope in Dublin Castle soon as blink. They're breeding like crazed badgers, they're ploughing the bogs and sowing the mountain tops, and we're trying to keep them *alive*.

BRACKEN: So what do you suggest?

CREIGHTON: Let them eat fish.

BRACKEN: They don't have a fishing industry.

CREIGHTON: Well, there you are, you see.

BRACKEN: They don't have the capital.

CREIGHTON: So what do *you* suggest?

BRACKEN: It's obvious.

CREIGHTON: Oh yeah?

BRACKEN: Yeah, here's what we do. We fold the island roughly along the Lagan valley, tear off the top bit and tack it on to Scotland, then tow the rest out towards the Arctic circle and cut it loose. It'd be cheaper than soup kitchens.

CREIGHTON: You reckon?

BRACKEN: Sure. You see, the whole country's just an oversight – a regrettable error. It was never actually *intended*. Somebody just ought to blow the whistle and call the whole place off.

CREIGHTON: Nobody's got the spunk to say it outright. Nobody.

BRACKEN: Say what?

CREIGHTON: Just tell the truth for a change. Just face the fact that if Ireland's ever going to be a country rather than a sick joke it's got to shed its surplus population. Reshape the farms into economic-sized units. The landlords were too chicken to do it so the Distress is doing it for them.

DAINTON: A savage god.

CREIGHTON: Huh?

DAINTON: The divine plan for the salvation of Ireland. So why don't we help the place on a bit – breed a bit more typhus, cut out relief altogether? We're conspiring against the Almighty if we don't, aren't we?

CREIGHTON: Look, sonny, all relief does is shift the burden to the less deserving. We're just subsidizing shiftlessness.

DAINTON: We're trying to save lives.

CREIGHTON: If we had any guts we'd just let the thing take its course. But of course that wouldn't be *moral*. As though it hadn't gone beyond all that.

DAINTON: You're sick, Creighton.

CREIGHTON: No, just honest. We're just letting our precious little ethics stand in the way of history.

DAINTON: (*Rounding on him ferociously*) Have you the faintest idea of what it must be like to be hungry? Not just one empty belly, not just a thousand, but millions? Can you wrap your mind around that, Creighton? People shrieking, howling, bloating? Children who are just bags of bone? Don't you ever think of that when you tuck into your steak and onions?

CREIGHTON: God, no, How sick-making.

DAINTON: Well I do, Creighton. In fact I can't eat because of thinking about it, and I can't sleep either. Every time I close my eyes I see skeletons. Can you imagine what it must be like to watch your wife swell up and die? Or is that just another statistical exercise to you?

(MCCLINTOCK *appears suddenly in the doorway of his office. They all leap to their feet; he looks wildly around, grunts, then retires. The men relax.*)

BRACKEN: (*Sotto voce*) What's *he* after then?

CREIGHTON: Search me. Someone ought to hang a bleeding bell round his neck.

(*They return to work.*)

BRACKEN: You see, what I don't understand about this whole thing is why –

(MCCLINTOCK *suddenly reappears in the doorway; they leap to their feet once more. He advances slowly towards them.*)

McCLINTOCK: (*Scots accent*) 'The children of Gibeon, ninety and five. The men of Bethlehem and Netophah, an hundred four score and eight. The men of Anathoth, an hundred and twenty-eight. The men of Bethazmaveth, forty and two': the Book of Nehemiah, chapter seven, verses 25 to 28. (*Thrusting his face abruptly into* CREIGHTON'S) Well, sir?

CREIGHTON: Beg pardon, sir?

McCLINTOCK: The total, laddie. What is the total?

CREIGHTON: Er – I don't quite – I'm afraid I –

McCLINTOCK: How many men all told of Gibeon, Bethlehem, Netophah, Anathoth and Bethazmaveth?

CREIGHTON: I'm – I'm afraid I wasn't counting, sir.

McCLINTOCK: Come, come, my friend, this will never do. You must be a little more on the *qui vive*. For the night cometh in which no man shall calculate. How are we to compute the number of dysentery cases in the workhouses of Waterford if a simple biblical sum escapes you?

CREIGHTON: I'm sorry, sir.

McCLINTOCK: (*Turning to* BRACKEN *and raising his right hand*) You see this hand, Mr Creighton?

BRACKEN: It's Bracken, actually, sir.

McCLINTOCK: What do you see here, sir?

BRACKEN: Your hand, Mr McClintock.

McCLINTOCK: And what did this hand do?

BRACKEN: Crucified our beloved Saviour, sir.

McCLINTOCK: More exactly?

BRACKEN: Pressed the spear into his side and – and – gave it a – a –

McCLINTOCK: Gave it a *what*?

BRACKEN: A good sharp twist.

McCLINTOCK: (*Repeating with relish and enacting the gesture*) A good sharp twist. And in what condition, Mr Creighton, is this hand now?

CREIGHTON: Washed in the blood of the Lamb, sir.

McCLINTOCK: Precisely. Not the baa lamb, Mr Creighton, not the lamb of the mint sauce and cranberry jelly variety, not the lamb of the Lamb and Flag hostelry down the road from your humble lodging-house, but the Lamb of God. Blood stains, my boy, but blood purifies too. Two negatives make a positive. We're all wurrms, laddie, all wurrms. What is your opinion, Mr Bracken, of the doctrines of reprobation and unconditional election?

BRACKEN: I consider them to be most comfortable and worthy doctrines, sir.

McCLINTOCK: Splendid, splendid. And what is the matter with your feet?

BRACKEN: My feet, sir?

McCLINTOCK: (*Without looking at them*) Your feet, wee laddie. What ails them?

BRACKEN: Er – they're fine, thanks, sir. Doing just fine.

McCLINTOCK: No, they are not fine, Mr Bracken. Your feet are far from fine. Examine them, sir, if you would be so kind.

BRACKEN: Oh yes – I'm sorry, sir.

McCLINTOCK: Brown shoes, Mr Bracken. A violation of sartorial propriety. Once let the feet go to ruin and the rest of the man, both inner and outer, follows apace. The feet are the foundation of all virtue.

BRACKEN: Very good, sir, I'll see to it.

McCLINTOCK: (*To* DAINTON) And what is *your* opinion, sir, of the state of the public works in Ballydehob?

DAINTON: I – I think the public works in general leave much to be desired, Mr McClintock. In fact, sir, I think this whole terrible business –

McCLINTOCK: (*Without looking down*) You have a wee stain on your breeks, laddie. I trust it does not signify moral turpitude.

DAINTON: I think it signifies tomato soup, sir.

McCLINTOCK: The public works indeed leave something to be desired, Mr Dainton. What on this side of eternity does not? Ballydehob falls a little short of the beatific vision, would you not agree?

DAINTON: Yes, sir.

McCLINTOCK: Enlighten us, Mr Creighton, as to the deficiencies of the public works relief scheme in Ireland.

CREIGHTON: Too many idlers, sir.

McCLINTOCK: Exactly, my boy. Too many stout-limbed fresh-faced fellows who would be better employed tending their farms but who would rather leech on the long-suffering British taxpayer. Too many sleek-headed round-bellied rogues who wheedle their way into a little agreeable stone-breaking so as to earn the wherewithal to swill whiskey and abandon their bairns. Too many sharp picks and spades in the hands of churls and hot-heads posing as starvelings, and too many tender foremen's skulls within their reach. What is the cure for the potato blight, Mr Bracken?

BRACKEN: The cure, sir?

McCLINTOCK: Cure, remedy, panacea, sir. What ought to have been done to the potatoes when the blight first took hold?

BRACKEN: (*As though reciting a lesson*) The affected potatoes should have been grated very finely into a tub, the pulp washed and dried on a griddle over a small fire, and the resultant milky substance mixed with dried potato pulp to produce wholesome bread.

McCLINTOCK: Failing which, Mr Creighton?

CREIGHTON: An alternative plan would be to cut off the diseased parts of the potato, soak them in bog water, spread them with lime and salt, or treat them with chlorine gas manufactured by mixing vitriol, salt and manganese dioxide if these elements are conveniently to hand.

BRACKEN: Pardon me, Mr McClintock.

McCLINTOCK: What is it, laddie?

BRACKEN: Wouldn't that be sort of – poisonous, sir?

McCLINTOCK: Of course it would be poisonous! It would poison the blight and hence cleanse the potato. But none of this was put in hand, gentlemen, such is the darkness of men's hearts. Inform us of the present state of affairs, Mr Bracken.

BRACKEN: (*Reading from his notes*) N.D.S. still widespread especially along the western seaboard . . .

McCLINTOCK: N.D.S.?

CREIGHTON: Nutritional Deficiency Syndrome, sir.

McCLINTOCK: Ah.

BRACKEN: . . . resulting in exponential increase of T.A.D.s in west Clare and the Erris region of Mayo . . .

McCLINTOCK: T.A.D.s?

CREIGHTON: Terminal Alimentary Deprivation. Er – death, sir.

McCLINTOCK: Very good.

BRACKEN: . . . with reports of H.D.S.s in a number of P.R.s. . . .

CREIGHTON: Human Dietary Supplement. Ah – that's cannibalism, sir. In Peripheral Regions – er – that's to say, areas we've by and large . . .

McCLINTOCK: Written off.

CREIGHTON: Exactly, sir.

BRACKEN: One or two teething problems with the relief works, sir. Reports of starving mobs tearing up the roads they've been laying, corruption and favouritism on the public works, un- paid wages, one or two foremen dragged from their beds and beaten to pulp, famished chimps – I mean famished women and children unfit for labour, otherwise everything well in hand.

McCLINTOCK: There will be changes, gentlemen. There is too much bureaucracy at present. From now on, the whole process of setting up public works will be streamlined in the following manner. If there are those in a particular district not simply without food but in reasonable danger of – what is the phrase, Mr Creighton?

CREIGHTON: Terminal Alimentary Deprivation, sir.

McCLINTOCK: Exactly. Then these individuals shall come together in some suitable public forum and send a memorial to the Lord-Lieutenant in Dublin Castle requesting assistance. They will outline a scheme of works, which the Lord-Lieutenant will forward in due course to the Relief Commissioners. From here, it will go to the Board of Public Works in the relevant locality. Upon receiving this report, the Board of Works will decide whether or not to accept the application in question, and if they accept it will recommend an appropriate financial grant to the Lord-Lieutenant, who will in turn ask for the approval of the Treasury. In this way, gentlemen, we shall nip starvation in the bud. Anything further?

DAINTON: Sir, we're still getting urgent requests to open the food depots. The Relief Commissioners report men and women dying on their doorsteps.

McCLINTOCK: There will be no more food depots, Mr Dainton, and no more government charity. If there is evidence of absolute destitution, the more prominent and respectable members of the community should form themselves into a relief committee and raise private subscriptions.

DAINTON: But it's the relief committees who are writing in, sir. They have no money.

McCLINTOCK: Then they must redouble their efforts.

DAINTON: (*Moving to desk*) Mr McClintock, I have on my desk a memorandum from Skibereen –

McCLINTOCK: From *where*, Mr Dainton?

DAINTON: Skibereen, sir.

McCLINTOCK: (*Moving up close to* DAINTON, *hoarse whisper*) Do not – I pray you – do not – ever – EVER – use that – obscene – word again in my presence. You understand?

DAINTON: Yes, sir.

McCLINTOCK: So, my fine fellows, is there anything further we can accomplish? It is heartening to see the charitable work continuing apace. I have had a particularly glowing account of the activities of the L.I.S.E.R.P.I.

BRACKEN: Sir?

McCLINTOCK: Mr Creighton?

CREIGHTON: Ladies' Industrial Society for the Encouragement of Remunerative Labour among the Peasantry of Ireland.

McCLINTOCK: Indeed, to be sure. The good ladies have been fostering the fishing industry in the west by distributing fishermen's jackets and trousers. There is nothing like a uniform, gentlemen, to stimulate self-respect. The widow's mite, my friends, the widow's mite. Speaking of which, Mr Creighton, and mindful of the distressed folk of Swinford, there is a small quantity of Royal Navy broken biscuit left over from the food depot project. No doubt it would be appreciated over there.

CREIGHTON: You mean – free, sir?

McCLINTOCK: Don't be ridiculous, laddie. But cheap, certainly. And though we have closed the food depots, we will of course continue to supply Indian corn to the most destitute.

BRACKEN: There are a number of complaints about the corn, sir. It seems that the people are eating it unground and it's piercing their intestines. The pain is described as moderately agonizing.

McCLINTOCK: The corn is ground in Cork, sir. And cooked for seventy hours, no less.

BRACKEN: But it has to be ground twice, sir, to be quite – er – edible.

McCLINTOCK: A superfluous requirement, Mr Bracken. We are supplying wholesome food, not milk and honey. The swains of Ireland need to practise a spot of self-discipline. I myself, gentlemen, have been subsisting on one pound of Indian corn a day for the past fortnight. And I am at my desk until two or three in the morning. I trust you detect no diminution in my girth. (*Twirls coquettishly around with a sudden snort of laughter.*) Well, back to work, my brave lads.

DAINTON: May I have a private word with you, Mr McClintock?

McCLINTOCK: (*Genially bowing*) At your service, my friend. Pray step into my office.

(*They move into his office;* CREIGHTON *and* BRACKEN *exit.*) Now, my good sir, stand at your ease. Is it a moral or a metaphysical matter about which you wish to consult me?

DAINTON: Well, actually, sir, it's not exactly –

McCLINTOCK: I understand, my friend. (*Moving close to him*) At your age, Mr Dainton, my blood too ran hot. (*Places hand on his shoulder.*)

DAINTON: I don't think you quite –

McCLINTOCK: Hot, lad, hot. What do you see when you close your eyes, my boy? You can be truthful with me. Is it – undraped female flesh? Strange, is it not, how we pass our waking hours brooding upon ribs and rags, while sometimes at night it is tender flesh which holds us in thrall. Flesh ample and undulating, subtly flavoured and scented. It is the way with us menfolk, my young friend. There is daylight and there is night-time, but they do not mingle. There are bodies arched in agony and limbs arched in lechery, fingers that would caress another's cheeks and fingers that would cram them down a ravenous maw. We are all amphibious creatures, Mr Creighton – not least our womenfolk, all bright-eyed laughter above and stench and darkness below.

DAINTON: Dainton, sir.

McCLINTOCK: I beg your pardon?

DAINTON: Mr McClintock, I want to talk to you about the relief operation. We're not feeding the people.

McCLINTOCK: We are not meant to be feeding the people, sir. Feeding the people is not our first priority.

DAINTON: Then what is?

McCLINTOCK: To induce the people to rely first and foremost on their own powers.

DAINTON: In that case, sir, we are *en route* to creating a nation of self-sufficient corpses.

McCLINTOCK: Better to die proud than live a pauper.

DAINTON: We have to reopen the food depots, sir, before the whole nation perishes – or rises up in revolt, which will come to the same thing.

McCLINTOCK: My dear young man, there are several excellent reasons for not reopening the food depots, the most cogent of which is that they are almost empty. Would you wish the people to know that?

DAINTON: Then we have to restock them.

McCLINTOCK: We cannot supply food while there is still private trade.

DAINTON: Good God, sir, are we to sit here and calculate how much diarrhoea and bloody flux and dysentery a people can bear before it becomes necessary to provide them with food? We can buy in supplies as the Tories did. Nobody perished under Peel.

McCLINTOCK: Pouf! Nobody died under Peel because that little devil the blight bug had hardly begun its work. Peel sold the people cheap corn in the hope of keeping down prices. That's bad ethics and even worse economics. If we scare off the private traders, Ireland is done for.

DAINTON: So we let merchants grow fat on a famine?

McCLINTOCK: And what is wrong with profiting from a famine? It is as much a law of nature as suckling one's young or scratching an itch. We are civil servants, Mr Dainton, we must move with the times. Yesterday we were state interventionists, today we are free-marketeers. All things passeth away and withereth like grass. Prices must find their natural level, like God's good rain cascading to the valleys. Marketman and marketwoman he created them, yea verily so. In short, young sir, forget about Sir Robert Peel because he and his crew are out on their snouts, and if you don't mend your high-minded ways you'll be out with them.

DAINTON: But prices are rocketing, sir. They're way out of the reach of the peasants on the public works.

McCLINTOCK: And the higher they rise, the more the private traders will flood the country with food. It is the law of commerce, which is the law of nature, which is the law of God.

DAINTON: By which time they'll be trading with a society of skeletons. We're closing the food depots before public works have time to get started, and thousands are dying in the gap.

McCLINTOCK: Public works take time. Have you the slightest notion, Mr Dainton, of how magnificent an achievement it has been to cover Ireland from coast to coast with relief projects?

DAINTON: It is truly splendid, sir. But there is no point in such an enterprise if it is starved of funds.

McCLINTOCK: Anyone would think, Mr Dainton, that the role of a Treasury was to *spend* money. I am not my own master, sir, any more than you are. I am under the most fearful pressure from the Prime Minister.

DAINTON: Mr McClintock, bands of famished men are roaming the countryside like wolves. There are some 5,000 beggars on the streets of Cork alone. Men, women and children exhausted with hunger, utterly unused to manual labour, are walking 7 or 8 miles each morning through the snow, in the worst winter on record, to stand for 10 hours on the public works shaking with frost and fever, hardly able to hold a pick. And this for starvation wages which will not even buy them food!

McCLINTOCK: It is indeed most undesirable. These peasants would be better off tending their farms. There is a most frightful neglect of the harvest.

DAINTON: Can they work their farms with empty bellies till the harvest blooms – if it ever does again, which many of them take leave to doubt? And then see it taken in rent by the landlord?

McCLINTOCK: So what do you suggest, Mr Dainton? That the government demoralize a sullen people even further by handing out free cartons of caviare?

DAINTON: What is the point of the works, for heaven's sake? To build roads to nowhere, paths around nothing, piers which collapse at the first assault of the waves? When we could be draining the bogs and reclaiming the mountainsides?

McCLINTOCK: Roads are precious commodities, my boy.

DAINTON: Roads are the one thing that Ireland has enough of.

McCLINTOCK: The works cannot be profitable. Interfere with private enterprise and we are doomed.

DAINTON: They could pay a living wage.

McCLINTOCK: Pay a living wage to those clowns and there'll be breeding like rabbits in a warren. I hear the works are littered with cheap drinking shacks already. No doubt there is more copulation than conscientious labour.

DAINTON: But if the people don't get a living wage, how can we kick-start the food markets?

McCLINTOCK: You seem to forget, Mr Dainton that there is considerable distress in areas of our own nation. Are we to beggar Peter to pay Paul? Are our own respectable artisans to sink under a rabble of lice-ridden immigrants for whom no form of labour is too disgusting? It is hardly a way for the government to secure its re-election.

DAINTON: I thought Britain and Ireland were a united kingdom.

McCLINTOCK: So they are, so they are. But Galway is not Surrey, nor Longford Lancashire. We cannot hope to save Ireland, sir; we can hope only to mitigate her miseries somewhat – though not so thoroughly that she fails to draw lessons for the future.

DAINTON: I tell you, sir, that there is no alternative but to distribute free food. We should have done it long ago.

McCLINTOCK: The moral effects of such a policy, my dear fellow, would far outweigh the ravages of typhus. Better a swollen belly than a broken spirit. Besides, there is the question of the yams.

DAINTON: Yams?

McCLINTOCK: I still have a fancy that the importing of West Indian yams may prove a not wholly injudicious policy.

DAINTON: And how are the people to cook them?

McCLINTOCK: Indeed, indeed. There is scarcely a peasant woman in Ireland whose culinary arts extend beyond boiling a potato –

not that there's much call for that either these days. We could,
I suppose, provide written instructions for cooking the yams,
but no doubt the benighted yokels would die while trying to
decipher them. A God-forsaken race, Mr Dainton, to be sure.
My only regret is that I am a Gael myself.

DAINTON: They're already dying of eating Indian corn.

McCLINTOCK: They need simply to grind it, sir. And they can do it
with this. (*Whips from beneath his coat a small wooden hand-
mill and brandishes it aloft.*) You see? You put the corn in here
– churn it with this little handle – and out it pops there.
Simplicity itself. We could distribute one to every poor loon
in Ireland.

DAINTON: How much does it cost?

McCLINTOCK: A mere fifteen shillings.

DAINTON: You might as well hand out silver tankards.

McCLINTOCK: Mr Dainton, which side, may I ask, are you working
for?

DAINTON: I wasn't aware there were sides, sir. As I say, I thought we
were a united kingdom.

McCLINTOCK: This isn't the way to get on, you know, lad. The Chancellor will be sorely disappointed in you. Do you know how to
lick a stamp?

DAINTON: Sir?

McCLINTOCK: Lick, laddie, lick. Run your moist tongue over the
minty backside of a fresh young stamp. Because I believe
there's an opening for a sub-sectional supervisor in the Derbyshire Post Office. And if you carry on in this spirit I'll be
recommending you for it most warmly.

DAINTON: I understand, Mr McClintock.

McCLINTOCK: Back to work, then, my boy. And remember: 'And the
man whose hair is fallen off his head, he is bald; yet is he
clean. And he that hath his hair fallen off from the part of his
head toward his face, he is forehead bald, yet is he clean. But
if there be in the bald head or bald forehead a white reddish
sore, it is a leprosy sprung up in his bald head': Leviticus,
chapter 13, verses 40 to 42. You take my meaning, sir?

DAINTON: (*Bursting out*) No, pardon me, sir but I don't take your
meaning at all. A whole nation is dying on our doorstep and
all we can talk about is market mechanisms. People are piling
up like dead leaves, and we drivel on about interest-bearing
loans. Why don't we just feed them, for Christ's sake, and

have done with it? How can we let people starve just to prove a point in economics? You asked me what I saw when I close my eyes. Yes, I see flesh right enough, but not that kind of flesh. I see bodies shrivelled like monkeys, faces like claws, infants gibbering like old men.

McCLINTOCK: (*After a pause*) You are overwrought, Mr Dainton. We will consider sending you on vacation. Perhaps the Derbyshire air might purge you of these fantasies.

(*Exits.* DAINTON *turns to leave and encounters* MOLLY BYRNE.)

MOLLY: (*Beckoning him*) Hey, mister.

DAINTON: Who are you? What do you want?

MOLLY: (*Still beckoning*) Come over here, will you, sure I'm not going to eat you.

DAINTON: Who are you? How did you get in here?

MOLLY: Oh, I know my way around the shop.

DAINTON: You sound – Irish.

MOLLY: Well now, maybe that's because I am.

DAINTON: (*Coming closer*) Are you a – a refugee?

MOLLY: A refu-what?

DAINTON: Are you fleeing from the Famine?

MOLLY: I suppose you might say that.

DAINTON: Yes – yes, now I look at you you seem . . . worn . . . tired.

MOLLY: Ah sure it's a hard auld life down on the Dilly.

DAINTON: On the what?

MOLLY: Piccadilly.

DAINTON: Is that where you live?

MOLLY: Where I work. Sure it was either that or becoming a nun.

DAINTON: So what do you do?

MOLLY: What do you fancy?

DAINTON: Are you a nurse?

MOLLY: Getting warm.

DAINTON: Do you live on the streets, my good woman?

MOLLY: Well, more sort of off them, as you might say.

DAINTON: And you've come here for help?

MOLLY: In a manner of speaking.

DAINTON: The Treasury isn't the place to come for money, you know.

MOLLY: Oh, I pick up the odd few bob.

DAINTON: You must have known – horrors.

MOLLY: Oh I've known some horrors alright. There are one or two just down the corridor.

DAINTON: And you're so young – so young to have left home. How can I help you?

MOLLY: You could give me what's in your trousers if you like.

DAINTON: (*Feeling in his pocket and producing some money*) You're welcome to it.

MOLLY: Haven't you more than that in your trousers?

DAINTON: I'm sorry – that's really all I've got.

MOLLY: (*Placing her hand on his groin*) Oh I wouldn't say that.

DAINTON: (*Leaping back in horror*) Good God, woman, what – what are you doing?

MOLLY: Didn't your mammy ever tell you what it was for?

DAINTON: But you said . . . you said . . . you were Irish . . .

MOLLY: That's right, love. Don't you think we have them over there? Ah well, maybe you'd like to come back when you're a big boy. Bye for now.

(*Exits.* DAINTON *doubles up, retching slightly, then stumbles off, passing* CREIGHTON, *who gives him a puzzled look.* CREIGHTON *settles down to work, when* JANE ELGEE, *dressed in flamboyant Victorian style and carrying a bag, enters the main office.*)

CREIGHTON: (*Leaping to his feet with exaggerated enthusiasm*) Well stone the crows, if it isn't the Rose of Tralee! Back again, eh? You don't give up easily, do you? The top o' the morning to you, Miss Elgee, and what could I be after doing for you?

ELGEE: (*English accent*) I want to see the Chief Under-Secretary.

CREIGHTON: I'm afraid that's not possible.

ELGEE: Why not?

CREIGHTON: The Chief Under-Secretary passed away this very morning. Too much Indian corn, I understand. Pierced intestines, you know.

ELGEE: I'm not leaving here till he sees me.

CREIGHTON: Come on now, Jane love, don't be a drag. How about a potato juice over the road?

ELGEE: I'm not budging till he sees me.

CREIGHTON: He won't see you, sweetheart, and that's that.

ELGEE: How dare you call me sweetheart?

CREIGHTON: Because I'm a cheeky bastard.

ELGEE: Why won't he see me?

CREIGHTON: Because he knows what you're going to say.

ELGEE: What am I going to say?

CREIGHTON: You're going to tell him that the Irish are starving to death. Well he's heard that one already.

ELGEE: (*Sitting down on floor*) I'll wait here till he comes out. (*Opens bag.*) Don't worry, I've got plenty of food with me. You just get on with wiping out my nation, I won't disturb you.

CREIGHTON: OK, Jane, I was kidding you, he isn't dead. But he's not here – he's down at Westminster. And he won't be back today, so there's no point in hanging around.

ELGEE: He sleeps here, doesn't he? I can wait till bedtime.

CREIGHTON: You're not doing your cause much good, you know.

ELGEE: Neither are you.

(MCCLINTOCK *appears in the doorway of his office, sees* ELGEE, *gives a grunt and dives back in.*)

ELGEE: (*Running over to his office*) Mr McClintock, a word with you, sir! Mr McClintock!

CREIGHTON: (*Trying to head her off, dodging one another*) Come on, pet, be a sport, come on now, just calm down and –

ELGEE: (*Shouting*) Mr McClintock, this is my fifth visit to the Treasury on behalf of my delegation. Your discourtesy, sir, is abominable. My friends await your answer. Will you receive us or not?

CREIGHTON: (*Trying to pull her away*) For Christ's sake, woman, can't you see you're not wanted around here?

ELGEE: Take your hands off me, sir! How dare you lay your hands on me! (*Lies down suddenly across the threshold of* MCCLINTOCK'S *office.*) Very well then, you can either face me like a man or starve to death in there.

CREIGHTON: (*Stepping over her into the office*) Pardon me, madam. (*To* MCCLINTOCK) I think you'd better just come out and get it over with, sir; there'll be no getting rid of her otherwise.

MCCLINTOCK: But the woman is barking mad. How can I deal with a notorious madwoman? Is she armed?

CREIGHTON: Well, unless she has a pistol stuck down her bloomers . . .

MCCLINTOCK: They're all lunatics – trollopes and terrorists. What am I to say to her?

CREIGHTON: Just explain that we're doing a difficult job in very trying circumstances. Say that we're lavishing on Ireland all the aid we can muster.

MCCLINTOCK: But we're not!

CREIGHTON: This is no time for the truth.

ELGEE: Are you coming out, Mr McClintock? Or shall I come in there and drag you out?

CREIGHTON: One moment, sir. (*Comes out of the office.*) OK, Jane, you've made your point. Get on your feet like a good wee lass and I'll get the old man out here.

ELGEE: You promise?

CREIGHTON: Cross my heart and hope to starve.

ELGEE: Very well then. (*Gets to her feet and retreats.*)

CREIGHTON: (*Returning to office*) It's alright, sir, she's on her feet and promises to behave. Just have a quick word with her and she'll go quietly.

McCLINTOCK: You think that's advisable?

CREIGHTON: It may be inadvisable not to, sir. She's from an eminent family in Ireland; they could always make trouble.

McCLINTOCK: Oh, very well then, let's get it over with.

(*They emerge into main office.* McCLINTOCK *takes* ELGEE's *hand aloofly,* CREIGHTON *shadowing him like a bodyguard.*)

How do you do, Miss Elgee.

ELGEE: (*Mock-modest bow*) Delighted to meet you, Mr McClintock. Are you of the McClintocks of Kyleakin Abbey?

McCLINTOCK: I have that honour, madam.

ELGEE: Then I think my father once broke your brother's nose. On the playing fields, of course.

McCLINTOCK: It's conceivable, madam; you seem a spirited family. How can I be of service to you?

ELGEE: I am here in London with two colleagues from the *Nation* newspaper, with which you are of course familiar.

McCLINTOCK: (*Grimly*) Indeed I am.

ELGEE: Mr William Smith O'Brien and Mr John Mitchel. I believe that you are acquainted with Mr O'Brien.

McCLINTOCK: That is so. His niece is I think married to my wife's second cousin.

ELGEE: Small world, eh? (*Indicating* CREIGHTON) Is this gentleman going to prowl around you like a pickpocket for the rest of the afternoon?

McCLINTOCK: You may return to your duties, Mr Creighton, though I would appreciate it if you stayed close to hand.

CREIGHTON: Of course, sir. Just shout if you need me.

(*Wags warning finger at* ELGEE *behind* MCCLINTOCK's *back, shakes his head and exits.*)

ELGEE: We are here to make representations to the government concerning the Famine.

McClintock: The Distress.

ELGEE: And I've called on you four times already.

McClintock: We are, as you will appreciate, most fearfuly preoccupied. As you will have observed, every corridor of the building is crammed with extra desks.

ELGEE: Strange that so much industry should generate so much idleness.

McClintock: We do what we can, madam.

ELGEE: And when did you last visit Ireland?

McClintock: (*Pause*) I beg our pardon?

ELGEE: I was wondering when your labours last took you across St George's Channel.

McClintock: Ah – I have not yet had that pleasure.

ELGEE: You mean the destiny of Ireland lies in the hands of a man who has never clapped eyes on the place?

McClintock: And how, pray, would it profit either me or the Irish if I had? We are social engineers, madam – clinicians of starvation. If we were to think for one moment of real flesh and blood we would be overwhelmed.

ELGEE: So you have put yourselves in the dark.

McClintock: Of course. How else are we to carry out our work? Would you wish to be in the hands of a surgeon trembling with tenderness? My God, woman, do you think that we are insensible to your suffering? Do you imagine that we would be labouring as we are, with four hours' sleep each night, if all that meant nothing to us? Or are you complacent enough to imagine that you have a monopoly on human compassion?

ELGEE: I am aware of your distaste for monopolies. My country is dying of free trade.

McClintock: Oh, no doubt it is convenient for you to cast us as Gorgons. How consoling to lay all your ills at the door of the English! As though we prepared the potato bug in our laboratories and shipped it over in cannisters one dark night, to let it loose on the plains of Galway. It was Irish improvidence, not English misrule, which brought this disaster upon you. Did you expect to survive for ever on half an acre of land with seven children and a stone of potatoes per day?

ELGEE: You seem to forget, sir, that –

McCLINTOCK: Oh, you have need of your demons, Miss Elgee. Let me tell you this, though I doubt you will even hear it, borne aloft as you are by your own self-righteousness. The captain of a sinking vessel must use foresight, calculation, and this is bound to appear flint-hearted to those who are floundering. If he lowers the life-boats too soon, they will be dashed to pieces by the waves. How can this not seem like callousness to those shrieking out to be rescued?

ELGEE: Life-boats! You aren't even distributing life-belts.

McCLINTOCK: Oh, we are the hated ones, Miss Elgee, no doubt of that. We bloodless analysts with our slide-rules and abstractions, fiddling while Kerry burns. We tight-lipped technologists of human misery. How much more tempting to be warm-blooded, impulsive, to give without stint! And so to confirm the people in their present degenerate ways, and invite another such catastrophe on their heads in a few years' time. No one loves the physician who counsels amputation, my dear lady; what the patient wants is another little pill and a pat on the head, while the limb slowly rots. All this they will get from the true liars and scoundrels, those supposed friends of the people, compared to whom we cold-blooded old codgers are as shining angels.

ELGEE: Sir, the victims of your policies –

McCLINTOCK: Ah yes, the victims. How else have the Irish ever imagined themselves? Those poor hard-done-bys who murder landlords and bury their bailiffs alive. Those downtrodden wretches who mutilate cattle and terrorize women. I suppose the cause of that too lies in Brighton and Birmingham. There is indeed a stench in your country, Miss Elgee – a most foul one. But it is not the smell of typhus; it is the stink of a people in love with failure. And it is an odour repugnant to the nostrils of the Almighty. It is not fever, I tell you, but fecklessness, which has brought Ireland to this pass.

ELGEE: So we brought famine upon ourselves?

McCLINTOCK: You have wallowed in your own excess for too long. If you are not thoroughly purged, it will suck you under.

ELGEE: So your aim is to save the people by exterminating them?

McCLINTOCK: *We* do nothing, dear madam. We are merely the instruments of Divine Providence. In any case, my good lady, you are hardly of the people yourself. There is not, as far as I know, much malnutrition in Merrion Square.

ELGEE: I can speak for the people. I can write for them.

McCLINTOCK: Ah yes, you are a poetess, I believe. The great Speranza. I mistrust poetry; it inflames men's passions.

ELGEE: That's why I write it.

McCLINTOCK: Words are slippery – promiscuous. Metaphor strikes at the root of social order. I have read your newspaper, madam: it is full of incendiary bombast.

ELGEE: Will you receive our delegation?

McCLINTOCK: So that you can hope to chill my blood with details of dysentery?

ELGEE: So that we can put the views of a mighty reform movement to you.

McCLINTOCK: Huh! The O'Connellites are finished, woman. What do you propose, to lead an army of scarecrows against the state?

ELGEE: (*Fumbling*) We propose . . . what we propose . . .

McCLINTOCK: Well, I shall consider giving you a hearing. I can promise nothing. Be good enough to return here for my answer in three days' time.

(CREIGHTON *enters*.)

ELGEE: Mr Secretary, Mr William O'Brien is, as you know, of noble birth. He is not accustomed to being kept waiting by civil servants.

McCLINTOCK: He may be an aristocrat over there, my good lady; over here he is just another colonial. And a contumacious one to boot.

ELGEE: So I am to return for a sixth time?

McCLINTOCK: Perseverance is all. Good day to you, madam. I thank you for what has been, I think, a most fruitful exchange of views. (*Bows, moves back into his office with* CREIGHTON.)

CREIGHTON: Jolly well done, sir.

McCLINTOCK: I held my own, you think?

CREIGHTON: Oh, absolutely, sir. Game, set and match, I'd say.

McCLINTOCK: Yes, I did do rather well, didn't I? Perhaps I *should* meet this shabby crew of conspirators. I'm beginning to enjoy these little jousts.

CREIGHTON: (*Obsequious chuckle*) Pleasant relief from paperwork, sir.

McCLINTOCK: Oh indeed, indeed.

CREIGHTON: (*Returning to general office, to* ELGEE) OK, Jane, you've had your say. Don't worry, I'll work on the old man, get him to meet your mates. You can count on me.

ELGEE: Please don't call me Jane.

CREIGHTON: Oooh, I like you when you're bolshie. How about that potato juice?

ELGEE: Stand out of my way, sir.

CREIGHTON: Come on, Janey, you can count on me, I'll bend the Governor's ear. But you'll have to be nice to me.

ELGEE: I said stand out of my way.

CREIGHTON: There's no need to be so prickly. I'm only trying to help. (*Tries to put arm around her waist.*) Come on, duckie, have a bit of mercy. Why don't you and me unite our two kingdoms?

ELGEE: (*Pushing him away*) How dare you insult me, sir. I command you to let me go.

CREIGHTON: (*Still holding her*) My word, we are stroppy today, aren't we? You know, you need me, sweetheart, if your little trip over the water is to pay dividends. You don't think your pals can just come in here swinging from the rafters any old time of day? (DAINTON *enters behind* CREIGHTON.) You and me together, though, we'll strike a blow for old Ireland.

ELGEE: Why don't we start with this? (*Knees him in the groin;* CREIGHTON *doubles up with a surprised grunt;* DAINTON *seizes him by the hair.*)

DAINTON: Get out of here, you scum. (*Throws him violently aside.*)

CREIGHTON: (*Picking himself up*) Well, if it isn't George Galahad himself. The leprechaun's friend, eh? I didn't know you were such a chimp-fancier, George. (DAINTON *moves threateningly towards him.*) OK, OK, I'm going – leave you two love-birds together. (*To* ELGEE) And you can tell your treasonable chums that they'll meet the Secretary over my dead body.

ELGEE: I can imagine no more delightful way of doing it. (CREIGHTON *exits.*)

DAINTON: Well done, Are you OK?

ELGEE: I'm fine.

DAINTON: I've been wanting to do that for years.

ELGEE: What, grab him by the hair?

DAINTON: No, knee him in the groin. What an animal. You mustn't think we're all like that, you know.

ELGEE: Why on earth should I think that?

DAINTON: Well you must hate the sight of us, surely.

ELGEE: Of course not. I'm just angry with myself for not tearing his throat out.

DAINTON: Creighton?

ELGEE: No, no, *he* doesn't matter. McClintock. He won; there's nothing we can do.

DAINTON: What do you mean?

ELGEE; Either you beat his brains out, in which case you're the savage he thinks you are, or you speak his language, in which case you're struck dumb. They teach us the Queen's English so they can gag us when they treat us like cattle.

DAINTON: I'm afraid I don't quite understand.

ELGEE: I couldn't *say* what I wanted to. I came to tell him that there are children in Ireland swollen to three times their natural size – children whose hair has fallen out of their head and begun to grow on their faces. I wanted to tell him that there are babies who suck their mother's nipple by daylight and chew her dead flesh by nightfall. He sees it as the work of Nature. Was it Nature which closed down the food depots when the harvest had failed? Was it Nature which refused to hold the harvest in '46, before relief had had time to arrive? (*Pause.*) You see – I can say it all to you.

DAINTON: I want to understand.

ELGEE: You'll do a better job if you don't.

DAINTON: I want to know how you feel about things – you and your friends. What's so strange about that?

ELGEE: So you can report it to the Chief Under-Secretary?

DAINTON: I detest the Chief Under-Secretary. I detest what I'm doing here. I think I'm going slowly mad. Can you imagine having to work with men who are bored by starvation? Who count up corpses and stifle their yawns?

ELGEE: Could I ask if you're an *agent provocateur*?

DAINTON: A what?

ELGEE: Oh well, if you have to ask I don't suppose you are.

DAINTON: I'm afraid my French is pretty awful.

ELGEE: You've certainly got a lot to learn.

DAINTON: I know; I'm shamefully ignorant. I was educationally deprived.

ELGEE: How do you mean?

DAINTON: They sent me to Eton and Christ Church.

ELGEE: Oh really? My brother was at Eton. Which house?

DAINTON: What does it matter?

ELGEE: Well, I'm pretty ignorant myself. I was going to tell McClintock that I'd seen men with typhus throwing themselves in the river to gain relief from their sores. That would have been a lie.

DAINTON: You haven't?

ELGEE: I've hardly been outside Dublin. In fact I've hardly been outside Merrion Square. I'm just an overgrown débutante, really.

DAINTON: And a poet, and an activist, and a tribune of the people.

ELGEE: You've read my poetry?

DAINTON: I read everything you write in the *Nation*.

ELGEE: You mean you take the *Nation* here?

DAINTON: Of course – for the same reasons you take *Hansard*. I know more about you than you think, Miss Elgee. I suppose you could say I'm a secret admirer.

ELGEE: Well, not so secret now.

DAINTON: No, indeed, not so secret now. Tell me about Ireland. Say something to me in Seltic.

ELGEE: In what?

DAINTON: You know: Seltic.

ELGEE: You mean Irish?

DAINTON: Yes. I'd love to hear you speaking your native tongue.

ELGEE: I am speaking my native tongue.

DAINTON: I mean the language of your own people.

ELGEE: This is the language of my own people.

DAINTON: Really?

ELGEE: Of course. Most of the Irish speakers are dead, or in Chicago.

DAINTON: I know it's stupid of me – it's just the idea of you saying something I can't understand. Something at once infinitely remote and unutterably close. Do you know what I mean?

ELGEE: How about *Too-dee-diddle-dee-dum-dee-do*?

DAINTON: No, no, I mean something *really* foreign. And then I could say something in English and you wouldn't understand me either.

ELGEE: Why not?

DAINTON: Because we could pretend that you only spoke Seltic.

ELGEE: Why?

DAINTON: I don't know; it's just the idea that thrills me somehow. Me talking to you and you talking to me and neither of us understanding a blind word the other says.

ELGEE: Have you seen anyone about this?

DAINTON: It would just sort of show up how we *do* understand each other deep down. You can understand each other in different languages.

ELGEE: Or misunderstand each other in the same language. The English and the Irish have been at it for years.

DAINTON: You must feel as though your tongue has been cut out.

ELGEE: Why should I feel that?

DAINTON: You know, being forced to speak English. Irish is so much more ancient.

ELGEE: So is gangrene. I'm not sure that's a recommendation.

DAINTON: I suppose you must think I'm an awful Romantic.

ELGEE: It had crossed my mind.

DAINTON: Do say something in Seltic!

ELGEE: *Cead mile failte.*

DAINTON: What does that mean?

ELGEE: It means – you have gentle hands.

(*They smile at one another, exit.*)

Black-out. We hear MCCLINTOCK'*s voice in the darkness.*

MCCLINTOCK: 'And one kid of the goat for a sin offering; beside the burnt offering, his meat offering, and his drink offering.

'And on the second day you shall offer twelve young bullocks, two rams, fourteen lambs of the first year without spot. These things ye shall do unto the Lord in your set feasts, beside your vows, and your freewill offerings, for your burnt offerings, and for your drink offerings, and for your peace offerings.'

(*Light gradually up on* MCCLINTOCK'*s face only, straining and twisted in the dark of his office.*)

What is your name? What is it? Is it Erin, or is it Wormwood? The womb of Erin is withered from too much childbearing, her brittle old dugs hang dry. Do you feel your womb shrivelling, Molly? Do you?

(*The lights have come up to reveal* MOLLY'*s face below* MCCLINTOCK'*s, as he takes her from behind over his desk.*)

This is my rod. You feel it, Molly? My rod to scourge you with – to cauterize your slimy wound, scour out the secret places of shame. It is God's little finger you feel here, woman. It is the tip of the Lord's finger within you, setting free the springs of the valleys, watering the vineyards, reclaiming the parched lands. (*Lights by now fully up on them.*) Are you aching, Molly, are you famished?

MOLLY: I can feel my belly hankering, sir. I can feel it filling.

McCLINTOCK: It is swelling with the staff of life. You're hungry, Molly? I'll put something in your belly. I shall be your sustenance, my sweet. These pure white drops of life will fall on your tongue like manna in the desert. The earth shall bear fruit once more. You shall eat the flesh of the Lamb. Blessed be the name of the Lord. (*Moans, cries out*) Blessed be God for ever.

Black-out

———————◆———————

ACT TWO

The Treasury again. The portrait of Queen Victoria has been replaced by a sketch of the potato bug. WILLIAM SMITH O'BRIEN, *distinguished, frock-coated, early-middle-aged,* JOHN MITCHEL, *younger, dressed like a Victorian version of a modern-day left-wing intellectual, and* JANE ELGEE, *are standing facing outwards in different directions.*

MITCHEL: (*After a silence; Ulster accent*) What are we to tell them?

O'BRIEN: The truth.

ELGEE: They know the truth. It's not as though they're ignorant.

O'BRIEN: Then why are we here?

ELGEE: To call an end to their madness.

MITCHEL: And how do you plead with madmen without speaking their gobbledygook? When I talk of Ireland in this place I can feel the words falling dead from my lips. They don't know where those words have been, what horrors they've supped. It's like Orpheus come back from the underworld.

ELGEE: Yes. Yes.

MITCHEL: Like signalling from separate planets – hoping a puff of smoke will be seen from Venus. We're on different time-scales. Ireland's gone back to the Middle Ages: it's lepers and lazars, monks and madmen all over again.

O'BRIEN: They're not an alien species. We're members of the same kingdom, subjects of the same monarch.

MITCHEL: And they still expect us to swing in trailing our knuckles along the ground.

O'BRIEN: You forget I have sat in their parliament, Mitchel.

MITCHEL: *Their* parliament, as you put it.

O'BRIEN: What are we here to do?

MITCHEL: We're here to make representations. How do you represent that which withers the tongue? Shall I say I have seen a woman in Ballina spewing up the flesh of her own child?

ELGEE: No, no, that just drives them to fury. We're dealing with men who think it's humane to be hard-hearted. They're all topsy-turvy.

MITCHEL: They are not of our species, O'Brien. You can talk to them no more than you could to a wood-louse. They under-stand violence and that's all – that's where translation ends.

O'Brien: No, don't you see, the horror of it is that they're decent men. They play with their infants, they have soft words for their wives. It's just that they suffer from a sickness of the mind known as dogma. We must purge them of it if we can, so that Ireland can stop dying of ideology.

Mitchel: They know what they're about. These are no well-meaning bunglers. When the British needed crops from us they needed men to till them; now that we're becoming a floating cattle farm, the two-legged Hibernian has become superfluous.

O'Brien: Ah yes, your conspiracy theory again.

Mitchel: You mean governments *don't* conspire to bring their enemies low?

O'Brien: Oh, there are conspiracies, to be sure, but no *grand* conspiracy – there doesn't need to be. You forget the role of accident and stupidity.

Elgee: We need to plan tactics, gentlemen, not talk philosophy. Mr McClintock may be a mite demented, but he is a shrewd sort of lunatic. What are we to say to him?

O'Brien: Let's first be honest with ourselves. The Repeal movement has collapsed, the Church is against us and we have 40,000 British troops on our soil. The peasantry is too fever-ridden to hold a pick, let alone a pike. Our only weapons are rhetorical ones, and they are rapidly rusting.

Mitchel: You always did look on the bright side, Willie.

Elgee: So where's our bargaining power?

O'Brien: We have no bargaining power. Except to offer ourselves as a bulwark against revolution.

Elgee: *Against* revolution?

O'Brien: Of course. Young Ireland still has influence with the masses; we must carry on appealing to the landlords to give leadership to the people.

Mitchel: My dear O'Brien, the landlords of Ireland have been the subject of more appeals than a cricket umpire. Our task is to ferment revolution, not call it off.

O'Brien: We assure the government that if they feed the people then we shall use our good offices to pacify them.

Mitchel: So we offer to head off a non-existent uprising in exchange for a few more bags of grain? Is this what they call the ancient Gaelic pride? Why don't we just offer them our daughters and have done with it?

Elgee: You want us to police our own people?

O'Brien: Whereas you propose, Miss Elgee, that we threaten insurrection?

Elgee: What do we have to lose?

O'Brien: Our liberty, for a start.

Elgee: You call this liberty?

O'Brien: Yes, I call it liberty to be standing in the Treasury rather than languishing in the Tower of London. Maybe I'm just eccentric.

Mitchel: Do you really expect them to relent now? They've stood by and let hundreds of thousands go under; they've listened to the howls of dying children and spoken of the sacred rights of property. They shrink from giving a crust to a beggar in case it destroys his self-respect. And do you think that they will leave off all this at the behest of a respectable Irish gentleman, a rabid extremist like myself and – saving your presence, ma'am – a green young girl?

Elgee: 'Green' is no insult to me, sir. As for 'girl', would Maeve and Deirdre have given away our parliament to the British?

Mitchel: Would Cuchulain have run a house in Merrion Square?

O'Brien: Come, come, my friends, let's not tear each other apart before the enemy can get at us. It's too ancient an Irish custom.

Mitchel: Look, we need to remember that in their eyes we're as much savages as anything that crawled out of the swamps of Sumatra with a bone through its nose. Oh, we speak their language since they forced it down our throats – but we're niggers enough for their purposes.

O'Brien: No, no: if we were that they'd be less nervous. What rattles them is that we're too close for cannibals and too remote to be civilized. If we threaten to act undemocratically, they'll certainly write us off as barbarians.

Elgee: But there *is* no democracy in Ireland. What other means do we have?

O'Brien: So we mutter about rebellion?

Elgee: Why not? Whenever did our people take history in their hands?

O'Brien: History, Miss Elgee, is the story of the victors. Do you wish our people to join them in their triumph?

Elgee: I wish them to affirm themselves again.

O'Brien: And what if they fail?

Mitchel: How can they fail? Even if they're defeated they'll have reclaimed their manhood.

ELGEE: I agree with all of that but the last word.

O'BRIEN: We have to use different weapons. Otherwise we're just a mirror image of them.

MITCHEL: We have no different weapons.

O'BRIEN: (*After a pause*) So what do we agree on?

MITCHEL: Not much.

ELGEE: Looks like business as usual.

> (CREIGHTON *has entered during this speech.* ELGEE *retires distastefully to one side.*)

CREIGHTON: Sir Hamish will see you shortly.

O'BRIEN: *Sir* Hamish?

CREIGHTON: The Chief Under-Secretary has been honoured for his efforts by Her Majesty. Perhaps before he comes in you might care to sketch out your views? Just a rough idea, of course.

MITCHEL: With pleasure. We are here, sir, to warn the British government that –

O'BRIEN: (*Interrupting*) Perhaps I may put in a word. We are practical men and women here, not moralists. We are not here to point the finger of accusation –

MITCHEL: Ha!

O'BRIEN: – but we believe it gravely mistaken, even so, to imagine that cheap government food will endanger the private markets.

CREIGHTON: We are not state interventionists, Mr O'Brien.

MITCHEL: You are when you choose to be. You intervened to alleviate a slump in Lancashire two weeks ago.

O'BRIEN: We are also most concerned that the public works are not paying a living wage.

CREIGHTON: Ah yes, the public works. Well, perhaps I can spare us some superfluous argument here. The public works are to be closed.

> (*Pause.*)

MITCHEL: Closed!

CREIGHTON: With all convenient speed.

O'BRIEN: But . . . but . . . how are the people to live?

CREIGHTON: The burden of relief will fall upon the Poor Law.

O'BRIEN: The Poor Law!

CREIGHTON: That's right. And a system of soup kitchens will be set in place.

O'BRIEN: Free soup?

CREIGHTON: Free to the destitute, yes. Not free otherwise.

MITCHEL: Ha, here's a turn-around indeed! I thought free food weakened the moral fibre.

CREIGHTON: It is an interim measure only.

MITCHEL: Interim! And if you can do it now, why pray did you not do it before and save thousands from the grave?

CREIGHTON: I see you are not averse to a spot of poetic licence, Mr Mitchel. It is a delightful trait in your people.

MITCHEL: So you've spent millions of pounds on a failed public works programme when you could have distributed free food from the start.

O'BRIEN: Will this soup be edible?

CREIGHTON: Of course it will. It is the creation of the distinguished French chef Monsieur Soyer.

O'BRIEN: Really? I wonder would he use it in his own restaurant.

CREIGHTON: The soup will be cheap, to be sure: 100 gallons can be made for one pound only. But nutritious, certainly – at least . . .

MITCHEL: At least for those not already so wasted that it will bloat their bellies and hasten their end.

O'BRIEN: Will the kitchens be in place before the relief works are closed down?

CREIGHTON: That won't be easy. We can't guarantee it.

O'BRIEN: In that case you will have a lot of extra corpses on your hands, and so fewer mouths to feed. Who is to bear the cost of this project?

CREIGHTON: The poor rate.

O'BRIEN: In the United Kingdom as a whole?

CREIGHTON: In Ireland alone.

(*Pause.*)

O'BRIEN: But that is unthinkable!

CREIGHTON: The Distress is a local responsibility, sir, not a national obligation.

O'BRIEN: But the workhouses are already overflowing – some unions are already almost bankrupt. There is no way the rate can be collected; the system will simply collapse.

CREIGHTON: I fear, Mr O'Brien, that if the more prosperous of your countrymen will not shoulder responsibility for their less affluent brethren, then they must be coerced into doing so.

MITCHEL: Just a minute: are we part of the same kingdom or are we not? Is the union of our nations to be set aside whenever it happens to suit your pocket?

CREIGHTON: If the landlords of Ireland have to pay the poor rate, they'll soon sift out the idlers and scroungers.

O'BRIEN: But the landlords are close to ruin! They've already raised more money for relief than Ireland has ever seen.

MITCHEL: And evicted more peasants than Cromwell.

CREIGHTON: (*To* O'BRIEN) You speak, of course, as a landlord yourself. I'm afraid the truth is, gentlemen, that the British taxpayer is growing a little weary of funding Irish improvidence, not least in the face of ingratitude and rebellion. There isn't a whole lot of good will left. Famine fatigue, you know.

O'BRIEN: Nonsense, sir! You have spent a mere fraction of what Ireland has contributed to the British Treasury over the years.

MITCHEL: And a pittance compared with what you spent to compensate the West Indian landlords for their slaves. Are we to be treated worse than niggers?

O'BRIEN: The Negroes of Antigua have raised money for us; so have the Choctaw Indians. Is our own government to do worse than them?

MITCHEL: Would the British be so niggardly if this disaster had struck in Surrey or Kent? Would you have allowed Dorking to silt up with skeletons, or have ghosts stalking the streets of Guildford?

O'BRIEN: And would the Queen have contributed a miserly five pounds to the relief fund?

CREIGHTON: Mythology, sir. Her Majesty contributed two thousand pounds. (*Indicates picture of famine bug behind him.*)

MITCHEL: Is that the image you serve, sir?

CREIGHTON: (*Looking round*) Whoops, sorry. They really ought to warn us when they change these things.

MITCHEL: Is it mythology that you allow ships to bear off our harvest to England while the people starve?

CREIGHTON: Imports to Ireland have considerably outweighed exports during the Distress. It wasn't that that caused the food shortage.

MITCHEL: There is no food shortage.

CREIGHTON: I beg your pardon?

MITCHEL: Famines are not caused by food shortages.

CREIGHTON: (*Sardonically*) I'm afraid your reasoning runs too deep for me.

MITCHEL: Famines happen because people can't buy what food is available. There would be quite enough food in Ireland if only the peasants didn't have to sell their crops to pay the landlord's rent.

CREIGHTON: The blight has destroyed 50 per cent of the potato crop. Do you call that food enough?

MITCHEL: And why do they have no food but the potato? Whose fault is that?

CREIGHTON: The people are distressed because they are poor. Is that our responsibility?

MITCHEL: Yes!
O'BRIEN: No, but – } (*together*)

CREIGHTON: . . . and because there are too many of them. It appears your peasants are unable to rein in their reproductive instincts.

MITCHEL: There is no overpopulation in Ireland.

CREIGHTON: Your reasoning once more eludes me.

MITCHEL: Ireland has too many people for *your* purposes, sir, not for her own.

CREIGHTON: And what are our purposes, pray?

MITCHEL: To turn the country into an offshore ranch. You need a few cowboys, not an army of crop gatherers.

CREIGHTON: Your people are squatting on barren land.

MITCHEL: They wouldn't need to if the big farmers would edge over a bit.

CREIGHTON: Is it our fault they don't?

MITCHEL: Who put the farmers there?

CREIGHTON: Ancient history, Mr Mitchel.

MITCHEL: Like the House of Lords?

CREIGHTON: We must move with the times.

MITCHEL: Then why not abolish the monarchy?

CREIGHTON: There is an absolute food shortage in your country.

MITCHEL: There would have been less if you had allowed us to hold the harvest.

CREIGHTON: A cosmetic move.

MITCHEL: For want of which thousands ended up in the churchyards. Anyway, who's talking about Ireland? I thought we were supposed to be a single kingdom.

CREIGHTON: So we are.

MITCHEL: Well unless my eyes deceive me there's enough food in the bread shops of Clerkenwell to keep Kerry afloat for a while.

CREIGHTON: What do you propose, sir – to carry it back with you in wicker baskets?

MITCHEL: I mean that there is quite enough food in the United Kingdom as a whole to feed our people. So why do you invite us into your parlour and then treat us like Hottentots?

CREIGHTON: The Distress is best handled as a local affair.

MITCHEL: The Famine.

CREIGHTON: What's in a name?

MITCHEL: Then I suppose I'm allowed to call Queen Victoria a greasy sow?

CREIGHTON: Watch your lip, sir.

O'BRIEN: Very well, then: if Ireland is to be autonomous, let us stop paying into your Exchequer.

CREIGHTON: The country must stand on its own feet, Mr O'Brien. We can prop her up no longer.

O'BRIEN: Then will you withdraw your troops?

MITCHEL: Will you restore our parliament?

O'BRIEN: Will you disestablish your church?

CREIGHTON: Since you speak of the Church, let me say that the United Kingdom can best be compared – if one may venture so sacred an analogy – to the Blessed Trinity.

O'BRIEN: I think your arithmetic's a bit awry, isn't it?

CREIGHTON: The three Persons of the Trinity are at once eternally united and utterly distinct. So it is with Britain and Ireland.

O'BRIEN: Is this a Treasury or a seminary?

MITCHEL: The comparison can be pressed further, sir. In both cases one of the partners gets crucified.

CREIGHTON: But only to rise again.

MITCHEL: Tell that in the graveyards of Donegal.

O'BRIEN: Why is the Secretary not here to receive us?

CREIGHTON: He has been lunching with the Prime Minister. Well, I say lunching, though no food but Indian meal has passed his lips this fortnight.

(MCCLINTOCK *enters, slightly the worse for drink.*)

O'BRIEN: Hmm. No *food*, maybe.

MCCLINTOCK: As you were, gentlemen, as you were.

CREIGHTON: I believe you know Miss Elgee, sir.

MCCLINTOCK: I do indeed. (*Bows stiffly;* ELGEE *nods coldly from a distance.*)

CREIGHTON: Sir Hamish McClintock, Mr John Mitchel. (MITCHEL *refuses to shake hands.*) And Mr William Smith O'Brien.

McClintock: (*Shaking hands with* o'brien) Mr O'Brien, how do you do. We are kinsmen of sorts, I believe.

O'Brien: We are indeed, Sir Hamish.

McClintock: Though I must confess I had forgotten that you were – er –

O'Brien: Irish?

McClintock: Precisely.

Elgee: (*Coming forward as* creighton *retires*) Mr O'Brien is a lineal descendant of Brian Boru.

McClintock: Aren't you all, aren't you all?

Elgee: Yes, but you see in his case the joke is that it's true.

O'Brien: Sir Hamish, perhaps we might begin by discussing the recent –

McClintock: (*Interrupting*) There is one root to the Irish crisis, gentlemen, and one root only – and that is the potato. (*Chuckles.*) You see my pun? *Root.* (*A chilly response from the Irish;* creighton *laughs perfunctorily.*) What we observe taking place in Ireland is the consequence of divine displeasure with the potato, and a divine desire to eradicate it. The great evil we have to contend with here is not the physical hardship of the Distress, but the moral evil of a selfish, perverse and turbulent people. Now the potato is in many respects an admirable phenomenon. Mr Creighton, enumerate its virtues for us if you would.

Creighton: (*Tonelessly, as though reciting*) Cheap, bountiful, nutritious, easy of access, ready to eat, simple to cook, hard to pillage, labour-saving, rich in protein and vitamins, a shield against scurvy, flowering in poor soil, the most versatile crop known to mankind, capable of being stored in the form of a well-fed pig.

McClintock: Excellent. And what else is the potato, Mr Creighton?

Creighton: The work of the devil, sir.

McClintock: The work of the devil indeed. Its cultivation requires little labour, and leads to a mindless, bovine existence, without aspiration or ambition. Those who tend it are left with too much time to engage in lasciviously reproducing themselves. They need to rise above this barbarous diet, and this the Almighty has taken in hand. It is awful to observe how he humbles the pride of nations. The sword, the pestilence and famine are instruments of his discipline, the canker worm and the locust are his armies. Famine, my friends, is the last, the most dreadful of Nature's resources. It is, so to speak, God's locusts at work on the body itself. The vices of mankind often finish the work of depopulation themselves. But should greed, sloth, dirt, idleness, perversion all fail, then Nature in her wisdom is at hand to step in with pestilence, epidemic and plague, while mighty famine stalks in the rear, and with one blow levels the population with what food is available.

(*Pause.*)

O'BRIEN: Holy God! And this is the man in charge of the relief operation!

(BRACKEN *enters and hangs around unobstrusively.*)

McCLINTOCK: We have the honour to labour on your behalf, sir. But the night cometh, Mr O'Brien, in which no man shall labour. In fact precious few of you over there have laboured for a good few centuries.

MITCHEL: Apart from the hangman and the military.

McCLINTOCK: They are God's instruments, like this plague of locusts sent to your land.

MITCHEL: Locusts wouldn't be so bad; you can fry them.

McCLINTOCK: God has turned his hinderparts to you, my friend. He has sickened of your idolatry, your incense stinks in his nostrils. Might not this plague be his vengeance for the grant voted by a Protestant parliament to that hotbed of popery at Maynooth? Who else but my own people – your people too, Mr Mitchel, as an Ulsterman – have kept faith with him in that dreary island? You and I understand each other well enough, sir: we are both absolute for the truth.

MITCHEL: You understand nothing of me.

McCLINTOCK: Who else but our own people have ever worked in Ireland, in the bustling weaving sheds of Armagh and the humming workshops of Fermanagh?

ELGEE: On land stolen from the Celt.

McCLINTOCK: And who, pray, did the Celt steal it from? Who were their Red Indians? Did the Celt wade ashore to find the island empty?

ELGEE: Sir Hamish, I think we have heard enough . . .

McCLINTOCK: It is good stout Scotsmen you need at the helm, once the Distress has cleared away your thriftless landlords. Men like yourself, Mr Mitchel.

ELGEE: Look, I see absolutely no point in –

McCLINTOCK: Silence, woman! I am doing the Lord's business here. Your kind was made for the ornamentation of mankind, for procreation and for obedience. Three in one he created them.

MITCHEL: Isn't that the Trinity?

McCLINTOCK: It's not material: all doctrines are one doctrine, all truths one truth. You may hate us, but you can't survive without us. Either you shall ride into the modern epoch on our backs, or you shall stick fast in the Dark Ages with your priestly cant and your mutinous tongues. There is no progress without pain, gentlemen: for every masterpiece, misery; for every cathedral a pit of bones. Out of evil springs good: I am told that young women in Ireland may now walk abroad freely at night, since the young men are all impotent. You may not love us, my friends, but you need us as the cripple needs his crutch. And we do not despise you for that – in fact the hearts of our people go out to you.

ELGEE: Is that why they portray us as apes in their cartoons?

McCLINTOCK: The English are very fond of animals. (ELGEE *gasps, near to exploding.*) We look upon that verdant island of yours, and we are moved in spirit. And if it takes a famine to drag you out of the Dark Ages into the modern world – if that be the Lord's unfathomable purpose in this affair – then, I say, his will be done.

ELGEE: (*Leaping on him with a cry of rage and tearing his hair*) It was you who did it! It was you who turned a blight into a famine! And now you have the gall to lay the blame on Providence. That's an obscenity, do you hear? An obscenity!

(O'BRIEN *and* CREIGHTON *try to pull her off, while* MITCHEL *tries to pull* CREIGHTON *off.*)

MITCHEL: (*To* MCCLINTOCK) You'll pay for this. You'll be paying for this with your blood down the generations.

(CREIGHTON *helps* MCCLINTOCK *to his feet and dusts him sedulously down.*)

McCLINTOCK: You can count yourself lucky that we don't hang you on the spot. It's what we usually do with subversive scum. (*Exits with* CREIGHTON. BRACKEN *stays lurking at the back. The Young Irelanders stand around in silence, recovering themselves.*)

MITCHEL: (*To* O'BRIEN) So you still think they're decent men?

O'BRIEN: I can't believe my senses. It's monstrous – unspeakable. And this from a civilized Englishman!

MITCHEL: They're barbarians, O'Brien. Just because you've lounged in the same clubs with them doesn't mean they're not savages. Well, that's it, then. We leave tonight.

O'BRIEN: And what do we do then?

MITCHEL: We rise up against them in Ireland.

O'BRIEN: More deaths. More pointless butchery.

MITCHEL: So you'd rather keep jawing to the butchers over here?

O'BRIEN: I don't know what I believe any more.

MITCHEL: Well, at least now, after what you've just heard, you credit the conspiracy theory?

O'BRIEN: No, I do not.

MITCHEL: You don't grasp the logic of it at all?

O'BRIEN: There is no logic.

MITCHEL: They're dumping relief on the Poor Law. That means the landlords will have to pay for their poorer tenants. Who can't afford to pay them rent anyway. So the landlords go bankrupt, the tenants get evicted, and you move in a new class of British businessmen who'll take over the land.

ELGEE: And where do the people go?

MITCHEL: Where they're heading already – to hell. Emigrating to the New World, or the next one. They're trying to evict a whole nation.

O'BRIEN: We don't know that. We don't know there's a conscious plan.

MITCHEL: Of course there's a plan.

ELGEE: So how do we get hold of it?

MITCHEL: We need somebody on the inside.

BRACKEN: *Cen fa gan an ceist a cur ar an dtaoiseach fein?*

O'BRIEN: What? Who's that?

MITCHEL: What did you say?

BRACKEN: You heard me. I said 'Why not ask the Chief?' Don't worry, I was only joking.

O'BRIEN: Who are you?

BRACKEN: James Bracken. I work here.

O'BRIEN: You're Irish?

BRACKEN: How did you guess?

MITCHEL: Where from?

BRACKEN: Donegal.

MITCHEL: Do they know that?

BRACKEN: No.

ELGEE: You don't sound Irish.

BRACKEN: Neither do you.

ELGEE: How did you end up here?

BRACKEN: I got myself a Cambridge degree and a brand new accent
– that was the hard bit.

O'BRIEN: Very commendable. I'm a Trinity man myself.

BRACKEN: What are you hanging around for? Why don't you just get
out?

MITCHEL: We're trying to prevent genocide.

BRACKEN: That's garbage. There are no plans for genocide.

MITCHEL: You'd hardly be telling us if there were.

BRACKEN: You're backing the wrong horse, Mitchel. You can't win
here and you can't win back home. Why don't you just jack it
in?

MITCHEL: Like you did?

BRACKEN: You're fighting for your nation. Well nations are becoming
as obsolete as the pyramids. The globe's being refashioned,
my friend; I'd advise you to move with the times.

O'BRIEN: Now there's an appeal with an ancient history!

ELGEE: You mean betray our country, like you've done?

BRACKEN: Rubbish. I never had anything to betray.

ELGEE: Oh, an Irishman will always find something.

BRACKEN: You're a fine crew to be obsessed with national identity.
One Protestant Celt, one republican Presbyterian and an
Anglo-Irish woman. Not a pure Gaelic papist among the lot of
you.

O'BRIEN: What does that matter?

BRACKEN: Exactly: what does it matter? Forget about nationhood, Mr
O'Brien, it never did anything for either of us. The Famine's
making an international race out of a benighted backwater
and all you can do is complain. We're all emigrés in one way
or another.

MITCHEL: I see you haven't lost your Irish talent for amateur
philosophizing.

BRACKEN: You heard the old man, didn't you? Do you really think
you're going to make a dent in that? What's your plan, hang
around so you can take more shit? Come back for your daily
dose of insults?

MITCHEL: Who are you anyway, Bracken?

BRACKEN: I haven't a clue. Who cares who I am? Why don't you lot
stop clinging to the past?

ELGEE: In that case why don't the British give up their Empire? Or is it only the Irish who are to be modernized into oblivion?

MITCHEL: Have you no ideals, man?

BRACKEN: Oh, I've nothing against ideals; it's just that they tend to end up skewering people's guts. Innocent people, mostly. That's how you lot'll end up – skewered on the sticky end of an ideal. An intellectual in politics is like a chimpanzee with a rifle. Why don't you just stick to writing poetry?

MITCHEL: Why don't you stick to exterminating your own people?

BRACKEN: Do you think you're going to up-end the British Empire with a few rusty pitchforks? You saw the Chief in action, Mitchel; what did you make of him?

MITCHEL: I think he's a lunatic on the loose.

BRACKEN: That's right. Half wizard administrator, half raving nutter. It's a madhouse here, you see – total unmitigated insanity. And it's as contagious as typhus. So why don't you all just shove off before you get infected?

O'BRIEN: Why don't you come with us, Mr Bracken?

BRACKEN: Oh no. I've come a long way, O'Brien; it would be tedious to turn back now. There are some frontiers one doesn't cross twice. (*Exits.*)

MITCHEL: Scum.

O'BRIEN: You think so?

MITCHEL: Don't you?

O'BRIEN: He told us to get back on the boat. That's what you're telling us too. So now who's crawling to the Treasury?
(MITCHEL *and* O'BRIEN *stare at each other.*)
Black-out. Lights up on ELGEE *and* DAINTON.

DAINTON: How did it go?

ELGEE: What, with McClintock? It was awful. I attacked him.

DAINTON: Physically?

ELGEE: Yes.

DAINTON: Gosh, I wish I'd done that.

EGLEE: I seem to be doing most of your brawling for you.

DAINTON: So what happens now?

ELGEE: We go back to Dublin. What's the point of staying?

DAINTON: Well, I shall miss you, Jane. (*Pause.*) Can we still see each other?

ELGEE: I don't know. (*Pause.*)

DAINTON: I can't hold out here much longer. I lie awake at night and see bodies falling from the skies like fading stars. I sit in committee meetings and feel sick in the pit of my guts.

ELGEE: This is your home, George.

DAINTON: England was never my home. I always felt a stranger here, even as a child. (*Clinging to her*) You've got to get me out of here, Jane. My skull's near to exploding, I get the shakes every night, you've got to rescue me. (*Shaking her*) I'm going to die here if you don't.

ELGEE: There's no home for you in Ireland, George. Ireland is emptying like a burning building – there's no home for anybody there any more.

DAINTON: Take me back with you.

ELGEE: Well that would be original, at least: you'd be the only man trying to get *into* the country. And what would you do when you got there?

DAINTON: I could help you in your work. We could take a cottage somewhere.

ELGEE: A cabin, you mean.

DAINTON: That's right.

ELGEE: And you could look after the pigs?

DAINTON: If I had to. I worked on a farm in the school holidays.

ELGEE: You'd probably have to give up your bed for them. Look, George, I'm not a simple country lass. There aren't any simple country lasses. I live in a big house in Merrion Square with a butler and a balustrade. I wouldn't know the difference between a pig and a black pudding.

DAINTON: I could do some political work. I want to help deliver your country, not destroy it. And I want to be with you.

ELGEE: George, I'm not sure you should think about me in that way.

DAINTON: What do you mean?

ELGEE: There's too much between us – too much history. Anyway, I'm not the domestic type; if I had a son I'm sure he'd be a disaster.

DAINTON: Jane, for pity's sake, one would normally expect –

ELGEE: George, these aren't normal times. We're all behaving like animals. Hunger has brought out the worst in us; we're no longer really human. People back home are glad to see someone else die so they can seize their bit of a farm. We can't afford kindliness any more – that's a privilege of the victor. We just have to see everything in terms of survival.

DAINTON: Including me?

ELGEE: Yes, including you.

DAINTON: So you've never had any feeling for me?

ELGEE: Feeling's a luxury we can't afford right now. At the moment politics is all that matters.

DAINTON: And what use is politics without feeling?

ELGEE: No use for us – it just tears us apart. Perhaps those of us who are fighting for humanity are the worst examples of it. You're a good man, George; you'd be out of place in Ireland.

DAINTON: I can't accept that people have to be brutal. That makes you no better than McClintock. Mitchel could be his twin.

ELGEE: No, that's not fair. You can't equate the viciousness of the ruler with the violence of the ruled.

DAINTON: If that's true, anything's permitted. I don't accept that. We have to be better than them, otherwise what right have we to oppose them?

ELGEE: What's true in England isn't true in Ireland, George. As I said, there's too much between us.

Black-out. MCCLINTOCK's *voice in the darkness in his office.*

McCLINTOCK: 'And his host, and those that were numbered of them, were thirty and two thousand two hundred. And those that were numbered of the camp of Ephraim were an hundred thousand and eight thousand and a hundred throughout their armies.' (*Lights up on his face.*) Thirty-two thousand and two hundred plus two hundred thousand and eight thousand and a hundred totals one hundred and forty thousand three hundred. It is not enough. How can that suffice? A mere morsel in God's throat. That will not appease him. Will that sate his hunger, Molly? (*Lights up on* MOLLY's *face beneath him.*)

MOLLY: No, sir, it will not be enough.

McCLINTOCK: What will not be enough?

MOLLY: One hundred and . . . fifty . . .

McCLINTOCK: Forty, woman!

MOLLY: . . . forty thousand and . . .

McCLINTOCK: Three hundred.

MOLLY: Three hundred.

McCLINTOCK: He could spear as many on a toothpick. What of a million then? Will a million deaths be enough, then, Molly?

MOLLY: Yes, sir.

McCLINTOCK: No no no no! I tell you, woman, not even a million will answer. For his arithmetic is infinite and his justice beyond calculation. Are you in a fever, Molly?

MOLLY: Yes, sir.

McCLINTOCK: The whole earth is shaking with it. And it must grow
worse before it is purged. We must pierce this abscess called
Ireland and gouge it clean of corrupt matter. We must pile
frenzy upon frenzy, so that it may come at last to crisis and
lash itself quiet. For no man's hand will stay it. Will a man's
hand allay your fever, Molly? Can you feel the finger of God
upon you? Can you, woman, can you?
Black-out. Lights up on Young Irelanders.

MITCHEL: So what's the point of waiting?

O'BRIEN: We must request one last interview. We owe it to the
people.

ELGEE: For what?

O'BRIEN: To persuade him to see reason.

MITCHEL: He does see reason. It's just that what's reasonable in
Whitehall is raving lunacy in Westport.

O'BRIEN: It would help, at least, not to offer violence to his person.

ELGEE: Oh fiddlesticks. He's ravishing our whole nation and you are
tender of his scalp!

MITCHEL: Perhaps, sir, you might bring yourself to be a little less of
the Smith and a little more of the O'Brien.

O'BRIEN: I will not be instructed in my duty as an Irishman by a
Scotch Presbyterian.

ELGEE: Mr O'Brien, I think we might at least try to –

O'BRIEN: Or for that matter by an Englishwoman.

ELGEE: Englishwoman!

MITCHEL: You speak of violence. After what we have witnessed here,
Ireland has no alternative but to rise up in arms. Are you
prepared to place yourself in the van of that, or are you the
kind of leader who will instruct his soldiers not to trespass
upon private property?

O'BRIEN: Rise up in arms! So that a gaggle of peasants already
dropping with dysentery may be finished off with British
bayonets?

MITCHEL: Better to fall as Irish soldiers than be slaughtered like
sheep.

O'BRIEN: This is wanton adventurism, sir.

MITCHEL: Do you know that there are families back home who board
themselves into their cabins so they can die unobserved? As
though they were *ashamed* of starving – as though it was
some dreadful social gaffe, some unspeakable *faux pas*. They

die as though starvation was a mortal sin. The whole country is shrouded in secrecy, with men and women crawling off into graveyards so as to die on sacred soil. And some of them still loyal to Victoria with their last breath! At least they could *make* something of their dying – at least they could perish as freemen rather than slaves.

ELGEE: How can they be free with empty bellies?

MITCHEL: Freedom, independence? I tell you, madam, I sometimes think they wouldn't recognize these things if they broke their shins on them in broad daylight. They'd be running off to the priest and the landlord to ask for instructions on how to use them. Wheedling and poor-mouthing and Your-Honouring their way to the grave. I was speaking in Dingle a few months ago about abolishing the landlords, and an old fellow in the crowd cried out, 'Ah sure now who would we pay the rent to, sor?' Sometimes I think they don't deserve to be free.

O'BRIEN: You sound just like McClintock. He sees God's hand everywhere, you see Westminster's.

MITCHEL: It takes one Scot to know another.

O'BRIEN: Independence indeed! As though we won't all die without British aid. This is the last moment to talk of autonomy.

MITCHEL: We're dying anyway. We might as well go out in style.

O'BRIEN: There are other remedies.

MITCHEL: Such as?

O'BRIEN: Emigration.

MITCHEL: I thought that was part of the problem.

O'BRIEN: I mean planned emigration – government-sponsored.

MITCHEL: So we should collude with the British to empty the island?

O'BRIEN: There is no such plot!

MITCHEL: Ireland is haemorrhaging like an open wound. Men are stealing turnips so as to get themselves transported. We need to staunch that wound, before the land is left to the stoat and the scarecrow.

O'BRIEN: We have no power to heal that wound.

ELGEE: Well there's something we have the power to do.

O'BRIEN: What's that?

ELGEE: We have the power to leave this place. And leave our illusions behind us.

O'BRIEN: We can't pull through without the British.

ELGEE: We can't pull through with them either.

MITCHEL: You know that's the truth, Willie. You know it.
> (*Pause.*)

O'BRIEN: (*Quietly*) Yes. Yes, I suppose we can salvage some truth, at least. Very well, we go back. Empty-handed. As we came.
> *Black-out. We hear* MOLLY's *voice in the dark, as lights slowly up on her face.*

MOLLY: And so the Famine came and went, like a rent in the texture of time, a warp in the fabric of space, leaving a huge silence in its wake. It was as though history had rumbled down upon the present like lava, and its hissing was finally quenched. And those who had survived crawled to the rim of the smoking crater, dragged themselves out and made a new beginning. And there were those whose tongues had been torn out by what they had witnessed, and those who consumed themselves with fury. But there were those of us who found our tongues for the first time, as the dead gave birth to the living.
> (*Lights up. Small changes in set to indicate some months later.* DAINTON *and* BRACKEN *writing at their desks.* CREIGHTON *enters with papers.*)

CREIGHTON: Here y'are, chaps, Constabulary reports. Sorry to break into your wet dreams. (*Distributes copies to* DAINTON *and* BRACKEN.) Come on now, get a move on, I promised to meet slaggy Sammy in Tufty's.

BRACKEN: How is the old scrubber? Still screwing that little tart from Bermondsey?

CREIGHTON: Nah, she couldn't keep her hands off the men for five minutes. She's back with Flash Harry.

BRACKEN: What, Henry Headbanger?

CREIGHTON: Too right. Seems he took her to that new club the other night – you know, the one where you're served by these big Zulu geezers clanking chains behind them.

BRACKEN: Slavers?

CREIGHTON: That's the one. They have girls up in the roof in this big net, writhing around starkers. Wrestling with snakes and all that.

BRACKEN: What, real snakes?

CREIGHTON: No, rubber jobs. But they do say that they'll slip the odd live python in there if you're willing to pay.

BRACKEN: Jesus.

CREIGHTON: Oh, it's a rough house right enough. Anyway, Sammy was pretty legless as usual and she wanted to get into the net with the tarts. Started stripping off and shouting about how she loved snakes. Well she should know, she married one.

BRACKEN: So what happened?

CREIGHTON: So she made head-banging Harry sort of hitch her up to the net, but he was pretty shit-faced too – in fact he was as tight as a gnat's arse stretched over a sugar bowl. So he fell over backwards and left her dangling from the ceiling in her knickers. She was a real hit – the manager offered her good money to do it every night.

BRACKEN: (*Reading report*) Seems like things are looking up in Ulster.

DAINTON: (*Reading*) But not in Connemara.

CREIGHTON: Ah well, you can't win them all. It's a reasonable percentage, as the man said about the good and the bad thief.

DAINTON: And there's cholera rife from coast to coast.

CREIGHTON: That's not our problem, old bean. Cholera's got nothing to do with food shortage, it comes from letting your hygiene go to hell. The chimps aren't dying of starvation, they're dying of disease – and that comes from lice, and lice comes from not bloody bothering to wash.

DAINTON: So you expect starving men to buy soap?

CREIGHTON: You've got to keep up your self-esteem. Otherwise we're all wurrms, all wurrms (*imitating* McCLINTOCK).
(McCLINTOCK *enters with papers in hand;* CREIGHTON *embarrassed; they all rise.*)

McCLINTOCK: As you were, gentlemen, as you were. A braw morning, my lads – good keen wee nip in the air. And how fares the great work?

CREIGHTON: Everything well in hand, sir.

McCLINTOCK: Splendid, splendid. I've just been reading here of the magnificent harvest in Ulster. The Poor Law inspectors report that they've never seen such a luxurious bloom. Not a trace of blight to be found.

DAINTON: But the blight has returned on the western seaboard, sir – and the demand for relief there is higher than this time last year. We're getting appeals all the time.

McCLINTOCK: Ah well, the west. Whenever did anything good come out of there? The future is with Belfast, Mr Dainton, not Ballyvaughan. And now, gentlemen, I have some good news for you all. In fact marvellous news, stupendous intelligence, tidings of great joy.

CREIGHTON: Has the Pope been assassinated, sir?

McCLINTOCK: Even better, Mr Creighton, even better. (*Dramatic pause.*) The Distress is over!

(*The men look at one another, stunned.*)

DAINTON: What?

CREIGHTON: Over, sir?　　　(*together*)

BRACKEN: Eh?

McCLINTOCK: Over, gentlemen. Perfected, concluded, consummated, complete. It remains only for me to congratulate you, my friends, on a task magnificently performed.

DAINTON: But Mr McClintock, this just isn't true. There are still some two and a half thousand deaths in Ireland every week. The Poor Law Commissioners are complaining that they have no funds to fight the cholera. How can you possibly declare –

McCLINTOCK: Enough, my dear sir! You touch on one or two imperfections. What conclusion is ever infallible? My meaning is surely evident. There are to be no more government funds for Ireland – and since the relief operation is consequently at an end, so, logically, is the Distress.

BRACKEN: Eh?

McCLINTOCK: For were there still substantial distress in Ireland, then it follows that we would strive to alleviate it; and since we are now discontinuing all such efforts, it can be inferred that there is no distress remaining to be alleviated.

(*Pause.*)

DAINTON: But the Famine is *not* over, sir!

McCLINTOCK: Mr Dainton, pray allow me to explain. The point where a phenomenon may be said to be over is not always simple to determine. When, for example, was the Renaissance over? At what exact hour of the clock? From when precisely do we date the end of the Middle Ages, or of the Enlightenment? When, pray, is my breakfast over? When I have devoured the last morsel of bacon? When I have thrown down my napkin and pushed back my chair? When the bacon is digested, or when it is excreted? You tread here, sir, on marshy metaphysical terrain. There are philosophical complexities at stake here, which I for one would not rush to unravel. If, say, I were to punch you in the throat, to descend for a moment

from the metaphysical to the mundane, when could this event
be said to be over? At the moment I remove my knuckles from
your windpipe? When the pain has finally subsided?

DAINTON: I can't believe that I'm hearing this. This is nothing short of
madness.

McCLINTOCK: How long, you may ask, does a historical event endure?
Would it not be plausible to reply: as long as it is *thought* to
endure? And is not this illustrated by the unhappy situation
which pertained in Ireland until very recently, indeed until
this very morning? As long as men and women believe that
there is a food shortage, they will abandon their farms and
throw themselves with indecent expedition on public charity,
thus ensuring that there is a food shortage indeed. Once these
poor wretches can be persuaded that the emergency is over,
they will recover their self-respect, attend to their smallhold-
ings and the emergency will be over in reality.

CREIGHTON: I'd never thought of it that way, sir.

McCLINTOCK: Mr Bracken?

BRACKEN: It's certainly – er – an ingenious notion, sir.

McCLINTOCK: Though not, I should say, of my own invention. It was
discovered by the greatest of Irish philosophers, Bishop
Berkeley, who taught us that to exist, and to be perceived to
exist, are one and the same. At least in Ireland.

CREIGHTON: There's a ring of truth to that, sir.

McCLINTOCK: And what do you say, Mr Dainton? Still languishing
among the sceptics?

DAINTON: Sir, the Irish landowners are driving their tenants from the
land in their thousands. They are seizing advantage of their
wretchedness to consolidate their estates. Are these poor
houseless people to be left to wither by the wayside?

McCLINTOCK: The Poor Law will care for the destitute.

DAINTON: Mr McClintock, you are as aware as I am that the quickest
way to kill a man in Ireland today is to send him into a
typhus-infested workhouse. There are men and women ready
to slit their throats rather than fester in the hideous squalor
which is state support.

McCLINTOCK: Sir, clearance and consolidation are the means by
which Ireland will be hauled from its Gothic gloom into the
nineteenth century. To prop up paupers is to oppose the
march of history. Are you determined that no good at all
should spring from this calamity? – that it should all have

been for nothing? Can you find no trace of God's finger in this misfortune?

DAINTON: I don't believe in a future which rolls forward on the corpses of the present.

McCLINTOCK: The future has never rolled on anything else.

DAINTON: Then I turn my back on it.

McCLINTOCK: You may cold-shoulder the future, Mr Dainton, but you can rest assured it will not ignore you. The choice is to stare it in the face or be blown into it backwards.

DAINTON: Well, there's no future for me here.

McCLINTOCK: That's to be sure. (DAINTON *collects one or two personal belongings from his desk.*) And where, sir, will you go? To Ireland?

DAINTON: I don't know. Maybe.

McCLINTOCK: You choose a bad time. The future you are fleeing is just about to hit them. Mark my words, they will scramble with unseemly haste to put all this behind them. The last thing they will want to do is remember, and you will just be an embarrassing momento. You will just be an indecent noise in their conspiracy of silence.

DAINTON: They'll remember. You've just destroyed the *pax Britannica* for the next century. As you said, the future will roll forward on dead bodies.

McCLINTOCK: And you, sir, will be eaten up with bitterness. A slower kind of starvation, but just as deadly.

(DAINTON *exits.*)

McCLINTOCK: And now, gentlemen, all that remains is to deal with the debt.

BRACKEN: Sir?

McCLINTOCK: The loans, sir, the loans to Ireland. They must be called in immediately; there is an appreciable amount of interest involved. This will be your final task, my friends.

CREIGHTON: May we enquire about your own future, sir?

McCLINTOCK: Indeed you may. I have been appointed to reorganize the Civil Service from top to bottom.

BRACKEN: Oh, congratulations, sir.

McCLINTOCK: I wouldn't applaud too soon if I were you, Mr Bracken. There will no doubt be a number of redundancies. I trust you gentlemen will not be among them. After that it appears I am to be posted to India for a spell, as governor of Madras. I imagine that after dealing with Ireland India will be child's play. (*Laugh.*) Yes, quite a challenge, gentlemen. I'm already eagerly anticipating the good work I can do there.

BRACKEN: I'm sure the Indians are doing just the same, sir.

MCCLINTOCK: Everything passeth away, and withereth like grass. Only truth and justice endure.

(*Exits.*)

CREIGHTON: (*Going over to back wall, uncovering the blackboard and wiping it clean*) Well, that's the end of that little game. What do you say to noughts and crosses?

END